UNIVERSALS IN LINGUISTIC THEORY

Edited by

Emmon Bach/Robert T. Harms The University of Texas at Austin

Contributing Authors

Charles J. Fillmore The Ohio State University

Paul Kiparsky Massachusetts Institute of Technology

James D. McCawley The University of Chicago

UNIVERSALS IN LINGUISTIC THEORY

Holt, Rinehart and Winston, Inc.

New York Chicago San Francisco
Atlanta Dallas Montreal
Toronto London

Universals in Linguistic Theory edited by
Emmon Bach and Robert T. Harms

Library of Congress Catalog Card Number: 68-26825
03-068935-X
Printed in the United States of America
90123   98765432

PREFACE

On April 13–15, 1967, a symposium was held at the University of Texas at Austin on the topic 'Universals in Linguistic Theory.' This volume represents the written record of that conference, which consisted in the presentation of the papers included in the volume in more or less their present form together with considerable discussion of a formal and informal nature that went on during the three days among the speakers, a number of visitors (including invited discussants), and local staff members. The formal discussions were taped with an eye toward their eventual inclusion in some form in the published record of the symposium. At the end of the sessions, however, the participants voted against printing any direct record of the discussion. It was decided to publish just the papers, as soon as the speakers had a chance to rework them and incorporate any reflexes of the discussion judged to be apposite, perhaps by way of footnotes. The main motive for this decision, as we understood it, was that the volume could be published more quickly in this way. The price of this decision was considerable, in our opinion, since a large part of the success of the symposium was due to the articulate and vigorous discussion that followed all of the papers. One participant, David L. Stampe (Ohio State), spoke on the notion of 'naturalness' and the evaluation metric in phonology, subsequently decided against publishing the views presented by him at the conference. The invited discussants were Edward S. Klima (M.I.T.), George Lakoff (Harvard), D. Terence Langendoen (Ohio State), John R. Ross (M.I.T.), Paul Schachter (U.C.L.A.), Richard Stanley (M.I.T.), György Szepe (Hungarian Academy of Sciences and Columbia), and William S.-Y. Wang (U.C. Berkeley).

As a group the papers can be characterized by pointing out several directions in which there appears to be considerable unanimity. First of all, it is obvious that in spite of wide divergence in detail the ideas and discussion reflected here are to be understood against a background of consensus on the basic goals and methods of linguistic theory as it has developed in the last decade, especially under the leadership of Noam Chomsky of M.I.T. One measure of this consensus and of the change in the thinking of many American linguists is the vague embarrassment that one feels about the very title of the volume. After all, no one organizes conferences on 'universals' in physics, or even organic chemistry. What is linguistic theory itself if not the attempt to discover what is common to all languages, what is essential in the notion 'natural language,' what are the limits within which languages can vary, what are the (universal!) terms by means of which this variation can be described? The change in the climate of linguistic opinion has been aptly epitomized in the opening words of Fillmore's paper. We would take issue with McCawley's initial apology. Every paper in the volume is concerned in one way or another with questions of general linguistic theory, that is by necessity with 'universals.'

We feel that a profound change has occurred in linguistic thinking in the last decade. It is no longer of any interest to describe one after another language 'anyhow' without regard to the relevance of the facts to general linguistic theory. As Ross put it, it makes no sense to talk about 'describing a language in terms of its own structure alone.' Toward the end of the conference, when it had become apparent that the general agreement did not encompass any currently explicitly formulated model, the question was raised: What should we be teaching our students? Langendoen's answer seems to us most apt: We should give them the ability to recognize an interesting linguistic problem when they see one, that is, one which throws some light—negative or positive—on our conceptions of what languages in general are like.

Along with this consensus on goals and methods, however, the papers and discussion gave an indication of rather far-reaching changes in the substance of current linguistic theory, and this seems to us to be the second striking similarity. At a time when a consolidation of thought is most evident, there seems to be a widespread dissatisfaction with many aspects of current theory, at all levels. This is altogether healthy and to be expected. Another way of stating the situation is to say that we are finding out new things about languages and Language. We mention briefly a few examples.

The two papers are involved mainly with syntax development, in quite different directions, and ideas about 'universal' base rules. Fillmore's contribution—the longest in the volume—represents the fullest development of his ideas about a universal underlying set of caselike relations that play an essential role in determining syntactic and semantic relations in all languages. It shows one of the virtues of looking at things from a fresh point of view in the way in which a number of relationships and problems are discussed which had hitherto gone unnoticed (see, for example, the section on 'inalienable possession'). Bach's paper starts from some problems in English syntax and tries to show how study in depth of one language leads us toward rather than away from 'universal grammar.' Both papers exemplify changing conceptions of the form and substance of syntactic theory and, to a certain extent, of semantic theory, and its relation to syntax. The latter theme is central to McCawley's paper, where the whole notion of (syntactic) 'selectional feature' is subjected to attack and various specific proposals are made that lead to changes both in semantic and syntactic theory. The culmination of this line of thought is reached in McCawley's 'Postscript' where the very notion of 'deep structure' as distinct from 'semantic reading' is abandoned. Finally, Kiparsky's contribution, which deals mainly with phonological problems, introduces a new dimension by asking: What can historical change tell us about the adequacy of linguistic theory? This question, we believe, opens up what will be one of the most significant directions of linguistic work in the next few years.

We expressed our regret above for the omission of direct records of the discussions that followed the papers. We would give a totally false picture of the symposium if we did not mention the contribution of Ross and Lakoff, who not only played a role as discussants but were kind enough to remain in Austin to devote approximately six hours to a presentation of some of their recent work. Allusions to this work are frequent in the published papers (see especially the final pages of McCawley's essay and his 'Postscript'). At the date of this writing, however, nothing is available in print (some aspects are prefigured in Lakoff, 1965). It may not be out of order to indicate roughly the direction of their thinking, which in many ways parallels ideas found in this volume. We hope that a detailed and authoritative account will soon be forthcoming in published form. The main point that we would like to mention is the development of 'deeper' and more abstract underlying structures than are to be found, say, in Chomsky's *Aspects of the Theory of Syntax*. We cite one example: the surface sentence *Floyd broke the glass* is composed of no less than eight sentences. The form of this underlying structure may be indicated by a quasi-paraphrase: *I declare to you that it past that it happen that Floyd do cause it to come about that it BE the glass broken.* Each form in capitals represents an abstract 'pro-verb,' with 'break' represented in the innermost sentence. The first is a 'performative' verb (Austin, 1962), the second represents the tense of the sentence, fourth the 'actional' character of the sentence, the fifth and sixth the causative and inchoative components of 'broke' and so on. Each can be justified on syntactic grounds. It is but a step, then, to the position represented in McCawley's 'Postscript' where these 'deep structures' are taken to be identical with the semantic representations of sentences. A considerable convergence of ideas became apparent during the conference.

We would like to thank all who helped to make the symposium a success, including not only the official participants but the many visitors and colleagues in the Department of Linguistics at the University of Texas at Austin, especially W. P. Lehmann, Chairman. Generous financial support was provided by the Excellence Fund's Visiting Lecturers and Consultants Account of the University of Texas.

E.B.
R.T.H.

Austin, Texas
August 1968

CONTENTS

UNIVERSALS IN LINGUISTIC THEORY

THE CASE FOR CASE[1]

Charles J. Fillmore   The Ohio State University

[1] I am grateful to the College of Arts and Sciences of the Ohio State University for releasing me from teaching duties during the winter quarter of 1967. I wish also to express my appreciation to George Lakoff (Harvard), D. Terence Langendoen (Ohio State), and Paul M. Postal (I.B.M.) for the many challenges and suggestions they have sent my way concerning the ideas of this paper. I may soon regret that I did not always follow their advice.

Speculation on language universals has not always and everywhere been viewed as a fully respectable pastime for the scientific linguist. The writer recalls a Linguistic Institute lecture of not many summers ago in which it was announced that the only really secure generalization on language that linguists are prepared to make is that 'some members of some human communities have been observed to interact by means of vocal noises'. Times have changed, it is a pleasure to report, and this is partly because we now have clearer ideas about what linguistic theories are theories of, and partly because some linguists are willing to risk the danger of being dead wrong.

Scholars who have striven to uncover syntactic features common to all of the world's languages have generally addressed themselves to three intimately related but distinguishable orders of questions: (*a*) What are the formal and substantive universals of syntactic structure? (*b*) Is there a universal base, and, if so, what are its properties? (*c*) Are there any universally valid constraints on the ways in which deep structure representations of sentences are given expression in the surface structure?

Concerning formal universals we find such proposals as Chomsky's, that each grammar has a base component capable of characterizing the underlying syntactic structure of just the sentences in the language at hand and containing at least a set of transformation rules whose function is to map the underlying structures provided by the base component into structures more closely identifiable with phonetic descriptions of utterances in that language (Chomsky, 1965, pp. 27–30). A representative statement on substantive syntactic universals is Lyons' assertion (1966, pp. 211, 223) that every grammar requires such categories as Noun, Predicator, and Sentence, but that other grammatical categories and features may be differently arranged in different languages. And Bach (1965) has given reasons to believe that there is a universal set of transformations which each language draws from in its own way, and he has shown what such transformations might look like in the case of relative clause modification.

Discussions on the possibility of a universal base (as distinct from claims about universal constraints on the form of the base component) have mainly been concerned with whether the elements specified in the rules of a universal base—if there is one—are sequential or not. A common assumption is that the universal base specifies the needed syntactic *relations,* but the assignment of sequential order to the constituents of base structures is language specific. Appeals for sequence-free representations of the universal deep structure have been made by Halliday (1966), Tesnière (1959), and others. Lyons (1966, p. 227) recommends leaving for empirical investigation the question of the relationship between the

1

underlying representation and sequential order, and Bach (1965) has suggested that continued investigation of the syntactic rules of the world's languages may eventually provide reasons for assuming specific ordering relations in the rules of a universal base.

Greenberg's (1963) statistical studies of sequence patterns in selected groups of languages do not, it seems to me, shed any direct light on the issue at hand. They may be regarded as providing data which, when accompanied by an understanding of the nature of syntactic processes in the specific languages, may eventually lend comfort to some proposal or other on either the sequential properties of the base component or the universal constraints which govern the surface ordering of syntactically organized objects.

Findings which may be interpreted as suggesting answers to our third question are found in the 'markedness' studies of Greenberg (1966) and in the so-called implicational universals of Jakobson (1958). If such studies can be interpreted as making empirical assertions about the mapping of deep structures into surface structures, they may point to universal constraints of the following form: While the grammatical feature 'dual' is made use of in one way or another in all languages, only those languages which have some overt morpheme indicating 'plural' will have overt morphemes indicating 'dual'. The theory of implicational universals does not need to be interpreted, in other words, as a set of assertions on the character of possible deep structures in human languages and the ways in which they differ from one another.

The present essay is intended as a contribution to the study of formal and substantive syntactic universals. Questions of linear ordering are left untouched, or at least unresolved, and questions of markedness are viewed as presupposing structures having properties of the kind to be developed in these pages.

My paper will plead that the grammatical notion 'case' deserves a place in the base component of the grammar of every language. In the past, research on 'case' has amounted to an examination of the variety of semantic relationships which can hold between nouns and other portions of sentences; it has been considered equivalent to the study of semantic functions of inflectional affixes on nouns or the formal dependency relations which hold between specific nominal affixes and lexical-grammatical properties of neighboring elements; or it has been reduced to a statement of the morphophonemic reflexes of a set of underlying 'syntactic relations' which themselves are conceived independently of the notion of 'case'. I shall argue that valid insights on case relationships are missed in all these studies, and that what is needed is a conception of base structure in which case relationships are primitive terms of the theory[2] and in which such concepts as 'subject' and 'direct object' are missing. The latter are regarded as proper only to the surface structure of some (but possibly not all) languages.

Two assumptions are essential to the development of the argument, assumptions that are, in fact, taken for granted by workers in the generative grammar tradition. The first of these is *the centrality of syntax*. There was a time when a typical linguistic grammar was a long and detailed account of the morphological structure of various classes of words, followed by a two- or three-page appendix called 'Syntax' which offered a handful of rules of thumb on how to 'use' the words described in the preceding sections—how to combine them into sentences.

In grammars where syntax is central, the forms of words are specified with respect to syntactic concepts, not the other way around. The modern grammarian, in other words, will describe the 'comparative construction' of a given language in the most global terms possible, and will then add to that a description of the morphophonemic consequences of choosing particular adjectives or quantifiers within this construction. This is altogether different from first describing the morphology of words like *taller* and *more* and then adding random observations on how these words show up in larger constructions.[3]

The second assumption I wish to make explicit is *the importance of covert categories*. Many recent and not-so-recent studies have convinced us of the relevance of grammatical properties lacking obvious 'morphemic' realizations but having a reality that can be observed on the basis of selectional constraints and transformational possibilities. We are constantly finding that grammatical features found in one language show up in some form or other in other languages as well, if we have the subtlety it takes to discover covert categories. Incidentally, I find it interesting that the concept 'covert category'—a concept which is making it possible to believe that at bottom all languages are essentially alike—was introduced most convincingly in the writings of Whorf, the man whose name

[2] Notational difficulties make it impossible to introduce 'case' as a true primitive as long as the phrase-structure model determines the form of the base rules. My claim is, then, that a designated set of case categories is provided for every language, with more or less specific syntactic, lexical, and semantic consequences, and that the attempt to restrict the notion of 'case' to the surface structure must fail.

[3] John R. Ross pointed out, during the symposium, that some syntactic processes seem to depend on (and therefore 'follow') particular lexical realizations of just such entities as the comparative forms of adjectives. Compared adjectives, in short, may be iterated, just as long as they have all been given identical surface realizations. One can say,

    i. She became friendlier and friendlier.
    ii. She became more and more friendly.

but not

    iii. * She became friendlier and more friendly.

is most directly associated with the doctrine that deep-seated structural differences between languages determine the essentially noncomparable ways in which speakers of different languages deal with reality (see Whorf, 1965, pp. 69 ff.).

One example of a 'covert' grammatical distinction is the one to which traditional grammarians have attached the labels *'affectum'* and *'effectum'*, in German *'affiziertes Objekt'* and *'effiziertes Objekt'*. The distinction, which is reportedly made overt in some languages, can be seen in Sentences 1 and 2.

1. John ruined the table.
2. John built the table.

Note that in one case the object is understood as existing antecedently to John's activities, while in the other case its existence resulted from John's activities.

Having depended so far on only 'introspective evidence', we might be inclined to say that the distinction is purely a semantic one, one which the grammar of English does not force us to deal with. Our ability to give distinct interpretations to the verb-object relation in these two sentences has no connection, we might feel, with a correct description of the specifically syntactical skills of a speaker of English.

The distinction does have syntactic relevance, however. The *effectum* object, for example, does not permit interrogation of the verb with *do to,* while the *affectum* object does. Thus one might relate Sentence 1, but not Sentence 2, to the question given in 3.

3. What did John do to the table?

Furthermore, while Sentence 1 has Sentence 4 as a paraphrase, Sentence 5 is not a paraphrase of Sentence 2.

4. What John did to the table was ruin it.
5. What John did to the table was build it.[4]

To give another example, note that both of the relationships in question may be seen in Sentence 6 but that only in one of the two senses is Sentence 6 a paraphrase of Sentence 7.

6. John paints nudes.
7. What John does to nudes is paint them.

There is polysemy in the direct object of 6, true, but the difference also

[4] This observation is due to Paul M. Postal.

lies in whether the objects John painted existed before or after he did the painting.

I am going to suggest below that there are many semantically relevant syntactic relationships involving nouns and the structures that contain them, that these relationships—like those seen in 1 and 2—are in large part covert but are nevertheless empirically discoverable, that they form a specific finite set, and that observations made about them will turn out to have considerable cross-linguistic validity. I shall refer to these as 'case' relationships.

1. Earlier Approaches to the Study of Case

Books written to introduce students to our discipline seldom fail to acquaint their readers with the 'wrong' ways of using particular case systems as universal models for language structure. Grammarians who accepted the case system of Latin or Greek as a valid framework for the linguistic expression of all human experience were very likely, we have been told, to spend a long time asking the wrong kinds of questions when they attempted to learn and describe Aleut or Thai. We have probably all enjoyed sneering, with Jespersen, at his favorite 'bad guy', Sonnenschein, who, unable to decide between Latin and Old English, allowed modern English *teach* to be described as either taking a dative and an accusative, because that was the pattern for Old English *tæcan,* or as taking two accusatives, in the manner of Latin *doceo* and German *lehren* (Jespersen, 1924, p. 175).

Looking for one man's case system in another man's language is not, of course, a good example of the study of case. The approaches to the study of case that do need to be taken seriously are of several varieties. Many traditional studies have examined, in somewhat semantic terms, the various *uses* of case. More recent work has been directed toward the analysis of the case *systems* of given languages, under the assumptions suggested by the word 'system'. A great deal of research, early and late, has been devoted to an understanding of the *history* or *evolution* of case notions or of case morphemes. And lastly, the generative grammarians have for the most part viewed case markers as surface structure reflexes, introduced by rules, of various kinds of deep and surface syntactic relations.

1.1 Case Uses

The standard handbooks of Greek and Latin typically devote much of their bulk to the classification and illustration of semantically different relationships representable by given case forms. The subheadings of these classifications are most commonly of the form 'X of Y', where 'X' is the name of a particular case and 'Y' is the name for a particular 'use' of X. The reader will recall such terms as 'dative of separation', 'dative of possession', and so on.[5]

Apart from the fact that such studies do not start out from the point of view of the centrality of syntax, the major defects of these studies were (a) that the nominative was largely ignored and (b) that classificatory criteria which ought to have been kept distinct were often confused.

The neglect of the nominative in studies of case uses probably has several sources, one being the etymological meaning ('deviation') of the Greek term for case, *ptôsis,* which predisposed grammarians to limit the term only to the nonnominative cases. The most important reason for omitting the nominative in these studies, however, is the wrongly assumed clarity of the concept 'subject of the sentence'. Müller published a study of nominative and accusative case uses in Latin, in 1908, in which he devoted 170 or so pages to the accusative and somewhat less than *one* page to the nominative, explaining (1908, p. 1) that *'die beiden casus recti, der Nominativ und der Vokativ, sind bei dem Streite über die Kasustheorie nicht beteiligt. Im Nominativ steht das Subjekt, von dem der Satz etwas aussagt'.*

The role of the subject was so clear to Sweet that he claimed that the nominative was the only case where one could speak properly of a 'noun'. He viewed a sentence as a kind of predication on a given noun, and every nounlike element in a sentence other than the subject as a kind of derived adverb, a part of the predication.[6]

On a little reflection, however, it becomes obvious that semantic differences in the relationships between subjects and verbs are of exactly the same order and exhibit the same extent of variety as can be found for the other case. There is in principle no reason why the traditional studies of case uses fail to contain such classifications as 'nominative of personal agent', 'nominative of patient', 'nominative of beneficiary', 'nominative of affected person', and 'nominative of interested person' (or, possibly, 'ethical nominative') for such sentences as 8 to 12, respectively.

    8. He hit the ball.
    9. He received a blow.
    10. He received a gift.
    11. He loves her.
    12. He has black hair.

[5] For an extensive description of this type, see Bennett (1914).
[6] Quoted in Jespersen (1924, p. 107).

The confusion of criteria in treatments of the uses of cases has been documented by de Groot (1956) in his study of the Latin genitive. Uses of cases are classified on syntactic grounds, as illustrated by the division of uses of the genitive according to whether the genitive noun is in construction with a noun, an adjective, or a verb; on historical grounds, as when the uses of the syncretistic Latin ablative case are divided into three classes, separative, locative, and instrumental; and on semantic grounds, in which there is a great deal of confusion between meanings that can properly be thought of as associated with the case forms of nouns, on the one hand, and meanings that properly reside in neighboring words.

De Groot's critical treatment of the traditional classification of Latin genitive case uses is particularly interesting from the point of view taken here, because in his 'simplification' of the picture he rejects as irrelevant certain phenomena which generative grammarians would insist definitely *are* of syntactic importance. He claims, for example, that the traditional studies confuse difference of *referents* with differences of case uses. Thus, to de Groot the traditional three senses of *statua Myronis* (the statue possessed by Myro—*genitivus possessivus;* statue sculpted by Myro—*genitivus subjectivus;* statue depicting Myro—genitive of represented subject), as well as the subjective and objective senses of *amor patris,* are differences in practical, not in linguistic, facts. From arguments such as this he is able to combine twelve of the classical 'uses' into one, which he then labels the 'proper genitive', asserting (1956, p. 35) that 'the proper genitive denotes, and consequently can be used to refer to, *any* thing-to-thing relation'. He ends by reducing the thirty traditional 'uses of the genitive' to eight,[7] of which two are rare enough to be left out of consideration, and a third, 'genitive of locality', is really limited to specific place names.

Benveniste (1962) replied to de Groot's analysis in the issue of *Lingua* that was dedicated to de Groot. There he proposes still further simplifi-

---

[7] From de Groot (1956, p. 30):

    I. adjunct to a noun
        A. proper genitive, *eloquentia hominis*
        B. genitive of quality, *homo magnae eloquentiae*
    II. adjunct to a substantival
        C. genitive of the set of persons, *reliqui peditum*
   III. conjunct ('complement') of a copula
        D. genitive of the type of person, *sapientis est aperte odisse*
    IV. adjunct to a verb
        E. genitive of purpose, *Aegyptum profiscitue cognoscende antiquitatis*
        F. genitive of locality, *Romae consules creabantur*
   IVa. adjunct to a present participle
        G. genitive with a present participle, *laboris fugiens*
    V. genitive of exclamation, *mercimoni lepidi*

cations of the classification. Noting that de Groot's 'genitive of locality' applies only to proper place names, that is, that it occurs only with place names having -*o*- and -*ā*- stems, in complementary distribution with the ablative, Benveniste wisely suggests that this is something that should be catalogued as a fact about place names, not as a fact about uses of the genitive case. Benveniste's conclusions on the remaining genitive constructions is quite congenial to the generative grammarian's position. He proposes that the so-called proper genitive basically results from the process of converting a sentence into a nominal. The distinction of meaning between 'genitivus subjectivus' and 'genitivus objectivus' constructions merely reflects the difference between situations in which the genitive noun is an original subject and those where it is an original object, the genitive representing a kind of neutralization of the nominative/accusative distinction found in the underlying sentences.[8]

At least from the two mentioned studies of uses of the Latin genitive, it would appear (*a*) that some case uses are purely irregular, requiring as their explanation a statement of the idiosyncratic grammatical requirements of specific lexical items, and (*b*) that some semantic differences are accounted for independently of assigning 'meanings' to cases, either by recognizing meaning differences in 'governing' words or by noting meaning differences in different underlying sentences. The suggestion that one can find clear special meanings associated with surface cases fails to receive strong support from these studies.

1.2   Case Systems

There are reasonable objections to approaching the case system of one language from the point of view of the surface case system of another (for example, Classical Latin) by merely checking off the ways in which a given case relation in the chosen standard is given expression in the language under observation. An acceptable alternative, apparently, is the inverse of this process: one identifies case morphemes in the new language within the system of noun inflection and then relates each of these to traditional or 'standard' case notions. To take just one recent example, Redden (1966) finds five case indices in Walapai (four suffixes and zero) and identifies each of these with terms taken from the tradition

---

[8] It must be said, however, that Benveniste's desentential interpretation is diachronic rather than synchronic, for he goes on to explain that it is on analogy from these basic verbal sources that new genitive relations are created. From *ludus pueri* and *risus pueri*, where the relation to *ludit* and *ridet* is fairly transparent, the pattern was extended to include *somnus pueri*, *mos pueri*, and finally *liber pueri*. The generative grammarian may be inclined to seek synchronic verbal connections—possibly through positing abstract entities never realized as verbs—for these other genitives too. (See Benveniste, 1962, p. 17.)

of case studies: -*č* is nominative, -*Ø* is accusative, -*k* is allative/adessive, -*l* is illative/inessive, and -*m* is ablative/abessive. Under each of these headings the author adds information about those uses of each case form that may not be deducible from the labels themselves. Nominative, for example, occurs only once in a simple sentence—coordinate conjunction of subject nouns requires use of the -*m* suffix on all the extra nouns introduced; accusative is used with some noun tokens which would not be considered direct objects in English; allative/adessive has a partitive function; and ablative/abessive combines ablative, instrumental, and comitative functions.

In a study of this type, since what is at hand is the surface structure of the inflection system of Walapai nouns, the descriptive task is to identify the surface case forms that are distinct from each other in the language and to associate 'case functions' with each of these. What needs to be emphasized is (*a*) that such a study does not present directly available answers to such questions as 'How is the indirect object expressed in this language?' (for example, the system of possible case functions is not called on to provide a descriptive framework), and (*b*) that the functions or uses themselves are not taken as primary terms in the description (for example, the various 'functions' of the 'ablative/abessive' suffix -*m* are not interpreted as giving evidence that several distinct cases merely happen to be homophonous).[9]

One approach to the study of case systems, then, is to restrict oneself to a morphological description of nouns and to impose no constraints on the ways in which the case morphemes can be identified with their meanings or functions. This is distinct from studies of case systems which attempt to find a unified meaning for each case. An example of the latter approach is found in the now discredited 'localistic' view of the cases in Indo-European, by which dative is 'the case of rest', accusative 'the case of movement to', and genitive 'the case of movement from'.[10] And recent attempts to capture single comprehensive 'meanings' of the cases have suffered from the vagueness and circularity expected of any attempt to find semantic characterizations of surface-structure phenomena.[11]

---

[9] These remarks are not intended to be critical of Redden's study. Indeed, in the absence of a universal theory of case relationships there is no theoretically justified alternative to this approach.

[10] This interpretation, discussed briefly in Jespersen (1924, p. 186), appears to date back to the Byzantine grammarian Maxime Planude.

[11] As an illustration of this last point, take Gonda's claim (1962, p. 147) that the Vedic dative is called for whenever a noun is used to refer to the 'object in view'. The vacuity of this statement is seen in his interpretation of

    vātāya kapilā vidyut (Patanjali)
     'a reddish lightning signifies wind'

as 'the lightning has, so to say, *wind in view*'.

The well-known studies of Hjelmslev (1935, 1937) and Jakobson (1936) are attempts not only to uncover unified meanings of each of the cases, but also to show that these meanings themselves form a coherent system by their decomposability into distinctive oppositions. The possibility of vagueness is, of course, increased inasmuch as the number of oppositions is less than the number of cases.[12]

The difficulties in discovering a unified meaning for each of the cases in a case system have led to the alternative view that *all but one* of the cases can be given more or less specific meanings, the meaning of the residual case being left open. This residual case can either have whatever relation to the rest of the sentence is required by the meanings of the neighboring words, or it can serve any purely caselike function not pre-empted by the other cases. Bennett tells us that Goedicke explained the accusative as 'the case used for those functions not fulfilled by the other cases'. The fact that Bennett, following Whitney, ridiculed this view on the grounds that *any* case could be so described suggests that Goedicke's remark must not have been very clearly expressed.[13] A different approach is taken by Diver (1964), who assigns the 'leftover' function not to a particular case as such, but to whatever case or cases are not required for a given realization of what he calls the 'agency system'. Briefly, and ignoring his treatment of passive sentences, Diver's analysis is this: A verb can have one, two, or three nouns (or noun phrases) associated with it, corresponding generally to the intransitive, normal transitive, and transitive indirect object sentence types, respectively. In a three-noun sentence, the nouns are nominative, dative, and accusative, the nominative being the case of the agent and the accusative the case of the patient; the dative, the 'residue' case, is capable of expressing any notion compatible with the meaning of the remainder of the sentence. The function of the dative in a three-noun sentence, in other words, is 'deduced' from the context; it is not present as one of a number of possible 'meanings' of the dative case.[14] In two-noun sentences, one of the nouns is nominative and the other either dative or accusative, but typically accusative. The nominative here is the case of the agent, but this time

---

[12] See, in this regard, the brief critical remarks of A. H. Kuipers (1962, p. 231).

[13] Bennett (1914, p. 195, fn. 1). I have not yet had access to the Goedicke original.

[14] The following is from Diver, 1964, p. 181:

> In the sentence *senatus imperium mihi dedit* 'the senate gave me supreme power', the Nominative, with the syntactic meaning of Agent, indicates the giver; the Accusative, with the syntactic meaning of Patient, indicates the gift. The question is: Does the Dative itself indicate the recipient or merely that the attached word is neither the giver nor the gift?

> Diver makes the latter choice. In particular, he states that 'knowing that *mihi*, in the Dative, can be neither the Agent (the giver) nor the Patient (the gift), we deduce that it is the recipient'.

the accusative (or the dative, whichever occurs) is the residue case. In a two-noun sentence, in other words, the accusative is not limited to the meaning of patient; it can express any number of other meanings as well. And, since it no longer contrasts with dative, it can be replaced by a dative. The choice between dative and accusative in two-noun sentences, since it is not semantically relevant, is subject to random kinds of free and conditioned variation.

Carrying the argument through, the noun found in a one-noun sentence can express any meaning relationship with the verb. The noun, though most frequently nominative, may be accusative or dative, but the choice is not based on meanings associated with these cases. When the noun is nominative its 'syntactic meaning' may be that of agent, patient, or anything else.

The inadequacy of Diver's treatment is clear. In the first place, it seems unlikely that, as used in his paper, the notions agent and patient are in any sense satisfactory semantic primitives. To agree that *imperium* in *senatus imperium mihi dedit* is the patient is nothing more than to agree to say the word 'patient' on seeing an accusative form in a three-noun sentence. For many of Diver's examples, his argument would have been every bit as convincing if he had said that an unvarying function is performed by the dative, but the role of the accusative depends on such matters as the lexical meaning of the verb. Furthermore, the 'couple of dozen verbs' which appear in two-noun sentences and which exhibit some kind of semantic correlation involving the supposedly non-significant choice of accusative or dative should probably not be set aside as unimportant exceptions.

Diver's proposal may be thought of as an attempt to identify the semantic contribution of cases seen as syntagmatically identified entities, while the positing of distinctive oppositions, in the manner of Hjelmslev and Jakobson, is an attempt to see the functioning of cases from the point of view of the concept of paradigmatic contrast. The latter view has been criticized by Kuryłowicz (1960, pp. 134, 141). The apparent contrast seen in Polish and Russian between accusative and genitive (partitive) direct object, as between 13 and 14

13. *Daj nam chleb*. 'Give us the bread!'
14. *Daj nam chleba*. 'Give us some bread!'

is not a difference in the syntactic function of the object nouns relative to the verb, but is rather a difference which falls into that area of syntax that deals with the effect of the choice of article, in languages having articles, on the semantic content of the associated noun. The fact that in Russian the difference is reflected as a difference in noun inflection does

not alone determine its character as a part of the case system proper of
the language.

The vertical contrast between locative and accusative nouns after
locative/directional prepositions, as in 15 and 16

    15. *On prygajet na stole.* 'He jumps (up and down) on the table.'
    16. *On prygajet na stol.* 'He jumps onto the table.'

is a difference that would be discussed in transformational grammar terms
as involving a distinction between prepositional phrases which are inside
and those which are outside the verb phrase constituent. That is, a
locative prepositional phrase which occurs outside the constituent VP is
one which indicates the place where the action described by the VP
takes place. A locative prepositional phrase inside the VP is a complement
to the verb. Inside a VP the difference between the locative and directional senses is entirely dependent on the associated verb; outside the
VP the sense is always locative.

Kuryłowicz discussed 15 and 16 in essentially the same terms. To him
the directional phrase *na stol* is 'more central' to the verb than the
locative phrase *na stole.* An apparent contrast appears just in case the
same verb may appear sometimes with and sometimes without a locative
(or directional) complement. There is thus no genuine paradigmatic contrast in such pairs as 13–14 or 15–16.

Kuryłowicz's own approach to the study of case systems brings another order of grammatical fact into consideration: sentence relatedness.
Cases, in his view, form a network of relationships mediated by such
grammatical processes as the passive transformation. The distinction between nominative and accusative, for example, is a reflection in the case
system of the more basic distinction between passive and active sentences. In his terms, *hostis occiditur* becomes the predicate *hostem
occidit,* the primary change from *occiditur* to *occidit* bringing with it
the concomitant change from *hostis* to *hostem.*

Nominalizations of sentences have the effect of relating both accusative and nominative to the genitive, for the former two are neutral-
ized under conversion to genitive, as illustrated by the change from
plebs secedit to *secessio plebis* (*genitivus subjectivus*) as opposed to the
change from *hostem occidere* to *occisio hostis* (*genitivus objectivus*).

The relationship between nominative and accusative, then, is a reflex of diathesis; the relationship of these two to genitive is mediated
through the process of constructing deverbal nouns. The remaining cases
—dative, ablative, instrumental, and locative—enter the network of relationships in that, secondarily to their functions as adverbials, they
each provide variants of the accusative with certain verbs. That is, there

are verbs that 'govern' the ablative (for example, *utor*), rather than the accusative for their 'direct objects'.[15]

1.3 Case Histories

In addition to studies of case uses and interpretations of the cases in a given language as elements of a coherent system, the literature also contains many historical studies of cases; and these, too, are of various kinds. Some workers have sought to discover the original meanings of the cases of a language or family of languages, while others have sought to trace case morphemes back to other kinds of morphemes—either syntactic function words or some kind of derivational morphemes. Still others have seen in the history of one case system a case system of a different type—with or without assumptions concerning the 'essential primitivity' of the earlier type.

A very common assumption among linguistic historians has been that case affixes are traceable back to noncase notions. The form which eventually became the Indo-European case ending representing nominative singular masculine, that is, *-s*, has been interpreted as the demonstrative **so* which had been converted into a suffix indicating a definite subject; and the **so* in turn is believed by some to have originated as a Proto-Indo-Hittite sentence connective (Lane, 1951). The same form has also been interpreted as a derivational morpheme indicating a specific individual directly involved in an activity, contrasting with a different derivational affix **-m* indicating a nonactive object or the product of an action.[16] Scholars who can rest with the latter view are those who do not require of themselves the belief that 'synthetic' languages necessarily have antecedent 'analytic' stages.[17]

---

[15] Kuryłowicz (1960, pp. 138–139, 144–147, 150). Also see Kuryłowicz (1964, pp. 179–181). Somewhat similar interpretations of the connections between case and diathesis are found in Heger (1966).

[16] See, for example, the statement in Lehmann, 1958, p. 190.

[17] The impression is sometimes given that the identification of the etymon of a case affix brings with it an account of the intellectual evolution of the speakers of the language in question. If the interpretation of **-m* and **-s* as derivational morphemes is correct, it does not follow that one has discovered, in the transition from the earliest function of these elements to their later clear caselike uses, any kind of 'abstraction' process or tendency to pass from 'concrete' to 'relational' modes of thought. Our methods of reconstruction should certainly make it possible to detect basic (that is, deep-structure) linguistic evolution if it is there to discover, but the etymology of surface-structure morphemes should not lead to assumptions about deep typological differences. What I mean is that the underlying case structures of Proto-Indo-European may have been just as precisely organized as those of any of the daughter languages, and that the changes that have occurred may have been entirely a matter of morphophonemic detail. From the preponderance of (derived) active nouns in subject position, one generation may have 'reinterpreted' the suffix as a marker of human subject and

A second kind of speculation on historical changes within case systems traces case systems of one kind back to case systems of another kind. Of particular interest here is the suggestion that the Indo-European case systems point back to an original 'ergative' system. Case typologies will be discussed in slightly greater detail below, but briefly we can characterize an 'ergative' system as one which assigns one case (the ergative) to the subject of a transitive verb and another to both the subject of an intransitive verb and the object of a transitive verb. An 'accusative' system, on the other hand, is one which assigns one case to the subject of either transitive or intransitive verbs and another (the accusative) to the object of a transitive verb. A common feature of ergative systems is that the 'genitive' form is the same as the ergative (or, put differently, that the ergative case has a 'genitive' function).

The connection of Indo-European *-s with animateness (the subject of a transitive verb is typically animate), the original identity of the nominative singular *-s with the genitive ending, and the identity of the neuter ending *-m with the masculine accusative form have led many investigators to the conclusion that our linguistic ancestors were speakers of an 'ergative' language.[18] It will be suggested below that, if such a change has taken place, it is a change which involves the notion 'subject'.

1.4   Case in Current
Generative Grammar

A hitherto largely unquestioned assumption about case in the writings of generative grammarians has been made explicit by Lyons (1966, p. 218): ' "case" (in the languages in which the category is to be found) is not present in "deep structure" at all, but is merely the inflexional "realization" of particular syntactic relationships'. The syntactic relationships in question may in fact be relationships that are defined only in the surface structure, as when the surface subject of a sentence (destined to assume, say, a 'nominative' form) has appeared as the result of the application of the passive transformation, or when the 'genitive' marker is

---

a later generation may have reinterpreted it as merely a marker for the subjectival use of a particular set of words—to state the possibilities in the most simple-minded way. The change, in short, may well have been entirely in the economies of bringing to the surface underlying structural features which themselves underwent no change whatever.

[18] See particularly Uhlenbeck (1901), where the *-m ending was identified as a subject marker and the *-s as the agent marker in passive sentences (a common interpretation of 'ergative' systems), and Vaillant (1936). Lehmann (1958, p. 190) finds the arguments unconvincing, noting for example that evidence of an 'ergative' ending cannot be found in plural nouns or in ā stem feminines.

introduced as an accompaniment to a nominalization transformation. One of Chomsky's few remarks on case occurs in a discussion of the peripheral nature of stylistic inversions; although case forms are assigned to English pronouns relatively late in the grammar, determined largely by surface-structure position, the stylistic inversion rules are later still. In this way it becomes possible to account for such forms as *him I like;* the shift of *him* to the front of the sentence must follow the assignment of case forms to the pronouns (see Chomsky, 1965, pp. 221 f.).

It seems to me that the discussion of case could be seen in a somewhat better perspective if the assignment of case forms were viewed as exactly analogous to the rules for assigning prepositions in English, or postpositions in Japanese.[19] There are languages which use case forms quite extensively, and the assumption that the case forms of nouns can be assigned in straightforward ways on the basis of simply defined syntactic relations seems to be based too much on the situation with English pronouns.

Prepositions in English—or the absence of a preposition before a noun phrase, which may be treated as corresponding to a zero or unmarked case affix—are selected on the basis of several types of structural features, and in ways that are exactly analogous to those which determine particular case forms in a language like Latin: identity as (surface) subject or object, occurrence after particular verbs, occurrence in construction with particular nouns, occurrence in particular constructions, and so on. The only difficulties in thinking of these two processes as analogous are that even the most elaborate case languages may also have combinations of, say, prepositions with case forms, and that some prepositions have independent semantic content. The first of these difficulties disappears if, after accepting the fact that the conditions for choosing prepositions are basically of the same type as those for choosing case forms, we merely agree that the determining conditions may simultaneously determine a preposition *and* a case form. The second difficulty means merely that a correct account will allow certain options in the choice of prepositions in some contexts, and that these choices have semantic consequences. Analogous devices are provided by the 'true' case languages, too, for example by having alternative case choices in otherwise identical constructions, or by having semantically functioning prepositions or postpositions.

The syntactic relations that are involved in the selection of case

---

[19] The suggestion is of course not novel. According to Hjelmslev, the first scholar to show a connection between prepositions and cases was A.-F. Bernhardi, in *Anfangsgrunde der Sprachwissenschaft* (Berlin, 1805); see Hjelmslev, 1935, p. 24.

forms (prepositions, affixes, and so forth) are, in practice, of two types, and we may call these 'pure' or 'configurational' relations, on the one hand, and 'labeled' or 'mediated' relations on the other hand.[20] 'Pure' relations are relations between grammatical constituents expressible in terms of (immediate) domination. Thus, the notion 'subject' can be identified as the relation between an NP and an immediately dominating S, while the notion 'direct object' can be equated with the relation that holds between an NP and an immediately dominating VP. Where the relation 'subject of' is understood to hold between elements of the deep structure, one speaks of the deep-structure subject; where it is understood to hold between elements of the (prestylistic) surface structure, one speaks of the surface-structure subject. This distinction appears to correspond to the traditional one between 'logical subject' and 'grammatical subject'.

By 'labeled' relation I mean the relation of an NP to a sentence, or to a VP, which is mediated by a pseudocategory label such as Manner, Extent, Location, Agent.

It is clear that if all transformations which create surface subjects have the effect of attaching an NP directly to an S, under conditions which guarantee that no other NP is also directly subjoined to the same S, and if it always turns out that only one NP is subjoined to a VP in the prestylistic surface structure, then these two 'pure' relations are exactly what determine the most typical occurrences of the case categories 'nominative' and 'accusative' in languages of a certain type. For remaining case forms, the determination is either on the basis of idiosyncratic properties of specific governing words, or on the basis of a 'labeled' relation, as when the choice of *by* is determined by reference to the dominating category Extent in the extent phrase of sentences like 17.

[20] The distinction would be more accurately represented by the opposition 'relations' versus 'categories', because when a phrase-structure rule introduces a symbol like Manner or Extent—symbols which dominate manner adverbials and extent phrases—these symbols function, as far as the rest of the grammar is concerned, in exactly the same ways as such 'intentional' category symbols as S or NP. This fact has much more to do with the requirements of the phrase-structure model than with the 'categorial' character of the grammatical concepts involved. In an earlier paper I discussed the impossibility of capturing, in a base component of a grammar of the type presented in Chomsky (1965), both such information that *in a clumsy way* is a manner adverbial (and as such represents an instance of highly constrained lexical selection as well as a quite specific positional and co-occurrence potential which it shares with other manner adverbials) and that it is a prepositional phrase. See Fillmore (1966a).

The *intention* on the part of grammarians who have introduced such terms as Loc, Temp, Extent, and the like into their rules is to let these terms represent relations between the phrases they dominate and some other element of the sentence (that is, the VP as a whole); nobody, as far as I can tell, has actually wished these terms to be considered as representing distinct types of grammatical categories on the order of NP or preposition phrase.

17. He missed the target by two miles.

In my earlier paper (Fillmore, 1966) I pointed out that no semantically constant value is associated with the notion 'subject of' (unless it is possible to make sense of the expression 'the thing being talked
about', and, if that can be done, to determine whether such a concept
has any connection with the relation 'subject'), and that no semantically
relevant relations reside in the surface subject relation which are not
somewhere also expressible by 'labeled' relations. The conclusion I have
drawn from this is that all semantically relevant syntactic relations between NP's and the structures which contain them must be of the
'labeled' type. The consequences of this decision include (a) the elimi-
nation of the category VP, and (b) the addition to some grammars of a
rule, or system of rules, for creating 'subjects'. The relation 'subject', in
other words, is now seen as exclusively a surface-structure phenomenon.

2. Some Preliminary Conclusions

I have suggested that there are reasons for questioning the deep-
structure validity of the traditional division between subject and predicate, a division which is assumed by some to underlie the basic form of
all sentences in all languages. The position I take seems to be in agreement with that of Tesnière (1959, pp. 103–105) who holds that the
subject/predicate division is an importation into linguistic theory from
formal logic of a concept which is not supported by the facts of language
and, furthermore, that the division actually obscures the many structural
parallels between 'subjects' and 'objects'. The kinds of observations that
some scholars have made about surface differences between 'predicative'
and 'determinative syntagms' [21] may be accepted without in any way
believing that the subject/predicate division plays a part in the *deep-
structure* syntactic relations among the constituents of sentences.

Once we have interpreted 'subject' as an aspect of the surface structure, claims about 'subjectless' sentences in languages which have superficial subjects in some sentences, or reports about languages which appear
to lack entirely entities corresponding to the 'subjects' of our grammatical
tradition, no longer need to be regarded as particularly disturbing. Unfortunately, there are both good and bad reasons for asserting that par-

---

[21] See, for example, Bazell (1949, esp. p. 8), where the difference is expressed in such
terms as 'degrees of cohesion', 'liaison features' found within the predicate but not
between subject and predicate.

ticular languages or particular sentences are 'subjectless', and it may be necessary to make clear just what I am claiming. A distinction must be drawn between *not having* a constituent which could properly be called 'subject', on the one hand, and *losing* such a constituent by anaphoric deletion, on the other hand.[22] Robins (1961), in his review of Tesnière (1959), accuses Tesnière of failing to isolate the subject from the rest of the sentence. To Robins, Tesnière's decision to allow the subject to be treated as merely a complement to the verb must be related to the fact that the subject is omissible in such languages as Latin. If it is true that the *omissibility* of subjects is what convinced Tesnière that they are subordinated to verbs, and if the nonomissibility in any language of the subject constituent would have persuaded him that there *is* a special status for 'subject' vis-à-vis 'predicate' in the underlying structure of sentences in all languages, then that, it seems to me, is a bad reason for coming up with what might be a correct analysis.

It seems best to have a place in linguistic theory for the operation of anaphoric processes, processes which have the effect of shortening, simplifying, de-stressing sentences which are partly identical to their neighbors (or which are partly 'understood'). It happens that English anaphoric processes make use of pronominalization, stress reduction, and also deletion, under conditions where other languages might get along exclusively with deletion.[23] Under some conditions, in languages of the latter type, the deleted element happens to be the 'subject'. The non-occurrence of subject nouns in some utterances in some languages is *not* by itself, in other words, a good argument against the universality of the subject/predicate division. There are better ones. Some of these have already been suggested, others are to appear shortly.

[22] The tagmemicists in particular, because of their notation for 'optional' constituents, have had to come to grips with this distinction. A 'tagmemic formula' may be thought of as an attempt to present in a single statement a quasi-generative rule for producing a set of related sentences *and* the surface structure (short of free variation in word order) of these sentences. If the formulas for transitive and intransitive clauses are expressed as i and ii respectively:

    i. $\pm$ Subj + Pred $\pm$ Obj $\pm$ Loc $\pm$ Time
    ii. $\pm$ Subj + Pred $\pm$ Loc $\pm$ Time

it is clear (*a*) that any clause containing just a Pred can satisfy either of these formulas, and (*b*) that the potential appearance of such constituents as Loc and Time is less relevant to the description of these clauses than is that of the constituent Obj. Pike draws a distinction, which cross-cuts the optional/obligatory distinction, between 'diagnostic' and 'nondiagnostic' elements of clauses; see, for example, Pike (1966, esp. Chapter 1, Clauses). Grimes, on the other hand, seems to suggest introducing the 'diagnostic' constituents obligatorily, allowing for their deletion under certain contextual or anaphoric conditions. See Grimes (1964, esp. p. 16 f.).

[23] For an extremely informative description of these processes in English, see Gleitman (1965) and Harris (1957, esp. Section 16).

By distinguishing between surface- and deep-structure case relation-ships, by interpreting the 'subject' and 'object' as aspects of the surface structure, and by viewing the specific phonetic shapes of nouns in actual utterances as determinable by many factors that are vastly variable in space and time, we have eliminated reasons for being surprised at the noncomparability of (surface) case systems. We find it partly possible to agree with Bennett when, after surveying a few representative nineteenth century case theories, he stated (1914, p. 3) that they erred in sharing the 'doubtful assumption . . . that all the cases must belong to a single scheme, as though parts of some consistent institution'. We need not fol-low him, however, in concluding that the only valid type of research into the cases is an inquiry into the earliest value of each case.

Greenberg has remarked that cases themselves cannot be compared across languages—two case systems may have different numbers of cases, the names of the cases may conceal functional differences—but that *case uses* may be expected to be comparable. He predicts, for instance, that the uses of cases will be 'substantially similar in frequency but differently com-bined in different languages' (1966, p. 98; see also p. 80). Greenberg's rec-ommendations on the cross-linguistic study of case uses were presented in connection with the 'true' case languages, but it seems clear that if a 'dative of personal agent' in one language can be identified with an 'ablative of personal agent' in another language, then the 'personal agent' relationship between a noun and a verb ought also to be recognizable in the so-called caseless languages on exactly the same grounds. If, further-more, it turns out that other grammatical facts can be associated with sentences containing the personal agent relationship, it would appear that the concepts underlying the study of case uses may have a greater linguistic significance than those involved in the description of surface case systems. These additional facts might include the identification of a limited set of nouns and a limited set of verbs capable of entering into this relationship, and whatever additional generalizations prove to be statable in terms of this classification. Higher level dependencies may be discovered, such as the limitation of benefactive phrases to sentences con-taining a personal agent relationship in their deep structure.

The question should now be asked, of course, whether we are justified in using the term *case* for the kind of remote syntactic-semantic relations that are at issue. There is among many scholars a strong feeling that the term should be used only where clear case morphemes are discoverable in the inflection of nouns. To Jespersen, it is wrong to speak of 'analytic' cases, even when there is no 'local' meaning in the preposition phrases, because cases are one thing and preposition-plus-object constructions are another (1924, p. 186). Jespersen's position is colored a little by his belief that the caselessness of English represents a state of progress for which we ought to be grateful.[24]

Cassidy, in his 1937 appeal to rescue the word *case* from abuse, wrote (p. 244):' "Case" will be properly used and will continue to have some meaning only if the association with inflection be fully recognized, and if stretching of the term to include other sorts of "formal" distinction be abandoned.' In a similar vein, Lehmann (1958) chides Hirt for suggesting that an awareness of cases had to precede the development of case endings—that there was, in other words, 'among the speakers of pre-Indo-European and Proto-Indo-European a disposition for cases' (p. 185). Lehmann continues (p. 185): 'We can account for Hirt's statement by the assumption that to him a case was a notional category, whether or not it was exemplified in a form. To us a particular case is non-existent unless it is represented by forms which contrast in a system with others.' The claim that syntactic relations of various types must exist before case endings could be introduced to give them expression would surely have gone unchallenged; what was offensive, apparently, was the use of the word *case*.

It seems to me that if there are recognizable intrasentence relationships of the types discussed in studies of case systems (whether they are reflected in case affixes or not), that if these same relationships can be shown to be comparable across languages, and that if there is some predictive or explanatory use to which assumptions concerning the universality of these relations can be put, then surely there can be no meaningful objection to using the word *case*, in a clearly understood deep-structure sense, to identify these relationships. The dispute on the term *case* loses its force in a linguistics which accepts the centrality of syntax.[25]

---

[24] Jespersen (1924, p. 179):

> However far back we go, we nowhere find a case with only one well-defined function: in every language every case served different purposes, and the boundaries between these are far from being clear-cut. This, in connection with irregularities and inconsistencies in the formal elements characterizing the cases, serves to explain the numerous coalescences we witness in linguistic history ("syncretism") and the chaotic rules which even thus are to a great extent historically inexplicable. *If the English language has gone farther than the others in simplifying these rules, we should be devoutly grateful and not go out of our way to force it back into the disorder and complexity of centuries ago.* [Italics added.]

[25] The universality of case as a grammatical category is affirmed in Hjelmslev (1935, p. 1). In a recent study from a Jakobsonian point of view, Velten (1962) reveals enough of the historical continuity of 'synthetic' and 'analytic' cases to suggest that the linguist has no right to assign cases and prepositions to different 'chapters' of the study of grammar. The deep-structure notion of cases may be thought of as involving an extension of the synchronic concept of 'syncretism'. The usual synchronic sense of case syncretism assumes the form of a decision to posit a case contrast that may not be expressed overtly in most contexts as long as it appears overtly in 'one part of the system'. (See Newmark, 1962, p. 313.) Deep-structure cases may simply be

We may agree, then, for our present purposes, with Hjelmslev, who suggests that the study of cases can be pursued most fruitfully if we abandon the assumption that an essential characteristic of the grammatical category of case is *expression in the form of affixes on substantives*. I shall adopt the usage first proposed, as far as I can tell, by Blake (1930), of using the term *case* to identify the underlying syntactic-semantic relationship, and the term *case form* to mean the expression of a case relationship in a particular language—whether through affixation, suppletion, use of clitic particles, or constraints on word order.

3.   Case Grammar

The substantive modification to the theory of transformational grammar which I wish to propose amounts to a reintroduction of the 'conceptual framework' interpretation of case systems, but this time with a clear understanding of the difference between deep and surface structure. The sentence in its basic structure consists of a verb and one or more noun phrases, each associated with the verb in a particular case relationship. The 'explanatory' use of this framework resides in the necessary claim that, although there can be compound instances of a single case (through noun phrase conjunction), each case relationship occurs only once in a simple sentence.[26]

It is important to realize that the explanatory value of a universal system of deep-structure cases is of a syntactic and not (merely) a morphological nature. The various permitted arrays of distinct cases occurring in simple sentences express a notion of 'sentence type' that may be expected to have universal validity, independently of such superficial differences as subject selection. The arrays of cases defining the sentence types of a language have the effect of imposing a classification of the verbs in the language (according to the sentence type into which they may be inserted), and it is very likely that many aspects of this classification will be universally valid.

Case elements which are optionally associated with specific verbs,

---

nowhere overtly reflected as affixes or function words. The notion we are after probably corresponds to Meinhof's *Kasusbeziehungen*. (See Meinhof, 1938, p. 71.) The Meinhof reference, which I have not seen, was quoted in Frei (1954, fn. p. 31).

[26] It follows that whenever more than one case form appears in the surface structure of the same sentence (on different noun phrases), either more than one deep-structure case is involved or the sentence is complex. If, for example, German *lehren* is described as a verb which 'takes two accusatives', we have reason to believe that in the deep structure, the two object nouns are distinct as to case. Often enough the language will provide evidence for the distinction, as in the occurrence of such passive sentences as *das wurde mir gelehrt*.

together with the rules for forming subjects, will serve to explain various co-occurence restrictions. For example, in 18 the subject is in an Agent relation to the verb; in 19 the subject is an Instrument; and in 20 both Agent and Instrument appear in the same sentence, but in this case it is the Agent which appears as the subject, not the Instrument.

18. John broke the window.
19. A hammer broke the window.
20. John broke the window with a hammer.

That the subjects of 18 and 19 are grammatically different explains the fact that the combined meaning of the two sentences is not produced by conjoining their subjects. Thus 21 is unacceptable.

21. * John and a hammer broke the window.

Only noun phrases representing the same case may be conjoined. Similarly, the fact that only one representative of a given case relationship may appear in the same simple sentence, together with the generalizations on subject selection and the redundancies which hold between cases and lexical features (for example, between Agent and animateness), explains the unacceptability of Sentence 22.

22. * A hammer broke the glass with a chisel.

It is unacceptable, in particular, on the interpretation that both *hammer* and *chisel* are understood instrumentally. It cannot represent a sentence containing an Agent and an Instrument, since the noun *hammer* is inanimate.[27]

The dependency that can be accounted for by making these assumptions is that the subject of an active transitive sentence must be interpretable as a personal agent just in case the sentence contains a *with* phrase of instrumental import. Apparent exceptions to this generalization can be seen to have different underlying structures. Sentence 23 looks like an exception, but by attending to the effect of the word *its*, the essential difference between 23 and Sentences 22 and 24 becomes apparent.

---

[27] The author is aware that in Sentence 18 one might be talking about what John's body did as it was tossed through the window and that in Sentence 19 one might be speaking metaphorically, personifying *hammer*. Under either interpretation Sentence 21 turns out to be acceptable, and under the personification interpretation, Sentence 22 becomes acceptable. What is important to realize is that these interpretations, too, are explainable by reference to exactly the same assumptions appealed to in explaining their 'face value' interpretations.

23. The car broke the window with its fender.
24. * The car broke the window with a fender.

Sentence 24 violates the conditions that have been discussed, but Sentence 23 is a paraphrase of Sentence 25 and may be interpreted as having the same structure as 25.

25. The car's fender broke the window.

What is suggested here is that Sentences 23 and 25 are agentless sentences containing *a possessed noun* as the Instrument (*the car's fender*). The rules for choosing a subject allow an option in this case: either the entire instrument phrase may appear as the subject (as in 25), or the 'possessor' alone may be made the subject, the remainder of the instrument phrase appearing with the preposition *with* (as in 23). The second option requires that a 'trace' be left behind in the instrument phrase, in the form of the appropriate possessive pronoun. A similar explanation is suggested for such sentences as 26 and 27, which are also interpretable as deep structurally identical.

26. Your speech impressed us with its brevity.
27. The brevity of your speech impressed us.

The superficial nature of the notion 'subject of a sentence' is made apparent by these examples in a particularly persuasive way, because in the possessor-as-subject cases, the 'subject' is not even a major constituent of the sentence; it is taken from the modifier of one of the major constituents.

In the basic structure of sentences, then, we find what might be called the 'proposition', a tenseless set of relationships involving verbs and nouns (and embedded sentences, if there are any), separated from what might be called the 'modality' constituent. This latter will include such modalities on the sentence-as-a-whole as negation, tense, mood, and aspect.[28] The exact nature of the modality constituent may be ignored for our purposes. It is likely, however, that certain 'cases' will be directly related to the modality constituent as others are related to the proposition itself, as for example certain temporal adverbs.[29]

The first base rule, then, is 28, abbreviated to 28'.

[28] There are probably good reasons for regarding negation, tense, and mood as associated directly with the sentence as a whole, and the perfect and progressive 'aspects' as features on the V. See for a statement of this position Lyons (1966, pp. 218, 223).

[29] In my earlier paper I suggested that sentence adverbials in general are assigned to the modality constituent. I now believe that many sentence adverbs are introduced from superordinate sentences (by transformations of a type we may wish to call 'infrajections'). This possibility has long been clear for unmistakable sentence adverbs like *unfortunately*, but there are also quite convincing reasons for extending the infrajection interpretation to adverbs like *willingly, easily,* and *carefully.*

28. Sentence → Modality + Proposition

28′. S → M + P [30]

The P constituent is 'expanded' as a verb and one or more case categories. A later rule will automatically provide for each of the cases the categorial realization as NP (except for one which may be an embedded S). In effect the case relations are represented by means of dominating category symbols.

The expansion of P may be thought of as a list of formulas of the form seen in 29, where at least one case category must be chosen and where no case category appears more than once.

29. $P + V + C_1 + \cdots + C_n$

Whether these formulas can be collapsed according to the familiar abbreviatory conventions is not at present clear. For our purposes we may simply think of P as representable by any of a set of formulas including $V + A$, $V + O + A$, $V + D$, $V + O + I + A$, and so forth. (The letter symbols are interpreted below.)

The case notions comprise a set of universal, presumably innate, concepts which identify certain types of judgments human beings are capable of making about the events that are going on around them, judgments about such matters as who did it, who it happened to, and what got changed. The cases that appear to be needed include:

Agentive (A), the case of the typically animate perceived instigator of the action identified by the verb.[31]

Instrumental (I), the case of the inanimate force or object causally involved in the action or state identified by the verb.[32]

Dative (D), the case of the animate being affected by the state or action identified by the verb.

---

[30] The arrow notation is used throughout, but this should not be interpreted as meaning that the proposal for a case grammar requires an assumption of a left-to-right orientation of the constituent symbols of the rewriting rules.

[31] The escape qualification 'typically' expresses my awareness that contexts which I will say require agents are sometimes occupied by 'inanimate' nouns like *robot* or 'human institution' nouns like *nation*. Since I know of no way of dealing with these matters at the moment, I shall just assume for all agents that they are 'animate'.

[32] Paul Postal has reminded me of the existence of sentences like

i. I rapped him on the head with a snake.

The requirement that instrumental NP's are 'inanimate' is the requirement to interpret i as having in its underlying structure something equivalent to *with the body of a snake*. The fact that there are languages which would require mention of a stem meaning 'body' in this context may be considered as support for this position, and so may the unacceptability, pointed out by Lakoff, of sentences like ii:

ii. * John broke the window with himself. (See Lakoff, 1967.)

Factitive (F), the case of the object or being resulting from the action or state identified by the verb, or understood as a part of the meaning of the verb.

Locative (L), the case which identifies the location or spatial orientation of the state or action identified by the verb.

Objective (O), the semantically most neutral case, the case of anything representable by a noun whose role in the action or state identified by the verb is identified by the semantic interpretation of the verb itself; conceivably the concept should be limited to things which are affected by the action or state identified by the verb.[33] The term is not to be confused with the notion of direct object, nor with the name of the surface case synonymous with accusative.

Additional cases will surely be needed. Suggestions for adding to this list will appear in various places below.

It is important to notice that none of these cases can be interpreted as matched by the surface-structure relations, subject and object, in any particular language. Thus, *John* is A in 29 as much as in 30; *the key* is I in 31 as well as in 32 or 33; *John* is D in 34 as well as in 35 and 36; and *Chicago* is L in both 37 and 38.

29. John opened the door.
30. The door was opened by John.
31. The key opened the door.
32. John opened the door with the key.
33. John used the key to open the door.
34. John believed that he would win.
35. We persuaded John that he would win.
36. It was apparent to John that he would win.
37. Chicago is windy.
38. It is windy in Chicago.

The list of cases includes L, but nothing corresponding to what might be called directional. There is a certain amount of evidence, as was mentioned above, that locational and directional elements do not contrast but are superficial differences determined either by the constituent structure or by the character of the associated verb. An example provided by Hall (39) suggests, by the occurrence of the pro replacement word *there*, that *to the store* and *at the store* are variants of the same

[33] In Fillmore (1966a) the neutral case was unwisely and misleadingly labeled 'ergative'.

entity, determined by the movement or nonmovement character of the associated verb.[34]

39. She took him to the store and left him there.

I have stated that A and D are 'animate' participants in the activity of the associated verbs, and I have also suggested that verbs are selected according to the case environments the sentence provides—what I shall refer to as the 'case frame'. There are, then, the two problems of lexical selection, that of the nouns and that of the verbs. Those features of nouns required by a particular case are to be specified by obligatory rules of the type such as the following, which specifies that any N in an A or D phrase must contain the feature [+animate]. (Recall the qualification of Footnote 30.)

$$N \rightarrow [+\text{animate}]/^{A,D} [X \underline{\hspace{1cm}} Y]$$

To take care quite generally of lexical features associated with specific cases, we may appeal to a rule which associates with each noun a

---

[34] Hall (1965).

The putative contrast between locational and directional expressions as well as the distinction between 'optional' and 'obligatory' locative expressions, as exemplified in Hall's examples i and ii, seem to point to the difference between elements which are 'inside the VP' and elements which are 'outside the VP'.

    i. John keeps his car in the garage.
    ii. John washes his car in the garage.

In our terms this would be equivalent either to determining whether there is a difference between an L as a constituent of P and an L as a constituent of M, or whether there can be two L elements within P, distinguished in terms of degree of selectivity of verbs. The highly restricting L selects verbs like *keep, put,* and *leave,* but not *polish, wash,* and *build;* the weakly restricting L selects verbs like *polish, wash,* and *build,* but not *believe, know,* or *want.*

However this distinction is interpreted, the second or 'outer' L is in some respects similar in its 'selectional' properties to what might be called the *benefactive* case B. B, too, is involved in the selection of verbs in the sense that some verbs do not accept B modification (* 'He is tall for you'); but the restriction here may have more to do with *dependency relations between cases* than with dependencies directly connected with the verb. It appears, in fact, that those verbs which allow 'outer L' and B modification are precisely those which take agents. I have no ideas on how these dependencies can be stated, but it would appear that the second L and the B can appear only in sentences containing A's.

Thus the *regime direct* versus *regime indirect* interpretation of the difference between iii and iv

    iii. *Il demeure à Paris.*
    iv. *Il travaille à Paris.*

may have simply to do with the fact that the subject of iv is actually an A. Both the specific verb and the occurrence of an 'outer L' are determined by the presence of an A. See, in this connection, Bazell's discussion (1949, p. 10) of Gougenheim's review of de Boer's French syntax.

label identifying the case relation it holds with the rest of the sentence. Such a rule might associate with every noun under L the feature [+locative], for example. Since abstract nouns such as *idea* cannot serve as heads of L expressions, they will be marked [−locative].[35]

The insertion of verbs, on the other hand, depends on the particular array of cases, the 'case frame', provided by the sentence.[36] The verb *run,* for example, may be inserted into the frame [_____ A], the verb *sad* into the frame [_____ D], verbs like *remove* and *open* into [_____ O + A], verbs like *murder* and *terrorize* (that is, verbs requiring 'animate subject' and 'animate object') into [_____ D + A], verbs like *give* into [_____ O + D + A], and so on.

In lexical entries for verbs, abbreviated statements called 'frame features' will indicate the set of case frames into which the given verbs may be inserted. These frame features have the effect of imposing a classification of the verbs in the language. Such a classification is complex not only because of the variety of case environments possible within P, but also because many verbs are capable of occurring in more than one distinct case environment. This last fact can be represented most directly by allowing facultative representation of cases in the frame-feature expressions.

The word *open,* to take a familiar example, can occur in [_____ O], as in 40; in [_____ O + A], as in 41; in [_____ O + I], as in 42; and in [_____ O + I + A], as in 43.

40. The door opened.
41. John opened the door.
42. The wind opened the door.
43. John opened the door with a chisel.

The simplest representation of this set of possibilities makes use of parentheses to indicate the 'optional' elements. The frame feature for *open* may thus be represented as 44.

44. +[_____ O (I) (A)] [37]

---

[35] By allowing highly restricting lexical features to be associated with given case units we have returned to that extension of 'cases' to 'adverb forms' proposed by Bopp, Wüllner, and Hartung. Some adverbs, on this view, are really nouns capable of 'taking' only one case form. Since deep structure cases are in fact all 'defective' to some extent, with respect to the nouns which they accept, such a concept as *inflectional scope* no longer provides a clear demarcation between 'case forms proper' and 'adverbs'. See the discussion of this question in Hjelmslev (1935, p. 40).

[36] I am adhering, in this discussion, to the Postal-Lakoff doctrine, which I find thoroughly convincing, that adjectives constitute a subset of verbs.

[37] Case frames are represented in square brackets, with 'underline' indicating the position of the element with respect to which the expression is an environmental frame.

Other verbs having this same feature are *turn, move, rotate,* and *bend*.

For a verb like *kill* it is necessary to indicate, expressing it in familiar terms, that it takes an animate object and either an animate or an inanimate subject, and that if there is an animate subject, an instrument phrase may also co-occur. The frame feature for *kill*, in other words, will have to specify that either an Instrument or an Agent must be specified, and both may be specified. If the linked parentheses notation can be introduced to indicate that at least one of the linked elements must be chosen, the frame feature for *kill* can be given as 45.

45. $+[\underline{\hspace{1cm}} D\ (I{\backslash}A)]$

The verb *murder,* on the other hand, is one which requires an Agent. Its frame feature differs from that of 44 and 45 because the element A is obligatorily present. It is given as 46.

46. $+[\underline{\hspace{1cm}} D\ (I)\ A]$

The environmental subclassification of verbs is sensitive to more than the mere array of cases in *P*. Since one of the cases may be represented by *S* (an embedded sentence), verbs are also subclassified in terms of whether the O element is a sentence. By convention we shall interpret the symbol O in frame features as indicating NP's, and the symbol S as indicating an O to which an S has been embedded.

The frame feature $+[\underline{\hspace{1cm}} S]$ characterizes such verbs as *true, interesting,* and so forth; the feature $+[\underline{\hspace{1cm}} S + D]$ is common to such verbs as *want* and *expect;* verbs like *say, predict* and *cause* appear in the frame $[\underline{\hspace{1cm}} S + A]$; and verbs like *force* and *persuade* are insertable into the frame $[\underline{\hspace{1cm}} S + D + A]$.[38]

Verbs are distinguished from each other not only by specification of the case frames into which they can be inserted, but also by their transformational properties. The most important variables here include (*a*) the choice of a particular NP to become the surface subject, or the surface object, wherever these choices are not determined by a general rule; (*b*)

A frame feature is represented in square brackets with '+' or '—' in front, indicating that the set of case frames represented by the expression within the brackets is that which will (if the feature is marked '+') or which will not (if the feature is marked '—') accept the lexical item with which the feature is associated.

[38] It should be pointed out that descriptions of embedded sentences as *it + S* realizations of the category NP in 'subject/object' grammars must somehow guarantee that this particular expansion of NP is limited to the subjects of intransitive sentences and the objects (direct or oblique) of transitive sentences. All such restrictions are rendered unnecessary by the decision to limit complement S to the case element O.

the choice of prepositions to go with each case element, where these are determined by idiosyncratic properties of the verb rather than by a general rule; and (c) other special transformational features, such as, for verbs taking S complements, the choice of specific complementizers (*that, -ing, for to,* and so forth) and the later transformational treatment of these elements.

The use of parentheses in expressing the frame features, together with the transformational introduction of subjects, makes it possible to reduce the number of semantic descriptions in the lexicon. The semantic interpretation of a P will introduce all information provided by specific case relationships represented in the P, allowing such information to be omitted from the semantic descriptions of verbs. In the case of verbs having the feature 44, as we have seen, certain related transitive and intransitive verbs need not be given separate semantic description. This point may be further demonstrated with the English verb *cook*. The frame feature of *cook* is presumably something like 47

47. $+[\underline{\qquad} \text{ O (A)}]$

and an idiosyncratic transformational feature of the verb is that just in case the A is present and the O is some NP representing a typical NP for the verb (that is, something like *food* or *a meal*), the O element may be deleted. The semantic description of the verb will do no more than identify a particular activity having a result of a particular kind on the object identified by the O element. The same semantic entry, in other words, will account for the use of *cook* in all of the sentences 48–50.

48. Mother is cooking the potatoes.
49. The potatoes are cooking.
50. Mother is cooking.

Instead of saying that the verb has three different meanings, we can be satisfied to say that there is a certain variety in the case frames which accept it, and that it is one of the 'deletable object' verbs. The fact that A is obligatorily animate and that O is unspecified for animateness accounts for the fact that if we can read Sentence 49 as ambiguous, it is because we can accept certain violations of grammatical requirements in 'personifications' of the type we have learned in nursery school, whereas if we accept 50 as in fact ambiguous, it is because we are acquainted with the range of activities found in human societies.

The example with *cook* shows that the lexicon need not contain as many semantic entry *tokens* under the present proposal as it would in a subject/object grammar.[39] It will now be shown that this same flexibility makes it possible to reduce the number of semantic entry *types*, for now it is feasible to show that some syntactically different words are in fact semantically identical (with respect to that aspect of their meanings which is independent of the contribution of the associated cases). This may be true for verbs like *like* and *please*, to give the example that comes most quickly to mind. These words may be described as being synonymous. Each has the frame feature +[_____ O + D]; they differ only in their subject selection features. The verb *like*, in fact, has in its history the subject selection feature possessed by *please*.

The verb *show*, to give another kind of example, might well have the same semantic representation as *see*, differing from it only in that the frame feature for *show* contains an A where that for *see* does not. The verbs *kill* and *die* appear to be related in a similar way.

51. *see* (+[_____ O + D]) versus *show* (+[_____ O + D + A])
52. *die* (+[_____ D]) versus *kill* (+[_____ D (I)A]

We have seen, then, instances of synonymy where there are identical frame features but different subject selection features, and instances of synonymy where there are frame feature differences depending on whether a particular case category was present or absent. We may now turn to examples of synonymy where the difference is in the choice of one case or another.

It will be recalled that both A and D are animate. The semantic descriptions of certain verbs may refer to the animateness of the associated noun, independently of whether the 'source' of the animateness is A or D. That is, the semantic representation of certain verbs may specify a

[39] It may appear that facultative representation of cases in frame features has the advantages it does in English because there are so many verbs which can be used transitively or intransitively in the same form. It is a language-particular coincidence that English uses the same form in these words. The identification of transitive and intransitive *open*, or transitive and intransitive *cook*, is justified because the semantic characterization of the verb is the same in all of the uses discussed. (We must distinguish between the semantic characterization of a verb and the semantic interpretation of sentences containing the verb. In the latter case, all of the co-constituents and the semantic role they play as determined by their cases are taken into account.) Wherever that condition can be satisfied, facultative representation is called for. It will turn out that for some languages the occurrence or nonoccurrence of one of the 'optional' cases will have an effect on the verb. If, for verbs of the type [_____O (A)], the appearance of the A determines a variant of the verb different from that when A is missing (distinguishing the 'transitive' from the 'intransitive' use of the 'same' verb), or if the absence of the A requires some additive element (for example, a 'reflexive' morpheme) not needed when the A is expressed, these facts can be provided transformationally. See Hashimoto (1966). (By extending the range of acceptable surface variants of verbs under these conditions to suppletion, it may even be possible to interpret the contrasts exemplified in 51–53 below as surface lexical variation.)

relationship or a process associated with the necessarily animate participant in the state or activity identified by the verb. The relation of *hear* and *listen* to the necessarily animate NP is the same in both cases; the difference in the semantic interpretation of the P's containing them is determined by the semantic contribution of the associated cases and by the fact that the frames that contain *hear* are [_____ O + D] and those that contain *listen* are [_____ O + A]. The fact that in the case of *listen* the relationship is understood as involving the active participation of the person identified as A is due to the presence of A, not to a special meaning of *listen*. The same distinction can be seen between *see* and *know,* on the one hand, and *look* and *learn,* on the other.

53. *see, know* (+[_____ O + D]) versus *look, learn* (+[_____ O + A])

This latest point leads one to those properties of English verbs with which Lakoff (1966) associates the terms 'stative' and 'nonstative'. The question we need to ask is whether Lakoff's features are primitives in the lexical entries for verbs, or whether they permit reduction to concepts of the type I have been outlining. Lakoff has noticed that the 'true imperative', the progressive aspect, the occurrence of benefactive (B) phrases, and *do so* substitution occur only with 'nonstative' verbs. His discussion suggests that one must assign 'stative' and 'nonstative' as features on verbs and then guarantee that B phrases are permitted only with 'nonstatives' (put the other way around, one must guarantee that the presence of a B expression allows only for the selection of 'nonstatives'), that the imperative transformation can be applied only if the verb is 'nonstative', and so on. The treatment that I prefer is implicit in what I have already presented. The transformation which accounts for the 'true imperatives' can apply only to sentences containing A's, and the occurrence of B expressions (and 'outer L's') is dependent on the presence of an A. The progressive aspect can only be chosen in association with particular case frames, for example, those containing A's. No special features indicating stativity need be added to verbs because, if this suggestion is correct, only those verbs which occur in P's containing A's will show up in these sentences anyway.[40]

3.5 Surface Phenomena

To recapitulate, our discussion so far has suggested that the deep structure of (the propositional component of) every simple sentence is

[40] The *do-so* evidence is not so easy to interpret in this way. Still, the connection between 'nonstative' verbs and verbs that can 'take' A is too compelling to be simply wrong.

an array consisting of a V plus a number of NP's holding special labeled relations (cases) to the sentence. These relations, which are provided for categorially, include such concepts as Agentive, Instrumental, Objective, Factitive, Locative, Benefactive, and perhaps several others. Complex sentences involve recursion through the category Sentence under the case category Objective. Verbs are subclassified according to the case environments which accept them, and the semantic characterizations of verbs relate them either to specific case elements in the environment or to elements containing features (such as animateness) introduced as obligatory accompaniments of particular cases.

This section will deal with some of the ways in which deep structures of the type proposed in this essay are converted into surface representations of sentences. The various mechanisms involve selection of overt case forms (by suppletion, affixation, addition of prepositions or postpositions), 'registration' of particular elements in the verb, subjectivalization, objectivalization, sequential ordering, and nominalizations.

A surface case system may be related to the set of underlying cases in a variety of ways. Two deep cases may be represented in the same way in the surface structure, as when D and O direct objects are both represented with the 'accusative' case in many languages (where the determining factor may be occurrence immediately after the verb at some stage of derivation). A and D may be represented by the same overt form, where the determining factor may be case-linked animateness. Or the superficial form of a case element may be determined by an idiosyncratic property of some governing word.

The rules for English prepositions may look something like this: the A preposition is *by;* the I preposition is *by* if there is no A, otherwise it is *with;* the O and F prepositions are typically *zero;* the B preposition is *for;* the D preposition is typically *to;* the L and T (for time) prepositions are either semantically nonempty (in which case they are introduced as optional choices from the lexicon), or they are selected by the particular associated noun [*on the street, at the corner* (=intersection of two streets), *in the corner* (of a room); *on Monday, at noon, in the afternoon*]. Specific verbs may have associated with them certain requirements for preposition choice that are exceptions to the above generalization.[41]

The position of prepositions can be guaranteed either by having the

---

[41] The verb *blame,* for example, chooses ('governs') *for* for O and *on* for D. The O preposition is *at* for *look* meaning 'examine', *for* for *look* meaning 'seek', *to* for *listen,* and so forth. Changes in the original preposition assignment may be brought about by transformations: the rules which provide surface subjects and direct objects delete prepositions (replace them by zero), and the rules which form deverbal (= desentential) nominals convert some of the original case forms into 'genitive', either by replacing the assigned preposition with *of,* or, in some cases, by removing the original preposition and affixing the 'genitive' suffix.

case categories rewritten as *Prep + NP,* or by having *Prep* be one of the obligatory constituents of NP. I shall make the former choice, although the grounds for deciding one way or the other are not particularly clear. The 'universal' character of the base rules is kept intact by the assumption that prepositions, postpositions, and case affixes—semantically relevant or not—are all in fact realizations of the same underlying element, say *K* (for *Kasus*). We may regard all of the case categories as therefore rewritten as $K + NP$.

Every English sentence has a surface subject, if only formally so. For most combinations of cases there is a 'preferred' or 'unmarked' subject choice; for some there is no actual choice—the subject is uniquely determined. In general the 'unmarked' subject choice seems to follow the following rule:

54. If there is an A, it becomes the subject; otherwise, if there is an I, it becomes the subject; otherwise, the subject is the O.

Suppose, for example, that the base representation of a particular sentence is item 55:

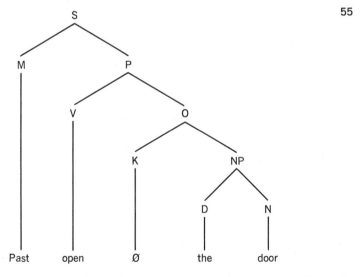

55

Since the sentence contains only one case category, it is obligatorily moved to the front (and hence directly subjoined to the category S) where it will later undergo subject-preposition deletion. There is a stage, in other words, where the form of the sentence in question is that represented in 56.

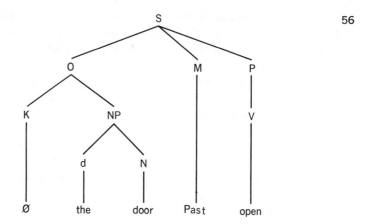

56

The subject-preposition deletion rule removes the preposition and deletes the case label. After application of the subject-preposition deletion rule, the form of the sentence is that represented in 57.

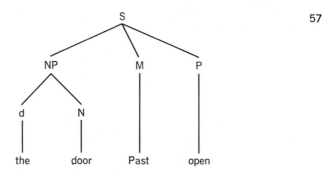

57

The final surface form, shown in 58, results from incorporation of the tense into the verb.

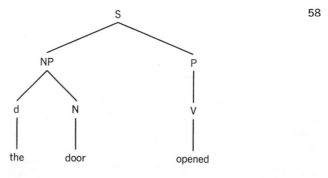

58

For a base configuration containing an A, a distinction must be made between the 'normal' and the 'nonnormal' [42] choice of subjects. The choice of the A as the subject, in accordance with the rule proposed in 54 above, requires no modification of the verb. The changes from 59 to 60 represent subject-fronting, those from 60 to 61 show subject-preposition deletion, and those from 61 to 62 indicate the effect of a third rule, object-preposition deletion.[43] The eventual surface structure of the sentence whose deep structure is 59 is 63.

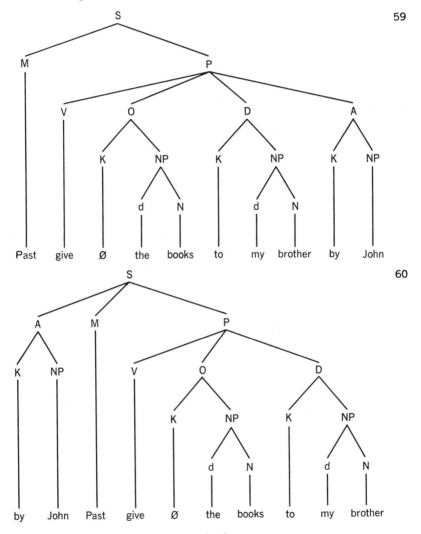

[42] The choice of terms is not to be taken seriously.

[43] Verbs are categorized according to whether they delete the preposition of the following case category, that is, whether they 'take on' a direct object. The object-preposition deleting property of a verb may be modified by a transformation.

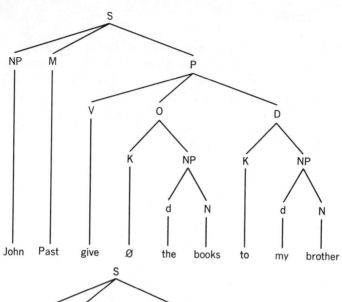

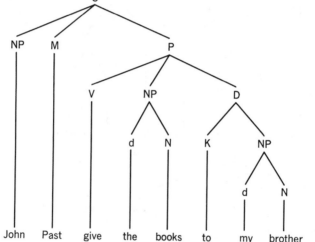

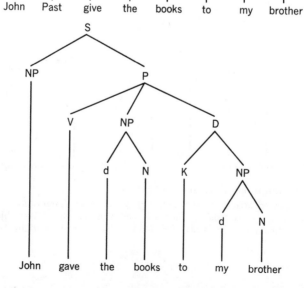

If it is noted that the verb *give* is one which, with A as subject, allows either O or D to become the direct object, an alternative surface form for 59 is 64 (assuming that case-label deletion occurs when zero K elements are 'deleted').

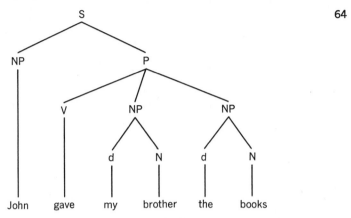

The 'normal' choice of subject for sentences containing an A, as stated in generalization 54 (which is a generalization for English), is the A. The verb *give* also allows either O or D to appear as subject as long as this 'nonnormal' choice is 'registered' in the V. This 'registering' of a 'nonnormal' subject takes place via the association of the feature [+passive] with the V. This feature has three effects: the V loses its object-preposition deletion property, it loses its ability to absorb the tense (requiring the automatic insertion of a *be* in the M constituent), and it must now be filled by a special 'passive' form (that is, *given*). The sequence 65 to 68 develops the choice of O as subject, and the sequence 69 to 73 shows the result of choosing D as subject.

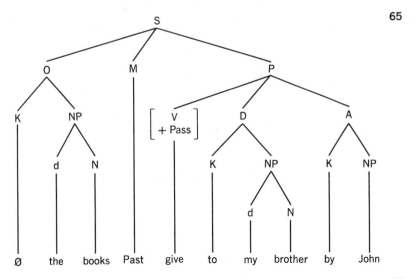

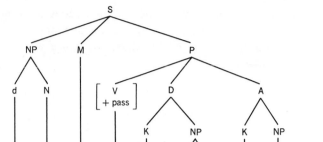

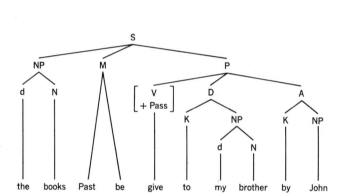

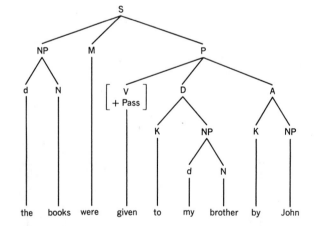

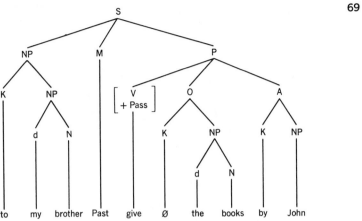

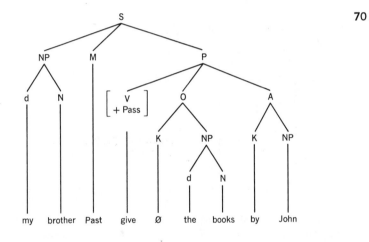

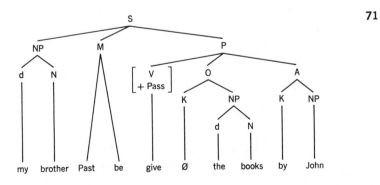

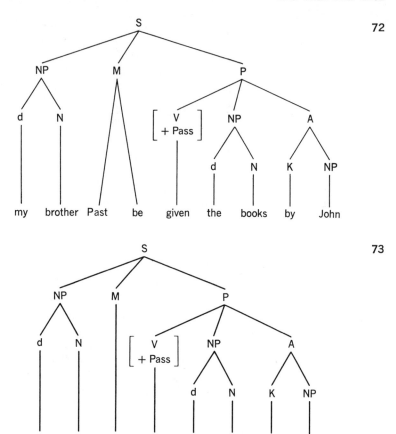

We have seen that where there is only one case category, its NP must serve as the surface subject. Examples 59 to 73 have shown ways of dealing with sentences containing more than one case category where one designated case could provide the subject without effecting any change in the V, or others could do so as long as a 'record' of this decision was attached to the V.

For many of the verbs which 'take' more than one case category, the one which contributes the subject is indicated by the verb itself. Of the verbs which are accepted into the frame [_____ O + D], *please, belong, interesting*, and others choose O as subject, and *like, want, think*, as well as others, choose D.[44]

---

[44] As mentioned above, by regarding the differences here as representing no more than idiosyncratic facts about the syntactic properties of these verbs, we can accept historical changes like those with *like, want*, and *think* from verbs of the type which choose O to verbs of the type which choose D to be merely a matter of detail in the subject-selection processes in our language. In other words, we do not need to agree with

Sometimes subjects are created not by moving one of the case elements into the 'subject' position, but by *copying* a particular element into
that position. This seems to be a consequence of the positional treatment
of subjects in English and to be related to the use of purely formal subjects.[45]

Copying for pro replacement can be illustrated with *that* clauses.
The 'verb' *true* occurs in the frame [_____ S], that is, as in Configuration
74.

74

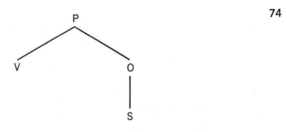

Since there is only one case element, it is obligatorily the subject. The
context requires that the complementizer *that* be provided for the embedded sentence. By subject copying, 76 is derived from 75.

75

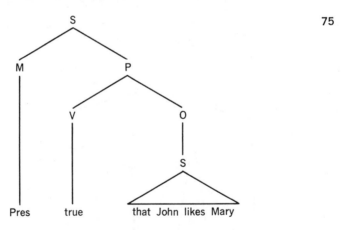

Jespersen when he describes the change in English from the use of expressions of the
type 'him like oysters' to those of the type 'he likes oysters' as reflecting a change in
the 'meaning' of the verb *like* from something like 'to be agreeable to' to something
like 'to take pleasure in' (Jespersen, 1924, p. 160). The change seems merely to be a
result of the inter-influencing of the two surface processes of choosing the first word
and establishing verbal concord.

[45] From the fact that there may be only one case in a simple sentence, it becomes possible to allow all subjects to be formed by a copying transformation. Sentences with
two copies of the same NP in the same case undergo one of a number of changes: the
second copy is either deleted or replaced by a pro form, or the first copy is replaced by
a pro form.

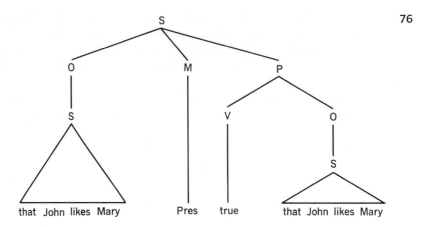

The structure of 76 undergoes either second copy deletion, yielding 77, or first copy pro replacement, giving us 78.

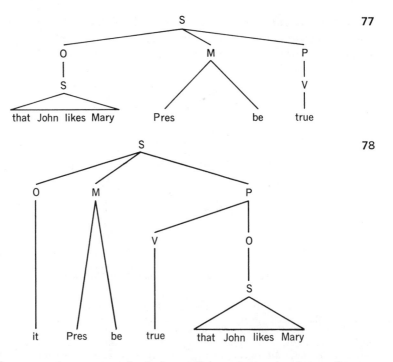

Verbs expressing meteorological conditions have the frame feature +[——— L]. Choosing *hot* in that frame, we can construct the sentence whose deep structure is represented by 79. From 79 we get, by subject copying, item 80. By second copy deletion (and subject-preposition deletion) item 80 becomes 81; on the other hand, if the first copy is replaced by its pro form (in this context, *it*), the resulting sentence is 82.[46]

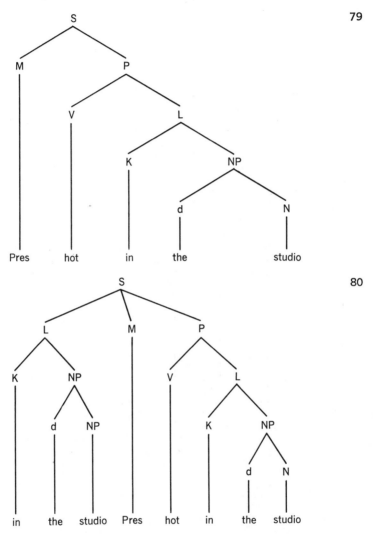

[46] It is likely that the correct analysis of subject copying is a little different from this. There is considerable evidence that when the first copy is replaced by its pro form, the second copy is actually outside of P, that is, that it is 'extraposed' in the sense of Rosenbaum. If this is true, then since the sentences having undergone extraposition must be created in two steps anyway, it is likely that the sentential subjects are formed in the usual way—not by copying—and that they are later extraposed, leaving behind, in the subject position, a 'trace' in the form of expletive *it*.

The examples and the analysis of meteorological verbs are adapted from Langendoen (1966).

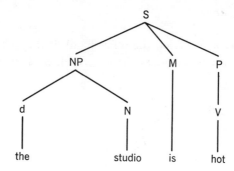

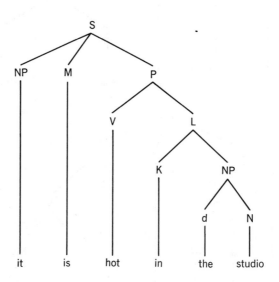

Under certain conditions, a first copy L may be replaced by an expletive *there*. The case frame [_____ O + L] may be filled by a blank verb (that is, zero). This situation (of verbless sentences) may call for the introduction of the element *be* into the M constituent, which is a process we have already seen to be necessary for verbs which are adjectives as well as for verbs which have been modified through addition of the feature [+passive]. For verbless sentences of the type [_____ O + L], the 'normal' subject choice is O. Thus from 83 we get 84, and eventually 85.

83

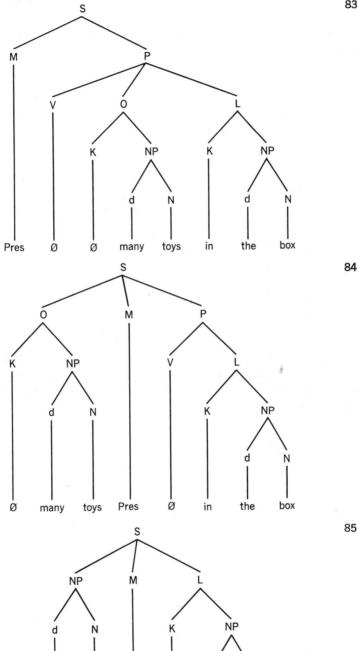

84

85

45

An alternative subject choice, through subject copying, is the L. Thus from 83 we might get 86.

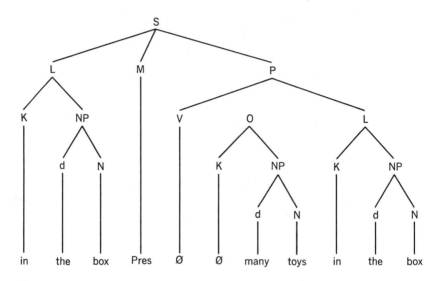

The pro form for L in verbless sentences is expletive (unstressed) *there*. The result of modifying 86 by pro replacement of the subject L is 87; extraposition of the second copy L, as suggested in footnote 45, has been carried out in 87.

87

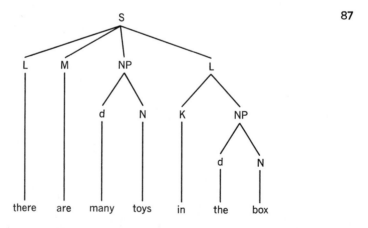

An alternative to replacing the first copy L by expletive *there* is to retain the L NP as subject. This decision requires the regular pronominalization of the repeated NP. It further requires modification of the verb: the hitherto empty V position is filled with the function verb *have*.[47] Since *have* is a V, it is capable of absorbing the tense, making the addition of *be* to M no longer necessary. The result of choosing the first L as subject results, through subject-preposition deletion, *have* insertion, object-preposition deletion, repeated NP pronominalization, and tense affixation, in 88.

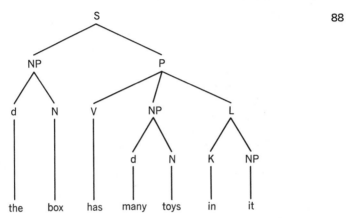

88

The general position I am taking on the verb *have* is that in verbless sentences (that is, when the V constituent is present but lexically empty) *have* is obligatorily inserted just in case the subject is an NP which is not from the case O. The most obvious case is that of the empty verb in the frame [_____ O + D], a context which in English requires D to be the subject, resulting in the typical *have* sentences. Other languages, for example, French, seem to have contexts in which the subject choice is optional—situations where *X a Y* is in a paraphrase relation with *Y est à X*. Other languages, for example, Estonian, do not have anything equivalent to the verb *have*.[48]

Some languages have subjectivalization processes; and, as I have suggested for English, there seems to be an analogous objectivalization process which has the superficial effect of bringing a particular nominal element into closer association with the verb.

The formal rather than purely notional character of the direct object was noticed by Jespersen. His examples (1924, p. 162) show intra-language paraphrase relations like that between 89 and 90, and cross-language differences like that between 91 and 92.

[47] For a recent argument on the transformational introduction of *be* and *have* in all of their occurrences, see Bach (1967). For a more adequate treatment of existential sentences than I have presented, see especially Lee (1967).

[48] Another situation for introducing *have* to account for connections between such pairs of sentences as i and ii is discussed below in the section on inalienable possession.

    i. My knee is sore.
    ii. I have a sore knee.

89. present something to a person
90. present a person with something
91. furnish someone with something
92. *fournir quelque chose à quelqu'un*

When such phenomena were examined by Hall, she took one form as basic, the other as derived. 'Derived subjects', in her analysis, are possible just in case there is no 'deep subject'; 'derived objects', on the other hand, have the effect of displacing the original deep-structure object and attaching a *with* to it. Her examples include 93–94 and 95–96.

93. John smeared paint on the wall.
94. John smeared the wall with paint.
95. John planted peas and corn in his garden.
96. John planted his garden with peas and corn.

Hall provides rules which move the locative element (*the wall* or *his garden* of 93 and 95 respectively) into the direct object position by a transformation which also attaches *with* to the former direct object.

From the point of view taken here, it would be just as easy to say that both *on the wall* and *with paint* were initially provided with prepositions (as L and I case elements), the verb *smear* having the property that whichever of these elements is chosen as 'direct object' must fall next to it and must lose its preposition. (In other languages, the process might be expressed as converting an original case specification to 'accusative'.)[49]

[40] There are semantic difficulties in treating subject and object transformationally, in the sense that different choices are often accompanied by semantic differences of one sort or another. These differences are more on the order of 'focusing'—to be as vague as possible—than anything else, and do not seem to require positing 'subjects' and 'objects' in the deep structure. The 'focusing' difference may be extremely slight, as in the pairs i–ii and iii–iv, or it may have somewhat more 'cognitive content' as in the pairs v–vi and vii–viii.

    i. Mary has the children with her.
    ii. The children are with Mary.
    iii. He blamed the accident on John.
    iv. He blamed John for the accident.
    v. Bees are swarming in the garden.
    vi. The garden is swarming with bees.
    vii. He sprayed paint on the wall.
    viii. He sprayed the wall with paint.

Sentence vi seems to suggest, while v does not, that the whole garden has bees in it everywhere; and viii suggests, while vii does not, that the entire wall got covered with paint.

To the extent that other grammars make use of derived subjects and derived objects—which is the only alternative, within subject/object grammars, to treating verbs like *spray, blame, open, break* as involving elaborate and unexplained examples of homonymy—the semantic difficulties are just as great for them as they are for case grammar. Since the 'semantic effect' of the transformations in question is so different in kind from the semantic role of the case relations themselves, and since the latter are not affected by these processes, I am inclined to tolerate the reintroduction into

Subjectivalization, where it occurs, results in a neutralization of underlying case distinctions to a single form, usually called the 'nominative'.
Objectivalization, where it occurs, neutralizes case distinctions to a single
form which, where it is distinct from the form assigned to subjects, is
traditionally termed 'accusative'. A third process which has the effect of
effacing deep-structure case distinctions is the formation of nominals
from sentences. The case modifications under nominalization transformations usually involve what is called the 'genitive'.

The brief mention above of situations in which there was an S embedded to the case category O suggested the ways in which case grammar
must deal with verb and adjective complementation. A second source
of embedded sentences is within the NP itself. The rule for NP may be
stated as 97.

97. NP → N (S)

Where the N is an ordinary lexical item and the adjunct S contains
a co-referential copy of the same N, the result is an NP consisting of
a noun modified by a relative clause. One of the most obvious sources
of 'genitive' is from relative clauses built on sentences which, by themselves, would have assumed the form X *has* Y. The N in the modified NP
is the same as the N contained in the D of the adjunct sentence, and the
V is empty. Thus, from 98 we get 99 by deleting the repeated noun, the
tense, and the 'empty' verb and reattaching the D to the dominating NP.

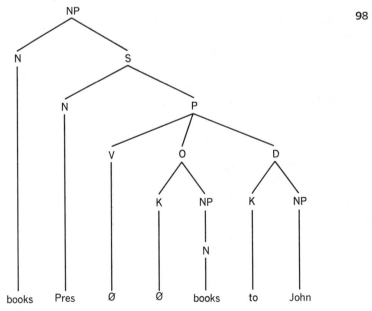

98

grammatical theory of transformations which have semantic import (of this highly
restricted kind).

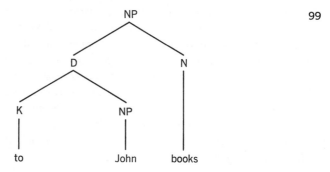

99

A D subjoined to an NP has its case marker modified—in this case to the sibilant suffix. Note 100.

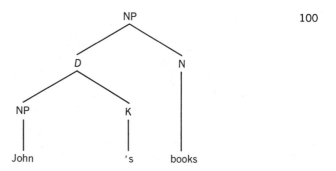

100

The 'true possessive' construction—resulting either in an NP of the form *X's Y* or *Y of X* in English—has as its source a sentence which by itself would have the form *X has Y*. The fact that in some languages there are instances of adnominal D not modified to the 'genitive' (*dem Vater sein Haus,* 'dative of possession') supports the view that conversion to genitive is a matter of the surface structure.

The interpretation of deverbal nouns which seems most satisfactory to me is that, except for the purely productive cases, the derivation of a noun from a verb is a matter of historical, not synchronic, fact. The synchronic reality is expressed by indicating that a given noun has a particular kind of relationship to a specific verb (or set of verbs), and that some of these nouns may, others must, appear in the NP frame [——— S].

That is, instead of having a synchronic process for producing such words as Latin *amor* from its associated verb, what is needed is the classification of such a word as an abstract noun having a particular kind of relationship with the verb *amo*.[50] Nouns having this kind of special

[50] This treatment allows for the inclusion of nouns which lack etymological connections with their related verbs. We might wish to indicate for *book* a connection of the in-

relationship to specific verbs can take part in a process which introduces into the NP elements which 'originally' depended on the associated verb. The processes in question frequently have the effect of converting the form of the subsidiary NP's to the genitive.[51] Thus the noun *amor* when qualified by a sentence of the form *deus amat . . .* yields *amor dei;* when it is qualified by a sentence of the form *deum amat . . .* the result is again *amor dei.* The D and O forms, in other words, are equally reduced to the genitive, and when only one noun is involved, potential ambiguities result.[52]

4. Some Remarks on Language Typology

The view of universal grammar which is emerging is something like this: In their deep structure, the propositional nucleus of sentences in all languages consists of a V and one or more NP's, each having a separate case relationship to the P (and hence to the V). The most straightforward

---

tended kind with the verb *write,* thus accounting for the ambiguity of *your book* between 'the book which you own' (ordinary relative clause modification) and 'the book which you wrote'.

[51] Exactly what universal constraints there are, if any, on the element to be converted to genitive is not at all clear. It appears that if there is only one element that shows up in the NP, it frequently takes the genitive form. Compare the ambiguous Sentence i with Sentences ii and iii.

   i. My instructions were impossible to carry out
      (*a*) so I quit.
      (*b*) so he quit.
   ii. My instructions to you are to go there.
   iii. * My your instructions are to go there.

In English it appears that if the conditions which allow the formation of the *of* genitive and the *s* genitive are satisfied by two different NP's in the associated sentence, multiple genitive constructions become possible, as in the following example borrowed from Jespersen.

   iv. Gainesborough's portrait of the duchess of Devonshire.

Japanese allows conversion to genitive in true relative clauses, as well as in the reduced relative clauses. A paraphrase of v is vi; *no* is the postposition most closely associated with functions which we would call 'genitive'.

   v. *Boku ga yonda zasshi.* 'I + subject + read − past + magazine'
      'the magazines I read'
   vi. *Boku no yonda zasshi.*

[52] Jespersen's suggestion that the ambiguity of *amor dei* is in the verb rather than the noun—the noun unambiguously identifying the subject, the verb being ambiguously either active or passive—must be understood as the hypothesis that only those NP constituents which are capable of conversion to surface subjects (with a given verb) may appear under genitive modification as modifiers of the deverbal noun. For English this may well be true. (Jespersen, 1924, p. 170.)

deep-structure commonalities between languages are to be sought at this 'deepest' level.

The lexical insertion rule for verbs is sensitive to the particular array of cases in the P. Since no distinction is needed between 'strict subcategorization features' and at least the highest level of 'selectional features' (because redundancy relations exist between cases and some lexical features, and because there is no 'subject' outside of a 'VP' whose features need to be dealt with separately), the lexical insertion rule for verbs can be a strictly local transformation which responds to nothing more than the cases which are co-constituents of V (with the exception, as noted above, that it must be known whether the O element is an NP or an S).

The criteria for typological classification that have suggested themselves so far in this study are these:

I. the presence or absence of modifications on the NP's as determined by the deep-case categories
    A. the nature of such modification (prepositional, affixal, or other)
    B. the conditions for the choice of particular case forms (which, when stated in their simplest form, constitute what is usually formulated as the 'case system' of the language)
II. the presence or absence of concordial modifications of the verb
    A. the nature of the concord (number agreement, incorporation of 'traces' of case categories, feature changes on V)
    B. the relation to subject selection (topicalization)
III. the nature of anaphoric processes
    A. type of process (replacement by pro form, deletion, de-stressing, replacement by unstressed variants, or other)
    B. conditions of application
IV. topicalization processes (where 'subject selection' may be thought of as a special case of topicalization)
    A. formal processes (fronting, modifying the case form, or other)
    B. the variety of topicalization processes in the same language
V. word order possibilities
    A. factors determining 'neutral' word order (nature of case categories, 'ranking' of noun classes, topic selection, or other)
    B. conditions determining or constraining stylistic variations on word order

It is important to realize that all of these typological criteria are based on superficial processes, and that there are no particularly good reasons for believing a priori that there will be much coincidence in the ways in which the different criteria sort out the world's languages.

4.1   The Bases for Determining Case Forms

The forms of the NP's in a P are determined on the basis of a variety of factors, one of which is the case category of the NP. Thus an NP under an I (that is, an instrumental noun) is assigned a particular form depending in whole or in part on the fact that it is under I.

Surface case forms of NP's are most elaborately developed in the personal pronouns. The study of the 'case' aspects of pronoun systems reveals a great deal about the variety of relationships that can hold between deep and surface cases.

Sapir's typological distinctions for Amerindian pronominal systems (1917b) can be expressed in case grammar terms quite simply. If we ignore whatever complications may exist in 'passive' constructions, and if we ignore all deep-structure cases except A and O, we can imagine sentences of the following three types given in their underlying propositional form:

(a) V + A   intransitive sentences with active 'subjects'
(b) V + O + A   transitive sentences with agents
(c) V + O   intransitive sentences with inactive 'subjects'

Since the V element is constant to the formulas, we can represent these three sentence types by presenting the case frames in three lines, as follows:

$$
\begin{array}{c}
\text{A} \\
101 \quad \text{O A} \\
\text{O}
\end{array}
$$

According to Sapir, then, there are languages which, like Yana, have only one form for pronouns in all four of these positions.

102

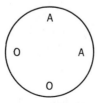

There are languages like Paiute that have a separate form for the O element in the transitive sentence, all others being the same. The two forms are traditionally called 'nominative' and 'accusative'.

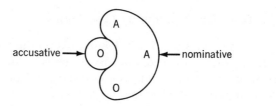

103

There are languages like Chinook which give one form to the A of transitive sentences and another to the remaining cases. The terms 'ergative' and 'nominative' are often given to a distinction made in this way.

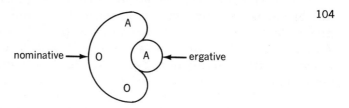

104

There are languages like Dakota which have separate forms for A and O; here the terms are usually 'active' and 'inactive'.

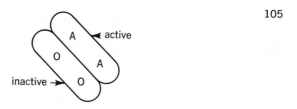

105

And, lastly, there is the situation found in Takelma, which has one form for the pronominal NP of intransitive sentences, and two separate forms for the A and O of transitive sentences. Thus:

106

What these observations are intended to suggest is merely that if I correctly understand Sapir's analysis of the pronominal systems of these languages, then the case concepts I have been discussing, together with the notion of clause types which various arrays of them define, provide the categorial and configurational information for determining the surface distinctions that are found in these languages.

4.2   Verbal Concord

There are these various ways, and possibly more, in which cases and case environments are involved in determining the case forms of NP's within a P. An additional factor is whether the given NP has been chosen as subject in languages having subjectivalization processes. Choosing subjects or topics is related to another aspect of the superficial structure of sentences, and that is verbal concord.

The choice of subject in English always has the effect of determining number concord (on those verbal and auxiliary elements capable of reflecting number concord). Apart from number concord, the choice of subject might involve modification of the verb to its passive form, or introduction of the verb *have*.

The information 'registered' in the V may have only to do with the choice of subject, as in English, or it may be more elaborate. Languages which 'incorporate' pronominal affixes into the V may do so for more than one NP at a time; or noun stems themselves from particular cases may be incorporated into the verbal expression.[53]

The subject selection rules discussed for English may be compared with the topicalization processes that are described for Philippine languages. The situation for Maranao has recently been described by Mc-Kaughan. One NP is chosen as topic for every sentence, and this choice is recorded in the following way: its original case preposition is replaced by *so,* and an affix is inserted into the V which indicates the case category of the chosen NP. There is apparently considerable freedom in the choice of topic. To take the verb meaning 'to butcher' (/*sombaliʔ*/), we find that when the topic noun is an original I, the verb takes on the prefix /*i-*/, as shown in 108; and when the topic is an original B, the suffix /*-an*/ is added to the V, as seen in 109.

107. som*ombaliʔ* so *mamaʔ* sa *karabao*
     'The man butchers the carabao.'
108. i*sombaliʔ* o *mamaʔ* so *gelat ko karabao*
     'It is with the knife that the man butchers the carabao.'
109. *sombaliʔ*an o *mamaʔ* so *major sa karabao*
     'It is for the mayor that the man butchers the carabao.' [54]

---

[53] Grammatical devices for providing concord of this type have been worked out for Mohawk by Paul M. Postal (see Postal, 1963).

[54] McKaughan (1962). The examples and the description of the relationships are from McKaughan, but a great deal of guessing lies behind my interpretation.

The choice of sentence subjects, or 'topics', from particular cases appears to be the most satisfactory way of accounting for the many types of voice modifications of verbs such as those described as middle, pseudo-reflexive, and so forth, in the Indo-European languages.

4.3   Anaphoric Processes

Anaphoric processes are best understood from the point of view of an extended concept of sentence conjunction. That is, every language has ways of simplifying sentences connected by conjunctions or subjunctions, and the processes used under these conditions seem to be exactly the same as those used in sentences connected in discourse. The grammarian's job, therefore, is to describe these processes as they work in sentences that are independently intelligible, and then to assume that utterances in connected texts or conversations can best be understood from the point of view of a shared knowledge of the language's anaphoric processes on the part of speaker and hearer.[55] The fact that in these anaphoric or reduced forms English uses pro-replacement under conditions that would call for deletion in some other language may thus be seen as a superficial difference between the two languages.

The point is important—and it was mentioned above in connection with 'bad' reasons for rejecting the universality of the subject/predicate division—because the absence of subjects in the final surface forms of sentences in some languages is seen by many scholars as having great typological relevance. The optional absence of NP constituents in languages with person-marker incorporation (for example, Chinook) has led scholars to claim that such languages lack the nexus relations that Europeans understand as 'subject' and 'object' but have instead what are described as 'appositional' relations between NP's and V's (see Sommerfelt, 1937). In languages without pronominal incorporation, a distinction is made by some scholars between true subject/predicate languages and those in which the so-called 'subject' is as much a 'complement' to

---

[55] In other words, the grammarian will describe the process by which i is converted to ii by noting the conditions under which repeated elements in conjoined sentences may undergo deletion and pro-replacement and under which conjoined sentences can have words like *too* and *either* added to them.

    i. Mary didn't want any candy and Mary didn't take any candy.
    ii. Mary didn't want any candy and she didn't take any either.

In contexts in which the information contained in the first conjunct of i is already understood by the addressee (by having just been spoken by him, for example), a speaker of English feels free to use the reduced form in iii.

    iii. She didn't take any, either.

There is no reason, it seems to me, to expect the grammar of a language to generate sentences like iii directly.

the V as is the direct object or any of the various adverbial elements. To Martinet, a subject is different from a complement only if it is 'constitutive of the minimal utterance' (1962a, pp. 61–62)—that is, only if it is obligatorily present in both full and anaphorically reduced utterances. In Japanese, the 'minimal utterance' lacks a subject, and hence, the argument goes, Japanese sentences lack the subject/predicate structure of sentences in our more familiar languages. To Martinet's disciple Saint-Jacques, this typological 'fact' about Japanese is regarded as excessively important. It is only by dint of considerable intellectual effort that the Westerner can achieve that liberation from familiar ways of thinking about language which is required for an understanding of the true character of Japanese. Or so Saint-Jacques tells us (1966, p. 36). It seems to me that language typology offers enough genuine excitements to make it possible for us to give this one up. The intellectual achievement of which M. Saint-Jacques speaks is that of knowing that when there is an 'understood' NP to deal with, some people replace it by a pronoun, others get rid of it.

4.4   Topicalization

The fourth criterion has to do with topicalization processes, devices for isolating one constituent of a sentence as 'topic', of bringing one particular constituent of a sentence into some kind of 'focus'. Where topicalization is distinct from processes for 'emphasizing' a constituent, we have much the same thing as what I have been calling 'subjectivalization', but which I shall now begin calling 'primary topicalization'. Primary topicalization for English involves position and number concord; stylistic changes involving stress assignment, late word-order changes, and possibly the 'cleft-sentence construction' fall into what might be called 'secondary topicalization'. From what I understand of McKaughan's account (1962, p. 47), primary topicalization in Maranao involves replacement of the original preposition associated with a noun by *so* and introduction into the V of an associated case indicator, while secondary topicalization involves moving an NP to which *so* has been added to the front of the sentence. One might refer to Oertel's study of the disjunct use of cases in Brāhmaṇic prose as a study of secondary topicalization.[56] I would imagine that all languages possess some means of carrying out

---

[56] 1936. Oertel distinguishes 'pendent' uses of a disjunct case, where the 'topic' is in the 'nominative' even if its original role in the sentence was not that of subject (comparable, I assume, to *he* in 'he, I like him'), and 'proleptic' uses, where the topic retains the original case form, is moved to the front of the sentence, and may or may not be resumed (in the form of a demonstrative) in the remainder of the sentence (comparable to *him* in *him, I like (him)*).

'secondary topicalization', but it may be the case that some lack the process of 'primary topicalization' (subjectivalization').[57]

The notion 'subjectivalization' is useful only if there are sentences in a language which offer a choice of subject. Languages described as not having passives, or languages described as only capable of expressing transitive sentences passively, apparently lack the grammatical process of primary topicalization.

This question leads naturally to the problem of the so-called 'ergative' languages. Recall that in the accusative type of pronominal system, the pattern was

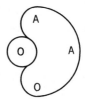

and that in the ergative type it was

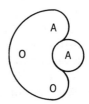

Now when languages of the accusative type have passive versions of sentences whose propositional form is [V O A], the case forms associated with the elements in the passive version are generally 'nominative' for the O and 'agentive' (realized as ablative, instrumental, or what have you, depending on the language) for the A. If passive sentences were introduced into our three-line diagrams and their active counterparts removed, we would get the pattern

[57] Jeffrey Gruber's recent study (1967) of topicalization in child language suggests that ontogenetically motivated (what I am calling 'secondary') topicalization precedes the use of formal subjects in English. It may be that when one device for topicalization becomes 'habitual', it freezes into a formal requirement and the language must then call on other processes for motivated topicalization.

Kenneth Hale (correspondence, 1967) reports that for Walbiri, an 'ergative' language of aboriginal Australia, there is apparently no 'subjectivalization' process, but any constituent may be repeated to the right of the proposition, the element inside the proposition being replaced by a pro form.

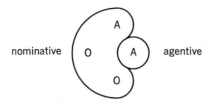

which is exactly like that for the regular assignment of cases in the ergative languages. This fact, plus the use of the term 'nominative' for subject-of-intransitive-*cum*-object-of-transitive in these languages, has led many scholars to identify the ergative case in ergative languages with the agentive case form found in passive sentences in accusative languages, and to conclude that the ergative languages are really 'passive' languages—languages in which transitive sentences can only be expressed passively.[58] For both of these systems, the case that has been given the name 'nominative' is frequently described as the 'subject' in a subject/predicate construction, and the 'ergative' element in the one instance and the 'accusative' element in the other are treated as verbal complements (see Trubetzkoy, 1939). The difficulty of determining the 'subject' in ergative languages has been described by Martinet (1962b, pp. 78 f.): Some scholars identify as subject the word which would be the subject in a translation of the sentence into French—that is, the nominative in intransitive sentences and the ergative in transitive sentences. Others regard the nominative as the subject in all sentences, thus giving transitive sentences a 'passive' interpretation. Lafon gives up on transitive sentences—he uses the term 'subject' only for intransitive sentences, saying of transitive sentences that they have no subject.

Vaillant, on the other hand, spoke of the northern Caucasian languages as having three types of verbs: (*a*) true intransitives, with subjects in the 'nominative'; (*b*) 'operative pseudotransitives', with 'pseudosubject' in the 'ergative'; and (*c*) 'affective pseudotransitives', with 'pseudosubjects' in the 'dative' (1936, p. 93). It seems quite clear that what he is dealing with are sentences having P's of the three types—[V O], [V O A], and [V O D]—where the surface cases for O, A, and D are 'nominative', 'ergative', and 'dative', respectively. It looks very much as if that is all there is to say. For my part I would much rather say of the ergative languages that they lack subjectivalization, than say either that all transitive sentences undergo obligatory passivization, or that some of their sentences contain true subjects while others do not.

[58] Note that even if there is a different form for the verb in [_____ O] and [_____ O + A] case frames, this cannot be interpreted as evidence of 'passivity'. As mentioned earlier, in languages not of the ergative type there may still be systematic variation of the same verb root depending on whether it is used transitively or intransitively.

The frequent claim that the ergative languages are more primitive than the accusative languages are (see Tesnière, 1959, p. 112), together with the assumption that the ergative construction is really a passive construction, has led such scholars as Kuryłowicz, Schuchardt, and Uhlenbeck to assume that the passive construction represents a more primitive concept in the evolution of language than that of the active transitive construction. Evidence mustered for this position includes the signs that pre-Indo-European was of the ergative type, and the fact that some languages have 'invented' *have*-like verbs in relatively recent times. The invention of *have* made it possible to give active expression to certain tense or aspectual forms which had remained unaffected by the general change from passive to active expression (as is seen, for example, in the circa third century shift from expressions of the type *inimicus mihi occisus est* and *mihi illud factum est* to transitive expressions using *habeo: inimicum occisum habeo* and *habeo illud factum* (see van Ginneken, 1939, p. 86)).

It seems very unlikely to me that syntactic changes of the type known from the present state of our knowledge are really capable of showing an intellectual evolution of a type as potentially significant as whatever might be understood as the transition from an essentially passive to an essentially active point of view. The connection claimed by van Ginneken between ergativity and the 'feminine' character of cultures with ergative languages is another that should be questioned.[59]

4.5 Word-Order Differences

The fifth criterion suggested for a language typology is that of word order. The variables that determine or constrain the freedom of word order in the languages of the world are very likely to have many important connections with the case structure of sentences; but this is an area which I have not examined at all.

---

[59] The following seems worth quoting in full (1939, pp. 91 f):

Nous sommes tous des hommes, et tous nous avons deux talents: les facultés plus actives de l'appétit et de la volonté, et les facultés plus passives des sensations et de l'appréhension; mais il est évident que les deux sexes de l'humanité montrent sous ce rapport une différence sensible.

L'ethnologie moderne, qui a écarté définitivement comme insuffisante la doctrine du développement uniforme, nous apprend cependant que le progrès de l'humanité a balancé presque toujours entre les cultures plus féminines ou plus masculines, dites cultures matriarcales et patriarcales. Ce sont toujours les cultures matriarcales très prononcées qui, comme le basque, ont un verbe transitif de nature passive avec comme casus rectus un patiens et comme casus obliquus un agens; mais les cultures patriarcales, comme l'indoeuropéenne ont un verb transitif de nature active, animiste et magique, avec un sujet au casus rectus et un objet au casus obliquus. Chaque peuple a donc le verbe qu'il mérite.

5.   The Grammar of Inalienable Possession

The preceding sections have contained an informal description of a syntactic model for language and a few demonstrations of the operations of this model of the sort that has come to be called 'restatement linguistics'. In the present section I shall attempt to show how a particular substantive modification of the rules will permit a uniform way of describing the interesting collection of grammatical facts associated with what is called 'inalienable possession'.

Every language, one can be sure, has nouns which express concepts that are inherently relational. Examples of inherently relational nouns in English are *side, daughter,* and *face*. One doesn't speak of a side, but of a side of something; one doesn't say of someone that she is a daughter, only that she is somebody's daughter; and although it is possible to speak of having seen a face, the word is typically used when referring to 'his face' or 'your face' or the like. The relational nouns most frequently discussed in the linguistic literature are names of body parts and names of kinsmen. My discussion here will concentrate on body parts.

5.1   The Data

5.1.1   Significant syntactic relationships exist between the dative and the genitive cases in all of the Indo-European languages; and in all but Armenian, according to Havers (1911, p. 317), the dative and the genitive case forms figure in paraphrase relationships of kinds that are highly comparable from language to language. The relationship is observed only when the associated noun is of a particular type. To take some of the modern German examples given by Havers, we observe that a paraphrase relation exists between 111 and 112 as well as between 113 and 114; but that of the two sentences 115 and 116, the latter is ungrammatical (as a paraphrase of 115).

111. *Die Kugel durchbohrte dem Feind das Herz.*
112. *Die Kugel durchbohrte das Herz des Feindes.*
113. *Er hat mir die Hand verwundet.*
114. *Er hat meine Hand verwundet.*
115. *Der Vater baute seinem Sohn ein Haus.*
116. * *Der Vater baute ein Haus seines Sohnes.*

It should be noted that *Herz* and *Hand* are the names of body parts, while *Haus* is not.

5.1.2   There are cases like the above where a given language exhibits in itself the paraphrase relationship, and there are also cases where it appears that one language has chosen the dative expression, another the genitive. Notice the following sentences, also from Havers (1911, p. 1).

117. My heart aches: *Mir blutet das Herz.*
118. Tom's cheeks burned: *Tom brannten die Wangen.*
119. She fell on her mother's neck: *Sie fiel ihrer Mutter um den Hals.*

5.1.3 There are adnominal (possessive) uses of dative constructions, particularly, it appears, when the possessive pronoun is also used with the possessed element. Here the most readily available examples are with kinship terms (Havers, 1911, p. 283).

120. *Dem Kerl seine Mutter.*
121. *Sa mère à lui.*

5.1.4 Many languages have separate possessive affixes for nouns that are obligatorily possessed (inalienables) and nouns that are optionally possessed (alienables). The difference in Fijian is apparently expressed by preposing the possessive morpheme to indicate alienable possession and suffixing it to indicate inalienable possession. Since the category 'inalienable' is a category of grammar rather than a property of real world objects (since, in other words, some objects grammatically classed as inalienable can in fact be separated from their 'owners'), the distinction can be seen most clearly if both methods of expression can be used with the same noun stem. Lévy-Bruhl gives a persuasive example of this situation (1916, p. 99): Fijian *uluqu* means the head which is now firmly attached to my neck, while *kequ ulu,* also translatable as 'my head', would refer to the head which, say, I am about to eat.

Languages may have separate morphemes for indicating alienable and inalienable possession, and they may have further distinctions among these morphemes depending on the type of inalienable possession (as Nootka, for example, suffixes -*?at-* to nouns representing physically inseparable entities, for example, body parts, but uses other means for kinship terms), or they may merely have a class of nouns incapable of occurring as free forms—noun stems requiring affixation of possession indicators.[60]

In all of these cases, it appears, the features in question are 'grammatical' rather than purely 'notional'. Discussions of inalienable possession almost always contain lists of nouns whose grammatical classifica-

---

[60] This last situation is sometimes described by saying that nouns are 'inflected for person' (see Manessy, 1964, p. 468).

The full variety of the treatment of inalienable possession in different Amerindian languages is catalogued in Sapir (1917a).

tion is the opposite of what one would notionally expect. Lévy-Bruhl (1916, p. 96) mentions a case where the word for 'left hand' functions as a body-part word grammatically, but the word for 'hand' does not. And Arapaho classifies 'louse' (or 'flea') among the inalienables (Salzmann, 1965, p. 139), a situation that invites people who like to speculate on these things to propose something or other on the Arapaho conception of 'self'.

5.1.5 Milka Ivić has recently discussed many instances of what she calls 'non-omissible determiners' (1962, 1964). Among the examples she cites are many that involve nouns of the type frequently included among the inalienables. The adjective cannot be deleted, for example, in the Serbo-Croatian expression in 122, for 123 is ungrammatical (1964, p. 477).

122. *devojka crnih očiju*, 'the girl with black eyes'
123. * *devojka očiju*

What is misleading about her discussion, it seems to me, is the decision to associate with the adjective the 'category of nonomissibility'. It is as if we wished to say, for the English Sentence 124, that there is something grammatically significant about the word *missing*, since its deletion results in Sentence 125 which is somewhat different in type from the original; put differently, Sentence 124 does not say the same thing that 126 does. What is genuinely important about 124 is its paraphrasability as 127 (or 128) and the fact that the construction exhibited by 124 is restricted to certain kinds of nouns. Note the ungrammaticality of 129.

124. I have a missing tooth.
125. I have a tooth.
126. I have a tooth and it is missing.
127. My tooth is missing.
128. One of my teeth is missing.
129. * I have a missing five-dollar bill.

5.1.6 Note that in Sentences 124 and 127, three things are involved: (*a*) a possessor (an 'interested person', to use the traditional term), (*b*) a body part, and (*c*) an attribute—(*a*) *me*, (*b*) *tooth*, and (*c*) *missing* respectively—and that the sentences provide alternate ways of ascribing the attribute to the possessor's body part. They are two distinct superficial ways of expressing the same relationship among these three concepts.

Using P, B, and A for *a*, *b*, and *c* above, we may represent the expression as seen in 124 as 130, and that as seen in 127 as 131.

130. P^{nom} *have* $[A \rightarrow B^{acc}]$
131. $[P^{gen} \rightarrow B]$ *be* A

The same element, in other words, which in some of the paraphrases mentioned above appeared in either the dative or the genitive case forms now appears as the subject of the verb *have*. Bally, in fact, speaks of the invention of the word *have* as fulfilling precisely the function of allowing the *personne intéressée,* which otherwise would have to appear either in dative or genitive form, to become the subject of a sentence. Examples of all three surface appearances of a first person possessor are given by Bally (1926, p. 75) as 132–134. Sentences 133 and 134 correspond to expression types 130 and 131 respectively; the expression type exemplified by 132 is given as 135.

132. *Mihi sunt capilli nigri.*
133. *J'ai les cheveux noirs.*
134. *Mes cheveux sont noirs.*
135. P^{dat} $[B^{nom}$ *be* A]

5.1.7 Henri Frei surveyed this variety of surface representations of the 'same' sentences and added a fourth type, a type intermediate, in a sense, between that suggested by Formula 135 and that of 130. His example was Sentence 136 (it also provided the title of his paper), which exemplifies the expression type we may wish to represent as 137.

136. *Sylvie est jolie des yeux.*
137. P^{nom} *be* $[A\ B^{oblique}]$.

Frei points out that the construction seen in 136 is related to the category of inalienable possession, since while 138 and 139 are acceptable sentences, 140 and 141 are not.

138. *Elle est fine de doigts.*
139. *Elle est bien faite des jambes.*
140. * *Elle est fine d'étoffe.*
141. **Elle est bien faite des vêtements.*[61]

---

[61] Frei (1939, p. 188). The expressions are limited to clear relational nouns, not only to body parts. Frei notes such phrases as 'des couloirs spacieux et *bas de plafond*' and 'libre de moeurs'. He beautifully demonstrates the distinctness of the sentences involving inalienable possession from overtly similar sentences of different grammatical structures with the contrast between i and ii below (p. 186).

   i. *La salle est pleine de visages.*
   ii. *La femme est pleine de visage.*

5.1.8 Since Frei sees this diversity as resulting from the attempt to 'condense' two judgments into one sentence—the two judgments that *P has B* and that *B is A* (in our terms)—he relates the constructions in question to the much discussed 'double subject' constructions of Japanese. In one type of this latter construction, two nouns appear before a verb or adjective, the first followed by the particle *wa* (indicating what I have called 'secondary topicalization'), the second by the particle *ga* (the particle of 'primary topicalization'). (Variations in the order and in the choice of particles do not change the status of the construction; the form described is the one most stylistically neutral.) The second of these nouns is of the inalienable type; the first identifies the object with respect to which the object identified by the second noun is 'inalienable'. The hackneyed example of the double subject construction is 142, a sentence which has 143 as a sort of forced paraphrase. In 143, the particle *no* is the particle whose functions are closest to those we would be inclined to label 'genitive'.

142. *Zoo wa hana ga nagai.* 'Elephant *wa* nose *ga* long.'
143. *Zoo no hana ga nagai.*

5.1.9 That expressions involving entities viewed as being closely associated with an 'interested person' have unique grammatical properties has also been observed in certain semantically unmotivated uses of 'reflexive pronouns' and the parallels one finds between these and various uses of the 'middle voice'. The connection with dative forms is seen in the fact that in some languages a kind of 'dative reflexive' is used in these special situations. Note 144 and 145.

144. *Se laver les mains.*
145. *Ich wasche mir die Hände.*

The connection between this use of the 'reflexive' and the category of inalienable possession is indicated by Bally, who points out that in item 146, *jambe* is the inalienable entity, while in 147 the word *jambe* can only (or, depending on my informants, can also) be understood as some independently possessed object, such as the leg of a table.

146. *Je me suis cassé la jambe.*
147. *J'ai cassé ma jambe.*

Notice that the *jambe* which does *not* have the possessive adjective is the one which is grammatically characterized as 'obligatorily possessed' (Bally, 1936, p. 68)!

5.2   Adnominal Datives

One way of introducing a possessive modifier of a noun has already been suggested: a sentence which could on its own assume the form 'X *has* Y' is embedded to NP. Since it is desirable for an embedded sentence to have a semantic interpretation that contributes to the meaning of the whole sentence, the sentence-embedding source of possessives is needed as an explanation for alienable possession. In other words, one is satisfied to have the meaning of 148 represented as a part of the meaning of 149, though we may reject such a relationship between 150 and 151.

148. I have a dog.
149. my dog
150. I have a head.
151. my head

A distinct method is required for introducing the possessive element in the case of inalienable possession, a method which reflects the fact that the relationship between the two nouns in 'inalienable possession' is not (*pace* Frei) a sentential relationship.

For the types of inalienable possession that we have considered so far—in which the relationship has always been to an animate or 'personal' entity—the solution is to say that some nouns obligatorily take D complements. This can be managed by adding to the grammar another way of writing NP, namely the rule in 152.

152. NP → N (D)

In the way that frame features for V's relate to environments of V's provided by the constituent P, frame features for N's relate to environments provided by the constituent NP. It was suggested above that N's which obligatorily take S complements are assigned the feature +[_____ S]. We may now add that N's which obligatorily take D complements are characterized as having the feature +[_____ D]; and these are the inalienably possessed nouns. The notation imposes a subclassification of nouns into those which require adnominal D (such as *son, child* in the meaning 'offspring', German *Mann* in the meaning 'husband') and those which reject adnominal D (such as *person, child* in the meaning 'very young person', *Mann* in the meaning 'man').

The two sources of possessive modifiers which the grammar now makes possible (adnominal D and adnominal S of a certain type) provide the deep-structure differences needed for determining the difference in the form of the possessive modifiers in those languages which make the distinction overt in that way. Where further distinctions are made (as between body parts and kinship terms), the information on which such distinctions need to be based may be included as lexical features of the N's themselves.

The general configuration of NP's containing D's, then, is that shown in 153.

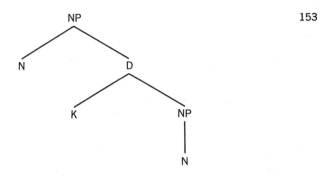

153

In some cases the adnominal D remains in the NP and in fact retains the surface features associated with D, as in 154; typically, however, a D inside an NP is changed to a genitive form, as in 155.

154. secretary to the president
155. the president's secretary

If determiners are universal,[62] then the expansion of NP must make provisions for them; but if they are not, then languages which have them will need 'segmentalization' rules of the type described by Postal (1966). At any rate, the determiners (which I represent as 'd') will figure in the various things that can happen to adnominal D. Sometimes, for example, when a D remains in the NP without undergoing genitive modification, certain of its features are copied onto the determiner so that the determiner may eventually assume the form of the appropriate 'possessive adjective'. This seems to account for such expressions as the possessive dative with kinship terms seen in some German dialects (recall 120) in Ossetic (see Abaev, 1964, p. 18).

5.3 Some Illustrations

The D constituent often need not remain in the NP: under some conditions it may be 'promoted', so to speak, from the status of a modifier of an N (which it is in the deep structure) to the status of a major

[62] I am inclined to think that they are. See Fillmore (1967).

constituent on the next higher level of the syntactic structure. This can
be seen in sentences having the base configuration [V + L + A]: just in
case the N under L is a body part, the D which in the deep structure is
subjoined to L is 'promoted' to become a constituent of P, yielding a
sentence superficially of the type [V + D + L + A].

The verb *pinch* is accepted into the case frame [_____ L + A], and
except when it has taken on the feature [+passive], it is a verb which
deletes the preposition of the following constituent. Let us consider sentences derivable from the deep structure seen in 156.

156

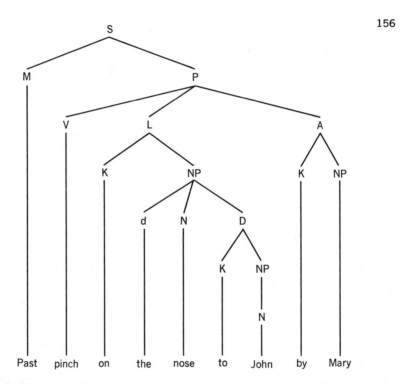

We shall see what happens to the sentence under four conditions: when
the D remains inside L and A becomes the subject; when the D remains
inside L and L becomes the subject; when the D is promoted and A
becomes the subject; and when the D is promoted and D becomes the
subject.

Whenever D remains inside NP (in this sentence), it is preposed to
the N and converted to its genitive form, displacing the original determiner. Since it is a personal noun, the K element assumes the form
of a genitive suffix. With nonpromoted D, in other words, 156 eventually becomes 157.

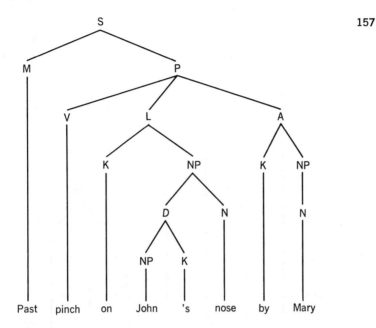

157

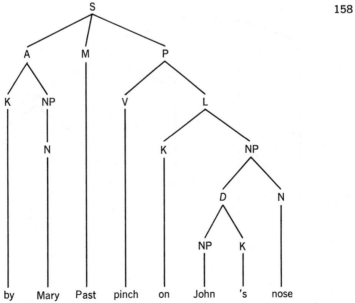

Diagrams 158–161 show the development from 157 when A is made the subject: the subject preposition is deleted and its case category is erased; the preposition after *pinch* is deleted and the case category L is erased; and the tense is absorbed into the V.

158

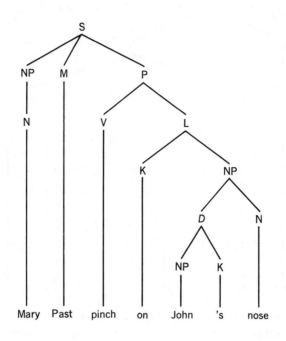

159

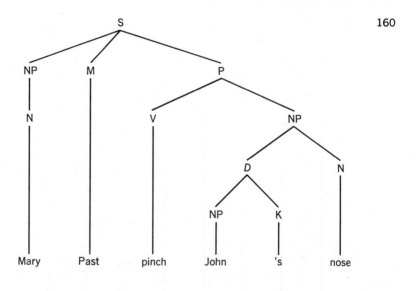

160

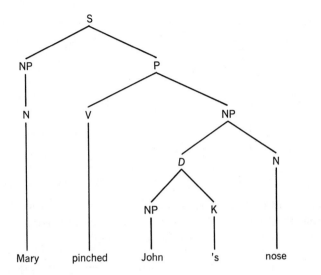

If the L of 157 is chosen as subject instead of the A, the result is 162. This choice of subject requires the V to assume the feature [+passive], which causes it to lose its ability to delete following prepositions and its ability to take tense affixes. The surface structure eventually resulting from 162 is 163.

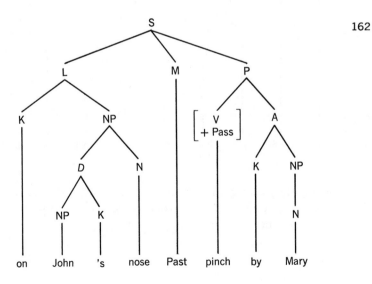

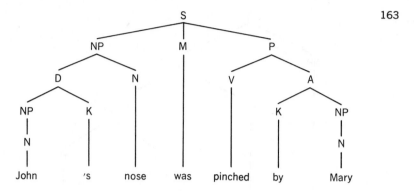

Backing up to 156, we may now see the consequences of 'promoting' adnominal D. When the D is removed from L and becomes the left-most case constituent in P, the resulting structure is 164.

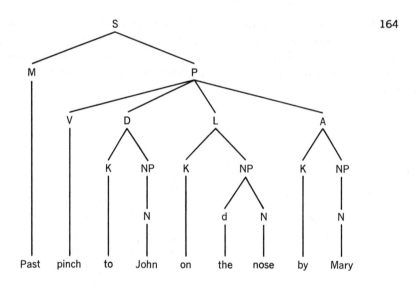

The possible subjects for 164 are the A or the newly promoted D. When the subject is A, we get 165, a structure which, on application of the rules we have learned, eventually becomes 166.

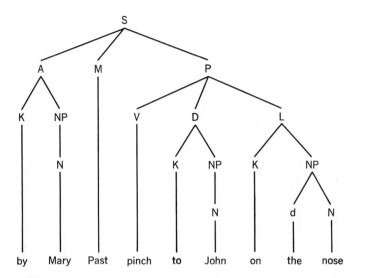

165

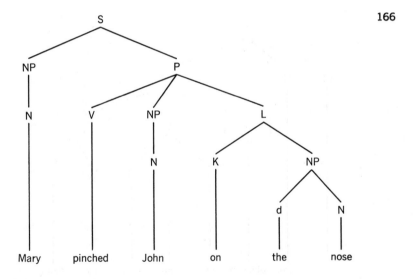

166

When D is made subject, on the other hand, we get 167; on applying the rules appropriate to a V with the feature [+passive], we eventually get 168.

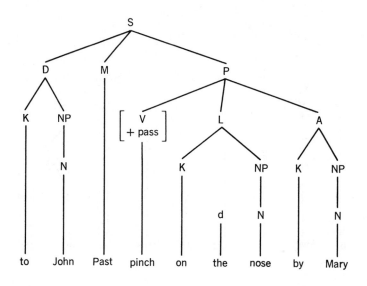

168

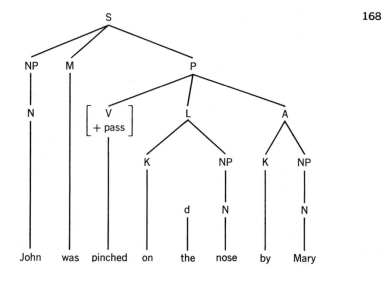

We may turn to the problem which interested Bally and Frei and examine the role of adnominal D in sentences which assign attributes to obligatorily possessed elements. The basic structure of such sentences can be illustrated by 169.

169

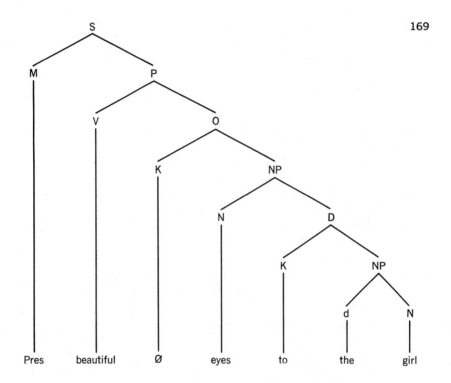

In languages which allow the D to remain in the NP, the D element is converted to its genitive form. In English this results in 170. Since 170 has only the form [V + O], the O is necessarily chosen as subject, and the result for English is 171.

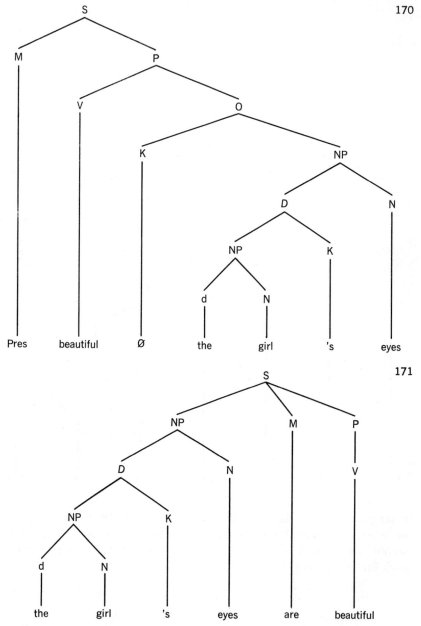

Notice that since the V is an adjective, it is incapable of 'absorbing' the tense,[63] so that it requires the provision of *be* within the M constituent.

[63] Stated more accurately, V's which are adjectives, passives, or progressives are incapable of absorbing the right-most affix in M.

Example 171 is a rendering of 170 in which the V is predicated on the O and the D is subjoined to the O. Thus it is analogous to our earlier Sentences 127 and 134 and is of the type indicated in 131.

Suppose next that the D of 170 does get 'promoted'. The result of introducing the D in this way as an immediate constituent of the P is 172.

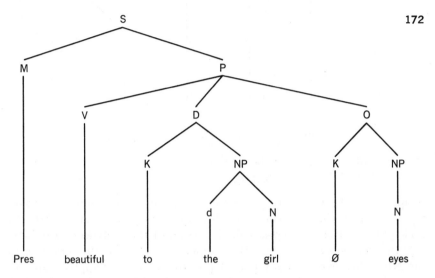

172

Some languages allow the O of Configuration 172 to become the subject and the D element to remain in the expected surface form for D, as in Sentence 132. Others allow the D element to undergo secondary topicalization when the O is subject, resulting, for example, in one case of the 'double subject' construction in Japanese (recall 142). The general expression type for sentences resulting from 172 when O becomes subject is suggested by the formula in 135 above.

Many languages allow the D to become subject. When this happens and there are no other changes, the O appears in some oblique case form. This is so because, since *beautiful* is not a true verb, the body-part word cannot be converted into an 'object'. The initial structure is seen in 173; it is one which is not typical of English, though it is perhaps seen in such expressions as those given in 174 and it may represent a stage in the derivation of a phrase of the type given in 175.

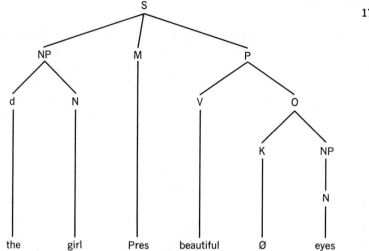

174. tall of stature, blue in the face
175. broad-chested, fat-legged

It appears to be the structural form underlying 136, whose expression type is given in 137. The construction is apparently quite rare in French; Frei speaks of it as a 'short-circuited' version of the sentences with *have*.

Another possibility, when D is subject, is to attach the adjective to the NP indicating the body part. I propose, in an unhappily quite ad hoc fashion, that this be done without removing the constituent label V. I believe there are some arguments for retaining at least an abstract V under P at all times. This constraint may turn out to be better motivated than it seems, for this structure appears to reflect what was needed in those languages which adopted a verb like *have*.

The structure I have in mind is that shown in 176.

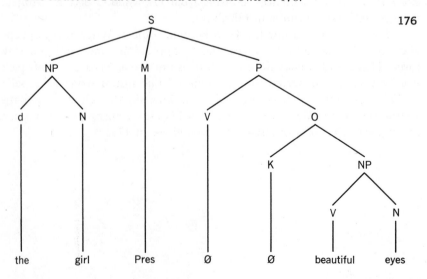

176

With the V under P vacant, a *be* must be added to the M in languages which allow structures of this type to become sentences directly. Notice that in this construction the modified body-part NP as a whole is 'in' some case form. The formula for this expression type has not yet been given; it would be something like 177.

177. P *be* $[A \rightarrow B]^{oblique}$

Conceivably this is the structure underlying such predicates as those shown in 178; the difference between predicates of the type in 137 and those of the type in 177 is seen in the Latin paraphrases of 179 and 180 respectively.

178. of tall stature; *di bello aspetto*
179. *aequus animo*
180. *aequo animo*

The last possibility, then, is to insert into the vacated V position the function word *have,* a verb which takes the modified body-part noun as its 'object'. In English, we have seen, this involves deleting the preposition. The result of modifying 176 in this way is 181.

181

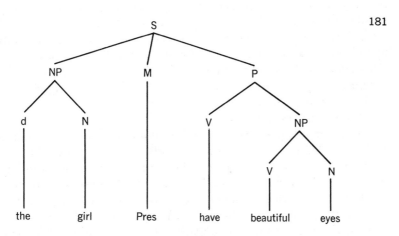

In short, it appears that the considerable surface variety found in sentences involving attribution of some property to an inalienable noun is to be accounted for by positing for universal grammar, in the spirit of Bach (1965), a set of recurrent transformations which each language uses somewhat in its own way. For sentences of the general structural type 182

182. $^\text{P}[\text{V}^\text{O}[\text{D} + \text{N}]]$

where V is an adjective and N is a body-part noun, the options are *a*
to *d* below:

(*a*) promote D
(*b*) choose D as subject
(*c*) copy adjective into body-part NP
(*d*) insert *have* into the vacated V

When *a* is not applied, the D becomes a genitive modifier of the body-
part N and the whole O becomes the subject. When *b* is not applied,
the O becomes the subject. When *c* is not applied, the 'short-circuited'
sentences of Frei are the result. Rule *d* is available only to languages
which have 'invented' *have*.

5.4 Further Remarks
on Inalienable Possession

If the feature of inalienable possession is to be treated as a universal
property of language, then either vocabulary items which are translations
of each other will be categorized alike with respect to alienability, or
the ways in which languages separately classify the 'same' things may
possibly reflect differences in the psychic make-up of the speakers of different languages. Many scholars have seen in the data on inalienabilia an
opportunity for the science of language to shed light on primitive men-
tality and on the possible range of man's concept of 'self'. Since the
differences appear more and more to be differences on the level of surface
structure, it may be advisable to wait some time before reaching any
conclusions on these matters.[64]

Adnominal D will certainly be needed for more than body-part nouns
and names of relatives. Directional indicators like *right* and *left* are
probably nouns of this type too. The reason that these words appear
typically without any personal reference in English and many other
languages is that they frequently refer to position or direction with respect to the speaker or addressee of the utterance, and there are simply
many situations in which an adnominal D does not need to be expressed
if it identifies speaker or hearer.

There are, too, many relational nouns which do not have a spe-

---

[64] For representative statements on the sociological relevance of the study of inalienable
possession, see Lévy-Bruhl (1916, p. 103), Bally (1926, p. 68 *et passim*), Frei (1939, p.
192), and van Ginneken (1939, p. 90). For a catalogue of noun classifications based on
grammatical differences associated with inalienable possession, see Rosén (1959, p. 268 f.).

cifically personal reference. We might wish to say that certain 'locational' nouns take an adnominal L. These nouns sometimes name parts of the associated objects, as in 183, and they sometimes identify a location or direction stated with reference to the associated object but not considered as a part of it, as seen in 184. 'Nouns' of the second type appear superficially as prepositions in English.

    183. corner of the table, edge of the cliff, top of the box
    184. behind the house, ahead of the car, next to the tower

6. Problems and Suggestions

There is a considerable residue of unsolved problems in the grammatical description of language phenomena, and it is disappointing though not surprising to realize how many of them remain unsolved under the formulation of grammar I have been suggesting. Those which come most quickly to mind are coordinate conjunction, nominal predicates, and 'cognate objects'.

6.1 Coordinate Conjunction

There may be a relationship between the ways in which languages deal with 'comitative' constructions and the phenomenon of coordinate conjunction of NP's. Put in case terms, there may be a relationship between conjunction of NP's and what one might wish to refer to as a comitative case. Jespersen noticed the parallels between *with* (a preposition which has a comitative function) and the conjunctor *and,* as in such pairs of sentences as 185 and 186 (1924, p. 90).

    185. He and his wife are coming.
    186. He is coming with his wife.

Japanese has separate devices for indicating sentence conjunction and NP conjunction, and the postposition used for NP conjunction is identical with the comitative postposition. In a conjunction of NP's, all but the last have the postposition *to.* The last one has the postposition appropriate for the case role of the whole NP. Compare 187 and 188.

    187. *Tanaka-san to Hashimoto-san ga kimashita.*
        'Mr. Tanaka and Mr. Hashimoto came.'
    188. *Hashimoto-san ga Tanaka-san to hanashimashita.*
        'Mr. Hashimoto spoke with Mr. Tanaka.'

Redden points out that in Walapai a sentence has only one noun in the 'nominative' case. Noun conjunctions are effected by having the 'ablative' suffix—the suffix with comitative function—on all but one of the nouns in a conjunction. Thus, in 189, /-č/ is nominative, /-m/ ablative.

189. /hàtθáùač hmáɲm/
     'the dog and the boy' (lit. 'the dog with the boy')

It may be that the rule in 190 is needed as an expansion rule for NP.

190. NP → NP + C

Using X as a cover term for the various case categories, 190 will produce such structures as 191.

191

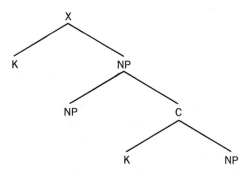

The case category C has a very special status, since the selectional constraints on nouns under C are those of the superordinate NP. What is needed, in other words, is a rule which imposes on any N under C the same redundant features that are associated with the dominating non-C case.

   A subjoined C under some circumstances must remain in the large NP. In languages which lack a generalized conjunctor, the case marker is simply that appropriate to C (the postposition *to* in Japanese, the suffix *-m* in Walapai); in languages which have a generalized conjunctor, this word replaces the case marker, in the way that *and* replaces *with* under certain conditions.

   The structure underlying 185 and 186, then, might be something like 192; we ignore the source of *his*.

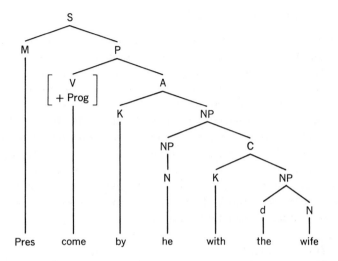

If the C remains inside the NP, the entire A becomes the subject, yielding Sentence 185; if the C is promoted, however, as in the structure shown in 193, it is left behind when the A becomes the subject, resulting in Sentence 186.

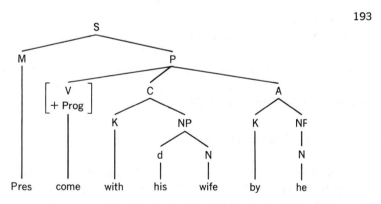

It is quite unlikely that the numerous problems associated with NP conjunction can be appreciably simplified through this approach, but that there is some connection between conjunction and comitative uses of NP's cannot be doubted. Lakoff and Peters (1966) have recently presented very persuasive arguments that the 'direction' of the relationship is the opposite of what I have suggested; that, in other words, comitative phrases are derived from NP conjunction rather than the other way around.

6.2 Nominal Predicates ·

Nothing that has been said so far suggests a way of providing for sentences of the *N be N* type. It is clear that they represent a distinct sentence type from those involving any of the case relations discussed above, though more than one case relationship may be involved in these sentences. (The terms *essive* and *translative* come to mind.)

Some nouns that appear in predicate position are restricted in their occurrence elsewhere. It might be possible to treat these nouns as, on one level, V's which are restricted to the form [_____ A]. Examples are words like *idiot, bastard,* and *fool.* The environment contains A because the subject is always animate and because the constructions exhibit selectional and transformational properties associated with V's having A's in their environment. Notice 194 and 195.

194. Don't be a fool.
195. He's being a bastard again.

This interpretation appears to account for the fact that we have sentences like 196, but not—with *idiot* used in this same 'evaluative' sense— 197.

196. John is an idiot.
197. An idiot hit the first homerun.

Further evidence that the word is properly treated as a V is found in the fact that these nouns may accept types of modification usually associated with adjectives, as in 198.

198. John is quite an idiot.

The serious problems are (*a*) with the use of words like *idiot, fool,* and so forth, in other contexts, as in 199, and (*b*) with the use of non-evaluative N's in predicate sentences, as in 200.

199. That rat swiped my lunch.
200. That boy is my nephew.

A new case category or two could be invented for the occasion, of course, but such matters as the requirement that subject and predicate NP's agree in number remain as serious as they ever were. Perhaps some solution is forthcoming along the lines of Bach's proposals elsewhere in this volume.

6.3 Cognate Objects

A difficulty of another sort is presented by the so-called 'cognate-object' constructions. These are constructions in which, at the very least, there is a high selectivity between a specific V and an 'object' N, and in which the V + N combination in one language might well be matched by a V alone in another.

Slightly modifying a recent analysis by Sandra Babcock (1966),[65] I would propose that there are contexts in which the case category F (factitive) may be left lexically empty, and that certain words classified as V's may be inserted specifically into frames containing dummy F's. These words may have associated with them special N representatives (for example, *bath*) and special pro-V's (for example, *take*). The rules that apply to dummy-F sentences are the following:

(*a*) Copy the N-representative of the V under the F.
(*b*) Replace the V by the designated pro-V.

The rules may have separate conditions of optionality for different V's. The cognate-object V *dream* may appear as a V in its own right, or it may appear in dummy-F sentences. As a cognate-object verb, it has *dream* as its N-representative and *have* as its pro-V; it is further specified as selecting either the preposition *about* or *of* for the O constituent and as not requiring Rule *b*.

When the N-representative associated with *dream* is copied into the F constituent, the result is Sentence 201; when the associated verb *have* replaces the V, the result is 202.

201. John dreamed a dream about Mary.
202. John had a dream about Mary.

With these devices, we may in fact consider extending the interpretation of cognate-object constructions in the following way. Some words may be treated as cognate-object V's even though the rule for replacing the pro-V is obligatory. The V *nightmare,* for example, might have *nightmare* listed as its N-representative and *have* as its pro-V. Thus, on applying Rule *a*, the structure in 203 becomes the intermediate structure in 204; on applying Rule *b*, 204 is converted to 205. Analogous uses of this device could possibly account for the connection between *suggest* and *make a suggestion, shove someone* and *give someone a shove,* and so

---

[65] Compare too the interpretation in terms of 'quasi transformations' found in Harris (1957, Section 30).

on, but many serious problems remain. In particular it is not obvious how
sentences like 206 and 207 can be dealt with in accordance with these
proposals.

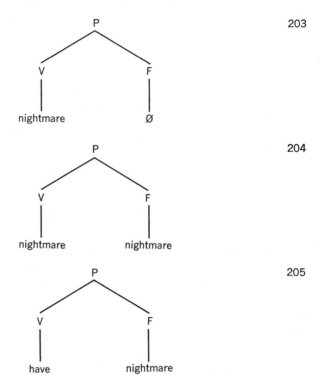

203

204

205

206. She made several ridiculous suggestions.
207. I had a terrible nightmare last night.

6.4   Other Problems

There are many issues for which I cannot even pretend to see solutions. The apparent connection between surface cases and 'partitive'
functions; the restriction of 'definiteness' in some languages to NP's in
particular surface-case relations (typically, the 'direct object'); the extreme variety of surface realizations of the same meaning (from the same
deep structure?) that Jespersen illustrates in connection with what he
calls 'rank shifting' (1924, p. 91), to name just a few.

The difficulties mentioned so far are empirical in nature, but many
formal problems exist as well. One of these is whether the permitted
arrays of cases under P need to be generated via phrase-structure rules,
since one of the most important functions of the PS rules has been that

of defining grammatical relations—that is, that of defining phenomena which are here partly treated categorially rather than configurationally. Related to this problem are the apparent dependency relations that exist *among cases*. It appears, for example, that the occurrence of B (benefactive) phrases in a sentence has more to do with whether the sentence contains an A than with independent specific properties of V's. One is almost willing to allow these facts to be expressed by a generative process which chooses a verb, then the cases required by that verb, then the other cases that are compatible with the cases originally chosen. The issue is not whether the permitted sequences can or cannot be generated by PS rules—there is no doubt that they can—but whether the kinds of co-occurrence or dependency relationships that seem to obtain might not be more efficiently stated in some other way. (Modifications of transformational grammar of the type introduced in Chomsky (1965) made it no longer necessary to use PS rules for subclassification of lexical categories or for the choice of lexical items. If the provision of syntactic relations of certain kinds must also be handled by some device other than PS rules, there is a chance that rules of this type may be abandoned altogether.)

Whether the cases should be represented as categories dominating NP's or in some other way is an issue which seems to me to be fairly wide open. One advantage of the categorial treatment is that NP's made subject and object may be said to have lost their 'original' case relation to the sentence (by the rule which 'erases' the case category whenever the case marker K has been deleted—that is, a 'node-razing' rule) with the result that their form can only be determined by referring to their 'pure relational' status. Thus it would appear that the surface distinction between labeled and configurationally defined relations on NP's may correspond to the traditional distinction between the 'concrete' and the 'grammatical' cases. (How the genitive figures in this distinction is not clear under either interpretation.)

Several people have pointed out to me the apparent convertibility of underlying representations in case grammar into objects which resemble dependency diagrams and tagmemic formulas. If the K elements are interpreted as constituents of NP's, then the case categories *unarily* dominate NP's. This makes them equivalent to *labels on the branches that link P with the various NP's that are directly related to it*. If the only function of the P is to provide a constituent in terms of which the NP's can be related to the V, one may just as well represent these relationships more directly by replacing the node P by the V. The result is no longer a diagram of constituent structure, since lexical elements are inserted into 'dominating' nodes; but it may turn out to be just as possible to represent the needed constituent organization of sentences from a 'stemmatic' diagram of the type used by Tesnière or Hays, as from a phrase-structure tree diagram.

There is an easy conversion from underlying representations of case grammar to 'tagmemic' formulas, too, as long as the case categories *unarily* dominate NP's. Or, for that matter, a case-grammar diagram could simply be read off as a tagmemic formula, as long as certain symbols were designated as function indicators. One can as easily say 'NP filling an A slot' as anything else. The crucial difference between the modification of transformational grammar that I have been suggesting and the typical tagmemic study is in the insistence here on discovering the 'deepest' level of the 'deep structure'.

7. Closing Words

One criticism of case grammar that has been brought to my attention is that it is too strongly motivated by semantic considerations. Many of the analyses have (hopefully) the result that certain semantic distinctions and interlanguage commonalities are revealed in fairly direct ways in the deep structures of case grammar, but, it has been argued, syntactic analyses should be based on syntactic data alone and on one language at a time.

The question arises whether there is a 'level' of syntactic description that is discoverable one language at a time on the basis of purely syntactic criteria. If it is possible to discover a semantically justified universal syntactic theory along the lines I have been suggesting, if it is possible by rules (beginning, perhaps, with those which assign sequential order to the underlying order-free representations) to make these 'semantic deep structures' into the surface forms of sentences, then it is likely that the syntactic deep structure of the type that has been made familiar from the work of Chomsky and his students is going to go the way of the phoneme. It is an artificial intermediate level between the empirically discoverable 'semantic deep structure' and the observationally accessible surface structure, a level the properties of which have more to do with the methodological commitments of grammarians than with the nature of human languages.

Nouns AND NOUN PHRASES[1]

Emmon Bach The University of Texas at Austin

[1] I am grateful to Charles J. Fillmore, James D. McCawley, Noam Chomsky, and Stanley Peters for comments on an earlier version of this paper.

1 Grammars of English traditionally maintain a sharp division between nouns, verbs, and adjectives. It is my purpose here to demonstrate that the differences between these 'parts of speech' exist only on a relatively superficial level and that the fundamental dichotomy underlying the distinctions is of a quite different sort. By saying 'sentences' rather than 'English sentences', I intend to suggest that the deep structures of sentences in different languages are identical; that is, I am subscribing to the idea of a universal set of base rules. Most of my arguments are drawn from English and I hope to show that my proposals can be justified purely on the basis of English evidence. The result is to posit deep structures for English sentences which look much less like their surface forms than heretofore.

There are several stages to my argument. In the first I shall try to show that nouns should be introduced into English sentences by way of relative clauses, that is, that noun phrases with nouns as their heads are exactly like noun phrases with verbs and adjectives (or their derivatives) as heads in their underlying form. This proposal leads then quite naturally, I believe, to the denial that there are any differences in the deep structures of phrases involving these three classes and to the postulation of a system involving three fundamental kinds of entities in the deep structure: sentences, terms, and predicates or 'contentives'. *Terms* are essentially involved in what we call noun phrases, while *contentives* correspond to the three major lexical categories of nouns, verbs, and adjectives. In working out the details of these proposals we are led to inquire about the role of referential indices in the structures underlying English sentences and then to the postulation of a system of variables and quantifiers much like those of the lower functional calculus, a system by means of which we can explain some recalcitrant facts about the interpretation of English sentences with indefinite noun phrases. A final stage of my argument will show the consequences of these proposals for our conception of the lexicon of a transformational grammar.

2 Let us begin by noting that any grammar of English will include among the sentences it specifies as well formed the following set:

1. I know someone who is working on English adverbs.
2. I saw something that was horrible.
3. I never speak to anyone who is a behaviorist.

Furthermore, optional rules will yield shorter versions of the first two sentences but not the third:

4. I know someone working on English adverbs.
5. I saw something horrible.

Yet we have the sentence

6. I never speak to a behaviorist.

Although 6 seems to be formally and semantically as related to 3 as 4 and 5 are to the first two, the only relation shown by current descriptions of English is a semantic one. A similar situation obtains in the following set of sentences:

7. I know someone who sells cactuses.
8. I know a seller of cactuses/a cactus-seller.
9. We noticed something that was irregular.
10. We noticed an irregularity.
11. I spoke to the one who was an anthropologist.
12. I spoke to the anthropologist.

That is, we have rules which derive nouns from underlying relative clauses containing adjectives and verbs and based on elements like *someone, something, the one,* but these rules specifically exclude relative clauses with predicate nominals.

The first points in favor of deriving nouns from relative clauses might then be those of simplicity and descriptive adequacy. If we simplify the rules so that the structure index does not mention adjectives and verbs, then our grammar will posit the same relationship between all of the pairs of sentences just quoted. Given present base rules, however, we would then be positing two different underlying structures for a sentence like 6—one in which it is directly generated in the base by well-known rules, the other in which it is derived by reduction of a relative clause. Although it is not assumed that sentences having different representations in the base must be interpreted differently, it is highly suspicious when our grammars allow two different routes to exactly the same sentence when there is no conceivable difference between them. The next step then is to postulate that all nouns (at least common nouns) are derived in one way, namely from structures of roughly the form

Det + one + S

where S is further developed into a sentence of the form

Det + one + Aux + be + Predicate nominal

or whatever the correct underlying form for such structures turns out to be. Such a decision actually simplifies the base rules and in this case simplicity leads to better descriptive adequacy.

The foregoing argument tends to show that we can derive nouns from relative clauses, that this will cost us nothing or less because of rules needed on independent grounds, and that such a decision accounts for relationships otherwise left unexplained. The next steps in the argument lead to a strengthening of the last statement. A number of facts show that there are very strong reasons for such an analysis, indeed, that, unless we are willing to accept a series of disconnected and ad hoc explanations rather than a single coherent one which follows directly from our analysis, we *must* derive nouns in this way.

I   The distinction between restrictive and nonrestrictive relative clauses is well known. Consider the two sentences:

13. Eskimos who live in igloos have lots of fun.
14. Eskimos, who live in igloos, have lots of fun.

Sentence 14 asserts both that Eskimos have lots of fun and that they live in igloos, while 13 makes the more modest claim that the class of fun-having objects contains wholly the class of igloo-inhabiting Eskimos. It is also well known that reductions of relative clauses maintain the semantic difference while erasing the formal difference. Hence it is possible to have ambiguities in phrases with preposed adjectives and the like (Jespersen, 1924, pp. 108 ff.).

15. The philosophical Greeks liked to talk.

Once we have accounted for the difference between restrictive and nonrestrictive relative clauses, we have also accounted for the differences between the two interpretations of sentences like 15. The analysis of nonrestrictive relative clauses from conjunctions of sentences seems to be reasonably clear in outline if not in detail, while that of restrictive clauses is clear in neither sense. However, whatever the details, no one would suggest a completely different explanation for restrictive and nonrestrictive adjectives. That is, there are numerous reasons for deriving most attributive adjectives from underlying relative clauses. The fact that the distinction between the two types of relative clauses is matched in adjective-noun constructions provides one more motivation for this analysis.

Consider now the sentence

16. The idiot called me up yesterday.

According to my suggestion 16 is to be derived from something like this: 'The one who is an idiot called me up yesterday'. But since relative clauses can be either restrictive or nonrestrictive it should also be possible to derive it from something like 'The one' (or perhaps 'he'), 'who is an idiot, called me up yesterday'. Hence, the sentence 16 should have at least two interpretations. This is in fact the case, as we can see by providing two settings: one in which Smith and Jones both know just one idiot and one of them tells the other 'The idiot called me up yesterday'; the other in which Smith asks Jones, say, 'Have you heard from Algernon lately?' and Jones answers 16.

This usage is to be distinguished, I believe, from the following: Smith and Jones have been talking about someone and then one of them says: 'The man is insane'. It does not seem reasonable to derive this from 'He, who is a man, is insane'. Rather this is a kind of quasi pronominal usage which must be explained in the larger context of pronominalization. It seems as if pronominalization is a process by means of which a second occurrence of a noun phrase is used anaphorically and can be changed in various ways just so long as the result contains some subset of the markers of the full NP, minimally those which distinguish the pronouns of a language (or possibly the null set).

It might be objected that sentences like 16 are rather limited since it is usually nouns with some sort of emotional overtones which are used in this way. Again suppose Smith asks Jones about Algernon. Sentences like 16 can be constructed easily with words like *dope, fink, angel,* but hardly *plumber, anthropologist, cook.* However, this argument turns out to be one in favor of our analysis rather than against it. Note that 16 comes ultimately from:

17. He called me up yesterday and he is an idiot.

This is a perfectly good sentence as are all those obtained by replacing *idiot* with *dope, fink,* and so on. But those formed with nouns from the second set are highly implausible:

18. He called me up yesterday and he is a plumber.

The following facts (pointed out by John R. Ross[2]) provide further support. In general, nonrestrictive relative clauses can have a truth value vouched for by the speaker and independent of the context in which they are inserted:

[2] At the La Jolla Conference on English Syntax, February 24–27, 1967.

19. I dreamt that Rebecca, who is a friend of mine from college, was on the phone.

Given proper conditions such sentences can be ambiguous (for instance, if we change 'is' to 'was' in the example above). Take now a sentence like this:

20. The district attorney said that the murderer had escaped.

Example 20 can mean either that the district attorney said 'X, who is the murderer, escaped' or that the D.A. said 'X escaped' and *I* say 'X is the murderer'. If we derive the phrase 'the murderer' from a relative clause we need no special statements to account for this fact. That is, the fact that this sentence is ambiguous follows from the more general fact that such sentences with nonrestrictive relative clauses are ambiguous.

It will be noted that all the examples above involve definite noun phrases. The facts seem to be relatively clear here.\Definite noun phrases can support both restrictive and nonrestrictive relative clauses.⌐ It has been claimed that indefinite NP's can support only restrictive relative clauses (Smith, 1964). If so, then we should expect no corresponding ambiguity in phrases involving nouns with the indefinite article. That is, if 21 but not 22 is possible, then we should expect no ambiguity in 23:

21. I saw someone who was an Eskimo.
22. * I saw someone, who was an Eskimo.
23. I saw an Eskimo.

Unfortunately, the facts seem to be rather cloudy here and the most that I can say is that they are approximately as cloudy for indefinite NP's without relative clauses as they are for those with relative clauses.

(**II** With few exceptions, every sentence in English can have both a negative and a nonnegative form.[3] We should thus expect to find several possible ways of negating sentences composed of several underlying sentences. This is in general true:)

24. I believe he said she was an Eskimo.

---

[3] Some exceptions are noted, for example, in Quang (1966). The fact that there are sentences of the form 'Asterisk nobody!' but neither * 'Not asterisk anybody!' nor * 'Don't asterisk anybody!' (*asterisk*₂, of course) lends credence to the idea that the negative element in the NP of such a sentence comes from an embedded relative clause and not from the outer 'sentence'.

To 24 correspond several negations, all of which can collapse to a single form (if we overlook some possible intonational differences) by attraction of the negative to the earliest part of the sentence:

25. I don't believe he said she was an Eskimo.

This may mean at least three different things:

26. It is not the case that I believe that he said she was an Eskimo.
27. I believe that he did not say that she was an Eskimo.
28. I believe that he said she wasn't an Eskimo.

As a matter of fact, possibilities for negation provide a good clue as to whether a sentence is composite or not. We note that the sentence

29. He promised to stop wasting so much time.

can have two negative versions

30. He didn't promise to stop wasting so much time.
31. He promised not to stop wasting so much time.

We connect these two negations to the negation of two of the underlying sentences. Similarly in the two sentences

32. He can't go to New Mexico.
33. He can not go to New Mexico.

we are led to consider the modal sentence to contain an embedded sentence. This is confirmed by the possibility of having two negatives at once:

34. He didn't promise not to stop wasting so much time.
35. He can't not go to New Mexico.

In addition to sentence (or 'nexus') negation, traditional grammarians speak of the negation of 'sentence elements' (Jespersen, 1924, pp. 329 ff.). This move is necessary to explain the fact that even supposedly 'simple' sentences can have several different negations.

36. Many of them didn't want to stop the bombing.
37. Not many of them wanted to stop the bombing.

The notion of negating a sentence element is suspicious on two counts. First, it is hard to understand exactly what could be meant by negating a noun, an adverb, or the like. Second, it would obviously be better to have a uniform account of negation than to posit two unrelated kinds, that is, sentence negation and 'element' negation. But if, as I have suggested, noun phrases all contain full sentences in their underlying forms, it is possible to provide just such a uniform account: all negations will come ultimately from the negation of a sentence. Let us examine a number of instances of negation to see how this suggestion might work out.

Consider the sentence

38. The professors signed a petition.

According to our account this sentence contains at least two embedded sentences ('at least' because 'petition' is probably complex already in the sense of 'petition to do something', for instance, it probably contains a further sentence). In underlying form this would look more like:

39. The ones who were professors signed something which was a petition.

There should then be three possible negations. And in fact there are:

40. The professors *didn't* sign a petition.
    Neg the ones who were professors signed something which was a petition.
41. The *professors* didn't sign a petition.
    The ones *Neg* who were professors signed something which was a petition.
42. The professors didn't sign a *petition*.
    The ones who were professors signed something *Neg* which was a petition.

Now, if we accept the idea of element negation we would of course expect to have three possible negations too. But then not only are we faced with the necessity to provide separate negative elements in every noun phrase (at least), but we must also explain the interpretation of these element negations. However, the interpretation of the sentences follows naturally from an account of sentence negation and the posited underlying forms for the three negated sentences. For instance, 42 does in fact mean that the professors signed something, but it wasn't a petition.[4]

The intonational facts seem to support this idea. Notice that in each case we can predict the point of prominent pitch and stress by looking at the original position of the negative element.[5]

It is worth pointing out that German has two possible versions for such sentences, namely:

43. *Die* Professoren *haben das Rundschreiben nicht unterzeichnet.*
44. *Nicht die* Professoren *haben das Rundschreiben unterzeichnet.*

Moreover, there are many English sentences in which the negative morpheme or some derivative is actually a part of the noun phrase:

45. None of the professors signed the petition.
46. No boys like to have their hair cut.
47. Only a fool would say such a thing. (A fool and no nonfool would say such a thing.)

III   Another set of facts provides support for the idea that nouns are derived from relative clauses. Since every sentence contains an auxiliary element we may ask whether there are any traces of such elements in ordinary noun phrases. Before answering this question, however, it is necessary to direct our attention to other reductions from relative clauses.

---

[4] In the discussion at the symposium, Charles J. Fillmore took exception to the analysis of negative sentences suggested here. He pointed out that there are in fact many more possible negations for the basic sentence underlying 39, for instance 'The professors didn't *sign* a petition'. He also suggested that there might be a more direct relation between the cited sentences and pairs of sentences like 'The *professors* didn't sign a petition but someone else signed a petition'. On the first point I must reserve judgment, since it is unclear just how many underlying sentences must be assumed to be present in even rather simple sentences (see the preface to this volume). I suspect that the disagreement about the second point involves a pseudo issue. There are various reasons for casting doubt on the notion that deep-structure NP's literally contain embedded sentences (see the discussion in 3, IV below), and it might turn out to be the case that the conjoined sentences cited by Fillmore and the sentences given above are merely different surface representations of a common deep (or better perhaps, 'flat') structure.

[5] It seems as if a number of further facts could be explained if we suppose that several negations can occur at once, or even that sentence negation is produced by a recursive rule S → Neg + S (or some analysis having this effect). If there is then a rule for negative absorption which cancels out pairs of negatives after the stress assignment rule, then we can eliminate the emphasis or accent element set up in current analyses of English. Thus 'The professors *did* sign the petition' would have a not unreasonable source in 'The professors didn't not sign the petition', and so on. Eugene Loos has pointed out (unpublished paper) that in Capanahua negation on a noun is recursive and produces a series of expressions of increasing intensity but alternating negativity: *he, not-he, not-not-he* (=he indeed), *not-not-not-he* (=someone else).

The usual rule for reduction of relative clauses with predicate adjectives is formulated in terms of deleting *WH Aux be.* Note first that such a deletion is inconsistent with current theory, since it is impossible to recover the nature of the elements included in *Aux.* That is to say, in the sentence

    48. I was watching the beautiful girl.

we do not know whether the auxiliary element which has been deleted from the underlying relative clause is Present, Past, or possibly even a modal. Now it is a fact of English that there are limits to the interpretation of such a phrase. Sentence 48 cannot for instance be reasonably related to

    49. I was watching the girl who must have been beautiful.

That is, even if the theory did not preclude such an unrecoverable deletion, an analysis which allowed free deletion of any auxiliary element would be descriptively inadequate. I propose that the possible sources for such a sentence are in fact just two. One is a hypothetical auxiliary element which I shall call 'narrative' tense, and the other the present tense.[6] By 'narrative' I mean a tense which takes on its values from the narrative context of the sentence in which it is embedded. The prediction of the actual shape of this tense in modern English is a difficult affair and one which I cannot go into here (even if I knew all the answers, which I am far from claiming). Most commonly it appears to be the *past* tense in nonpresent contexts, the *present* tense elsewhere. Note the following examples:

    50. The Russians will put a man on the moon who is well trained.
    51. Stalin made short shrift of those who didn't agree with him.
    52. I am watching a girl who is beautiful.

Sentence 50, for instance, does not mean that the man in question is well trained now; indeed, he may not even exist. (It is possible to argue that the *present* tense actually underlies all of these sentences, compare for instance the substitution of *past* for *present* in indirect discourse. If true, that simply pushes the difference back one step.) Examples of true *present* occur in the following:

[6] My thinking on the questions discussed here was substantially clarified by reading Kiparsky, forthcoming.

53. Stalin spared many a man who spits on his tomb today.
54. The Russians will enter a man in the Olympics who runs the mile in 3:56.
55. I used to know the girl who is so beautiful.

Now let us consider some examples of reduced relative clauses to see if we can detect any ambiguities that could be traced back to this source. Consider the sentence:

56. I knew the beautiful girl, when she still had braces on her teeth and hated boys.

The most likely interpretation of this sentence, perhaps, is that the girl is now beautiful but was not necessarily so when I knew her. But the other interpretation is also possible. So also, 48 most likely indicates a girl who was beautiful at the time of the narration, but it may be pulled into the other meaning by an appropriate expansion:

57. I was watching the beautiful girl while she was still an infant bawling in her mother's arms.

Let us look at some examples which show that the reduction cannot take place if one of the two tenses is not present in the underlying form of the relative clause:

58. I saw a girl who had been beautiful.
59. I doubt if there is a man who will be that clever when he is fifty.
60. I know the fellow who was living in that house.

For the last sentence, compare

61. I know the fellow living in that house.
62. I knew the fellow living in that house.

Similar observations can be made about other types of reduced relative clauses, such as possessive phrases:

63. We hadn't bought our house yet. (=the house which we have)
64. Our house was on 57th Street. (=the house which we had)

If we now turn to ordinary noun phrases we can readily see that exactly the same possibilities exist. Consider first the sentences:

65. Before I met my wife, she worked in a library.
66. When the mother was three years old, her family moved to Canada.

The ordinary interpretation of these sentences is that the persons designated by *my wife* or *the mother* are those which stand in that relationship *now* (that is, they are based on clauses with present tense). But the other interpretations are possible if vanishingly improbable (I might have married by mail, the mother might have been a prodigy). Consider also:

67. In order to run a four-minute mile, a man has to start training at the age of six.
68. While it was still a pupa, the butterfly often thought of becoming an aviator.

I have shown that there are sentences in which nouns must be assumed to come from relative clauses with a present tense. Next let us look at some examples which show that there are sentences in which the nouns must come from relative clauses with narrative tense:

69. I saw the house before it was bombed.
70. The pupa often dreamt of becoming a butterfly.

Finally, note that when a form of the auxiliary different from the two deletable tenses is present in the underlying form it remains:

71. We saw something which had been a soldier lying in the ruins.
72. I'm racking my brain for something which might be evidence for this claim.
73. I know someone who was a president of a university.

Once again, it would be possible to explain the various interpretations of nouns without recourse to the notion that they are based on underlying relative clauses, but to do so would be to miss the parallelism with the other kinds of reduced relative clauses. It is interesting to note that my analysis makes English seem much more like a number of 'exotic' languages, like Potawatomi, in which words corresponding to our nouns have tense /nčĭmanpən/ 'my former canoe' (Hockett, 1958, p. 238).

IV Two arguments ago I showed that my postulated analysis helped to explain some facts about negatives, while in the last section I have indicated some reasons for considering an auxiliary to be present in the underlying forms of noun phrases with nouns. Are there any other elements in noun phrases which can be explained more readily if we assume such an analysis? There are indeed.

Attributive adjectives are usually derived from underlying relative clauses with predicate adjectives. It has long been known, however, that many attributive adjectives cannot have such a source.[7] Thus, 'heavy smoker' and 'early riser' do not come from 'smoker who is heavy' (under the usual interpretation) or 'riser who is early' but from underlying structures in which the adjective is represented as an adverb: 'someone who smokes heavily', 'someone who rises early'. There are, however, a number of examples where there is no underlying verb from which to derive the noun. These cases can be explained in quite the same way as the examples just mentioned, if we derive nouns from underlying relative clauses. So for instance, 'I spoke to the former president' will not be derived from * 'I spoke to the president who was former' but from 'I spoke to the one who was formerly president'. Some other examples:

74. I saw the alleged killer.
75. You are a real dope.
76. He gave us the putative solution.
77. The precise causes of schizophrenia are unknown.
78. Folsom man lived in present-day Alaska.
79. The then president called me on the carpet.

---

[7] Werner Winter (1965) has used these and other exceptions to posited generalizations to launch a wholesale attack on the writers of transformational grammars. He himself cites earlier transformational studies which mention explicitly the problems raised in his article but writes, 'the implications for the general approach are not stated' (by those workers). It seems to me that the only implication that can be drawn is that there are further areas to be explained, a point which no one would deny. If we say that a class of expressions, say *adjective + noun*, is derived from another class of expressions, say *noun is adjective*, then finding examples of expressions in the first class which are not matched by expressions in the second class merely shows that the one class is not equivalent to the other. In this case, as was pointed out in the studies cited by Winter, the two classes overlap but neither is contained in the other. There are several ways to account for such facts, which are the rule rather than the exception. One can set up special features which prevent the operation of a rule or make it obligatory where it is otherwise optional, as in Lakoff (1965), where a general method for handling irregularities is developed. But it is more satisfactory to remove the exceptions by positing further general rules as is attempted here for one class of such exceptions to the standard analysis of attributive adjectives. The general problem is that of any empirical investigation, to find the regularities which underly as many and as varied facts as possible. Winter's mention (in his concluding footnote) of 'the crucial difference between the inductive approach of the empiricist and the deductive one of the theoretician' brings in a wholly empty and vicious dichotomy. This inappropriate opposition is reflected in the frequent attempt to set up some sort of division between 'descriptive' and 'theoretical' linguistics, as if there could be description without theory or theory without description.

It should be pointed out that the underlying forms of these relative clauses—'who was allegedly the killer' and so forth—are themselves problematical. It is likely that they come from several sources, most, perhaps, from composite sentences: 'somebody alleges that he is the killer'. But it is clear that at some point they will assume the form of a sentence with a predicate nominal and an adverbial and that they can then be treated just like the clear cases of adjectives from adverbs mentioned above.[8]

V   Consider next the nature of the predicate nominal itself, which I am proposing as a basis for the introduction of nouns. In early transformational studies of English it was assumed that the predicate constituent could contain among other things a noun phrase, but this noun phrase had rather peculiar properties when compared with other noun phrases. It could not freely contain pronouns or proper names (Lees, 1960, p. 14). Given the right type of noun, it had to agree in number with the subject of the sentence, since we have 'They are my friends' but not 'They are my friend' (as against 'They are a nuisance'). Moreover, the occurrence of definite noun phrases in the predicate was limited—there were heavy restrictions on the kinds of determiners allowed. If the predicate nominal is treated as an ordinary noun phrase it is possible to construct strange sentences under relative clause formation, pronominalization, and the like. That is to say, we have ordinary sentences like these:

80. John is a philosopher.
81. He is the person I was talking about.
82. The person I was talking about was John.

But the following are at best odd or marginal, or demand special interpretation, or stand in need of some expansion:

83. John is the philosopher.
84. John is this philosopher.
85. John is he (him).
86. A philosopher is John.
87. He is a philosopher, who studies metaphysics.
88. We saw a barn which something was.
89. She was an anthropologist, and he studies primitive cultures.

(In the last example, *he* is intended to refer to 'an anthropologist'.) Note also that the predicate nominal behaves differently from other noun phrases under question formation:

[8] In the discussion D. Terence Langendoen pointed out that the analysis suggested here explains neatly the ambiguity of phrases like *a good czar* as (1) 'a czar who is good' and (2) 'one who "czars" well' ('good as a czar').

90. What is she? An anthropologist.
91. Who said that? The fellow next door.

The peculiar properties of predicate nominals in sentences like 'He is an anthropologist' are sufficient to establish that these elements are not noun phrases. If we introduce ordinary nouns into noun phrases via relative clauses with just this element in them we will have automatically accounted for these properties. The only way in which pronouns and definite nouns (and names) can occur in the predicate is by way of a noun phrase consisting of a pronominal-like item (of a nature yet to be precisely determined) plus a further embedded sentence.

VI   A final argument for my analysis is a semantic one. Suppose I have a cat and no other pets and that I tell someone:

92. My marsupial scratched me yesterday.

Is this a true or a false sentence? If false, then its negation should be true:

93. My marsupial didn't scratch me yesterday.

But whether affirmative or negative it entails a false proposition, namely, that my pet is a marsupial, or that I have some other pet which is. The status of such a sentence is exactly like that of the well-known question: 'When did you stop beating your wife?' That is, it contains a sentence ('Something which I have is a marsupial') which is false and which must be subscribed to whether the outer sentence is false or true. Compare here the analysis of the sentence

94. Brutus killed a tyrant.

by the grammarians of Port Royal, which includes the underlying sentences 'Brutus killed someone' and 'That one was a tyrant' (Chomsky, 1966a, pp. 43 f).

3   I have shown so far that it is very easy to adapt independently needed rules of English to introduce nouns into sentences by means of relative clauses, that is, that the only occurrences of nouns in simple underlying structures of English will be in predications of the form 'Someone is an anthropologist', or the like. Further I have presented six rather disparate sets of facts which tend to show the correctness of this idea, in that the explanation for these facts follows directly from the posited analysis, whereas without this analysis it would be necessary to invoke

separate explanations for these facts (in so far as I can judge). It is in order now to take up in more detail the exact nature of the elements out of which surface noun phrases may be constructed.

In the foregoing discussion, I have used the form *one* in giving examples of underlying structures. It seems clear that something more abstract is needed. Let us note first that in order to keep both semantic interpretation and syntactic facts straight it is necessary to assume that this *one* like other referential nouns has some sort of referential index, say an integer (which might be written as a subscript). For instance, for the sentence

95. Someone drove downtown and robbed a bank.

we must assume an underlying structure in which the two occurrences of *one* have the same index (distinct from 'Someone drove downtown and someone robbed a bank').

Current theory has attempted to cope with notions like 'identity of reference' by means of a system of referential indexing as just indicated (Chomsky, 1965, pp. 145 f). Instead of using *one,* we might simply take the referential index as the underlying element. After all, in a sentence like

96. Someone drove downtown and that one robbed a bank.

the function of the two *one*'s is just to indicate this identity of reference (when taken with *some* and *that*). Further in the sentence

97. Someone is an anthropologist.

we must exclude such a referential index from the predicate nominal. It is only because of the collocation of *someone* and *an anthropologist* that we can be said to have *referred* to an anthropologist at all. I suggest that we replace concrete forms like one_1 and one_2 (or other pronouns) with a system of variables much like those used in symbolic logic. For convenience we can use x, y, z, and so on. Thus 97 would have an underlying form more like

98. Some x is an anthropologist.

While 96 would have the form

99. Some x drove downtown and x robbed a bank.

For a sentence like 100 we can readily provide an underlying form like 101:

> 100. Someone drove downtown and someone else (*or* some other one) robbed a bank.
> 101. Some x drove downtown and some y such that $x \neq y$ robbed a bank.

At first glance, such a use of variables seems to be little more than a notational change. If we take a further step, however, we shall see that there are strong reasons for adopting such a system.

It is natural to think about adapting a system of operators (quantifiers) like those used in logical systems and allowing these operators to function with the variables in the deep structures of sentences. The class of operators will include the more abstract elements underlying such forms as articles, *some,* and the like. We define the *scope* of an operator Q as the string dominated by the highest S to which Q is prefixed. If an operator Q is followed immediately by a variable x then we say that every occurrence of x within the scope of Q is *bound* by Q. Among the operators will be a *generic* operator, an *all* operator, a *some,* a *focus* or definiteness operator, a *question* operator, and the like. I shall now present several reasons why I believe such a system should be adopted in the base rules.[9]

I Consider the sentence:

> 102. She wants to marry a man with a big bank account.

This sentence is at least two ways ambiguous. On the one hand, it can mean that there is a certain man with a big bank account that she wants to marry; on the other, that she wants to marry an arbitrary man with a big bank account. In the following sentence, on the other hand, we have only one meaning:

> 103. She is marrying a man with a big bank account.

Now, rather than attributing the difference in interpretation of the

---

[9] In subsequent discussion George Lakoff (and later John R. Ross) made the claim that many elements considered operators here are in fact the verbs (or predicatives) of underlying sentences: 'All the men are here', for instance, would have roughly the structure '*It* the men are here + *All*'. I am not ready to admit that all operators are of this nature although it is quite possible that some are. In this connection Baker (1966) has discussed a number of the examples touched on here from a different point of view.

indefinite NP to the article, I would suggest that the difference resides in the placement and scope of the linguistic analogue of the existence operator (say *some*). We can paraphrase the two senses of 102 as follows:

104. There is a man with a big bank account that she wants to marry.
105. She wants there to be a man with a big bank account and that she marry him.

In the system I have been sketching here the deep structures of the two sentences x would have a form indicated roughly as

106. *Some x* [$_S x$ has a big bank account and she wants to marry x].
107. She wants [$_S some x$ [$_S x$ has a big bank account and she marry x]].

Another instance of such an ambiguity of scope is given in the example

108. He never charged us for one visit.

I do not believe it is possible to explain such ambiguities except by means of the notion of scope, because we find a systematic relationship between the number of interpretations and the number of embedded sentences (of the proper type). Thus the following sentence has three interpretations:

109. He said that she wanted to marry a man with a big bank account.

While the next one has four readings:

110. The Smiths claim Walter said Mary wanted to marry a Swede

as we can see by continuing the sentence in four ways:

111. . . . although they think he's Norwegian.
112. . . . although he thinks he's Norwegian.
113. . . . although she thinks he's Norwegian.
114. . . . because they're so dependable.

Now it is possible that one could explain these different readings (which are in principle limited in number only by the possibilities of embedding sentences) in some other way, but any such method will have to keep track of the number of different sentences involved and assign the varying interpretations in some way to the relationship between the indefinite NP and the embedding sentences. It seems to me that the proposal I have made does this in a natural way.

II Questions are explained usually with the help of two elements: a question marker Q, and some specifically marked, distinguished element (*someone* or the like). Yes-no questions involve Q alone (or possibly a sentence adverb, Katz and Postal, 1964, pp. 95f.), while WH questions involve both Q and the marked element. Both of these choices are optional in the base and independent of each other, in present analyses. The choice of questioned element cannot be left to a transformation under present theory, or else we would have the same underlying structure for semantically distinct sentences:

115. Who saw someone?
116. Who did someone see?

On the other hand, if some element is marked to be questioned and the general question marker, Q, is not chosen, then it is necessary to make some ad hoc provision to block strings like:

117. * He said that who was going.

The use of prefixed operators and variables allows this choice to be made in the base, and ill-formed sentences will be blocked by a general convention disallowing sentences with unbound variables. Thus 115 and 116 will have the underlying forms, respectively:

118. Q x x saw someone.
119. Q x someone saw x.

The same method can obviously be employed in describing the focus system of languages like those of the Philippines. The element to be focused can be identified by a variable attached to this operator in the deep structure.

III Next consider the fact that some elements that have been classed as determiners *must* be disassociated from the nouns with which they occur. Sentence 120 cannot have as its source a sentence like 121 but rather one like 122:

120. Every person loves himself.
121. Every person loves every person.
122. Every x such that x is a person loves x.

Sentence 121 is a perfectly good sentence but cannot be explained by the ordinary analysis since if the underlying form for the identical noun phrase is Det + N (with *every* as the determiner), it should reflexivize under identity of the object with the subject. But it is clear that it should have an underlying structure more like this:

123. For every x, y such that x, y are persons, x loves y.

In a similar way we can explain the difference between 124 and 125:

124. Some person loves himself.
125. Some person loves some person.

Note, by the way, that we can construct sentences with *every* that have scope ambiguities quite parallel to those discovered with indefinite noun phrases:

126. John told me that every rat had deserted the sinking ship.

That is:

127. Every rat was reported by John to have deserted the sinking ship.
128. John said: 'Every rat has deserted the sinking ship'.

Now let us look at some examples with other determiners. They follow exactly the same paradigm:

129. The man hates the man.
130. The man hates himself.
131. A boy killed a boy.
132. A boy killed himself.

Early transformational studies disallowed such sentences as 121 and 131 or made the rule optional. Later theory has introduced the idea of referential identity and made it a part of the condition for transformations like the reflexive. But sentences like 121 show that the condition of identical reference alone is not enough. After all the reference of phrases like *every man, all people,* and so forth, cannot be different under two occurrences in the same sentence. There are many similar examples:[10]

133. Everyone wanted to go.
134. Everyone wanted everyone to go.

[10] A number of similar examples were discussed by Paul Postal at the La Jolla conference referred to above.

IV I would like to claim that in every transformation including a condition, NP = NP, what is meant is *only* the identity of the referential index (or here variable). This amounts to saying that in a sentence where n identical NP's have been reduced or eliminated by deletion, pronominalization, and the like, we do not have $n + 1$ occurrences of the same NP in the deep structure, but only one (in some form) with $n + 1$ variables. To illustrate, under current theory 135 has a deep structure something like 136:

135. People who fool themselves want to fool themselves.
136. people$_i$ WH people$_i$ fool people$_i$ want IT people$_i$ WH people$_i$ fool people$_i$ fool people$_i$ WH people$_i$ fool people$_i$

The deep structure that I am proposing would be like 136 but with all the extra *people*'s stripped away, leaving just eight identical variables in their place.

The foregoing argument is strengthened considerably when we note that there are sentences which *cannot* be accounted for under current ideas about NP identity. Consider the sentence

137. A person should sometimes say 'No' to his children.

Given the analysis of pronominalization offered by Ross 1967 or Langacker (forthcoming), the phrase 'his children' contains in its deep structure a repetition of the NP underlying 'a person'. The second occurrence of this phrase is pronominalized to yield ultimately 'his'. There can be no doubt about the referential identity of 'his' and 'a person' (under one interpretation of the sentence). Thus it might seem that the condition NP = NP on pronominalization would be sufficient and necessary.

As Ross and Langacker independently showed pronominalization can take place not only from left to right as above, but also from right to left into an embedded sentence. What happens if we embed a modifying clause onto 'a person'—in particular, one which contains the underlying structure for 'his children'? Then we can have two versions of the sentence depending on whether we work from left to right or from right to left:

138. A person who doesn't want to spoil his children should sometimes say 'No' to them.
139. A person who doesn't want to spoil them should sometimes say 'No' to his children.

Both sentences are possible. Both support the same range of interpretations, including those in which 'them' and 'his children' and 'a person who doesn't want to spoil his children' and 'his' are coreferential, respectively. But the underlying structure for these sentences is embarrassingly deep. In 139 'them' is a pronominalization of 'his children', which itself contains a repetition of 'a person who . . .', which itself contains the underlying structure for 'his children', and so on ad infinitum. Or to put it in a formulation suggested by Paul Postal (correspondence), the analysis of pronominalization which depends on the condition NP = NP leads to the contradiction that an NP is identical with a proper part of itself.

I cannot claim that the system of variables suggested here is the only way out of this impasse. But the underlying structure for such a sentence can be given in a straightforward manner that does not lead to any such difficulty:

140. An x such that x is a person and x does not want x to spoil the y such that y are children and belong to x should sometimes say 'No' to y.

V   If we use quantifiers, variables, negative elements and the like to construct sentences, it should be possible to show that different results can be attained by arranging these elements in different orders in the deep structures of sentences; in some cases we should be able to show ambiguities that result when several possible arrangements reduce to the same surface form. We have already considered a number of such predictable results. But there are many more.

It is easy to construct logic-textbook examples of sentences involving the *all* operator and the *some* operator arranged in differing orders. Consider the sentence

141. Every man loves some woman.

Does this sentence have two meanings? If it does, then we have a case where two different orderings of operators will explain a fact about English that would be very difficult to explain otherwise. If it does not, then we can still exhibit sentences like the following to show two different results from differing orders of operators:

142. There is some woman that every man loves.

Here I would incline to consider the first sentence ambiguous because of cases like the following:

143. Every boy in town is wild about some girl on our block.
144. I know a woman that every man loves.

Consider now Quine's two sentences (1961):

145. I do not know every poem.
146. I do not know any poem.

It is of course possible to explain the difference by positing two different elements—*any* and *every*—and saying something (as does Quine) about the different characteristics of these items with regard to their scope. But the linguist must also account for the way in which these forms enter into sentences and be prepared to incorporate his statements about the interpretation of the sentences into a general theory of semantic interpretation. But we can, in fact, account for the difference very simply by means of two orderings of the *all* operator and the negative element:

147. Neg *all* x such that x is a poem I know x. (=145)
148. *All* x s.t. x is a poem Neg I know x. (=146)

The foregoing discussion was intended to be suggestive rather than conclusive. I believe that the facts presented are sufficient to indicate that a system of quantifiers and variables is worth exploring as a possible part of the base rules. It seems to me, further, that the linguistic analogue to the notion of binding variables by quantifiers might help explain the relations 'in construction with' and 'command' which have been discussed by E. S. Klima (1964) and Ronald Langacker (forthcoming), respectively. It goes without saying that the particular operators postulated for the base cannot be identified with the universal and existential quantifiers of logic. Thus, in normal usage and in contrast to the usual 'translations' of such sentences into artificial logical languages, 149 does not entail 150, while 151 does entail 152:

149. Men eat fish and John is a man.
150. John eats fish.
151. Some people have red hair.
152. Some people don't have red hair.

4   One can take, and various scholars have taken, quite disparate positions regarding the question of universals in linguistic theory. No one, I think, would seriously maintain the position that there are no universal concepts in linguistics whatsoever, since this would be tantamount to a denial of the possibility of any rational understanding of

language in general; that is, linguistics would be a discipline which had no subject matter apart from the study of individual languages, and even here it would be a complete mystery how knowledge about one language could throw light on another (as it does).

Let us juxtapose two extreme positions. We might say that the only universals are what have been called *formal* universals (Katz and Postal, 1964, p. 160; Chomsky, 1965, pp. 27–30). That is, the most that linguistics can say is that grammars of natural languages are chosen from a set of objects meeting certain purely formal specifications: there are such and such components, the rules in the various components meet certain formal conditions, and so on. But the elements occurring in these grammars are completely arbitrary from one language to another. This view is patently false, as is shown every time a field linguist encounters a new language. Given the logically or physically possible sets of elements available at all levels—phonological, semantic, syntactic— the similarities among languages are far more striking than their differences. No language utilizes a belch as a distinctive feature, or Pike's fourth possible initiator (the air chamber formed by the lower lip, the lower teeth, and the tongue) (Pike, 1943, p. 101). I am quite confident that no language has a word to denote the object consisting of a person's right limbs and left hemisphere. No language has a system of twenty-five major lexical categories, and none lacks a means of building up complex sentences out of smaller ones.

On the other hand, one could claim that languages all share exactly the same set of *substantive* elements. Note that as a hypothesis this is much better than a hypothesis that languages share no substantive elements. But once again it is too obviously false to merit discussion. The truth must lie somewhere between these two extremes. One frequent statement is that each language makes some undetermined selection from a stock of universal elements. This is a completely empty claim, of course, without an exhaustive specification of what these elements are. Otherwise, we can simply list all elements that have occurred in the descriptions of particular languages and say that this is a partial set of such universal elements awaiting completion as we describe more languages. Obviously, there is no way to refute the statement that the universal set of elements comprises simply those which have been postulated for individual languages and which might be postulated in the future.

Let us consider various hypotheses which could be made about the system of elements and rules in the base component (leaving aside the lexicon for the time being):

A. The base rules for any language are constructed out of a fixed set of elements.

B. There is a fixed set of universal grammatical relations such as *subject-of, object-of.* The rules of the base are constrained so as to express just this set of relations according to universal definitions.[11]

C. The actual rules of the base are the same for every language.[12]

These three hypotheses make increasingly strong claims about the part of linguistic theory which can be called universal grammar; that is, each hypothesis implies but is not implied by the ones preceding it in the list. And each hypothesis makes a different empirical claim about the innate linguistic capacity of the speaker of a natural language. Obviously, to present a convincing defense or refutation of any of these hypotheses would be to anticipate the linguistic research of the next few decades.

In case I have not yet betrayed my bias in favor of the last hypothesis, let me do so now and explain why I am a Universalist-Unitarian. First (to adapt an argument of James D. McCawley's about the ordering of the base rules, forthcoming *b*), no one has ever discovered two dialects of the same language which differ in essential ways in the base rules. Second, continuing research in depth on languages like English has resulted in sets of base rules that look increasingly abstract and less and less like the surface structure of English sentences.[13] I have presented some evidence on that point already. Third, research on widely different languages tends to throw light back and forth in unexpected ways. Finally, it seems that the best strategy for research is to adopt the strongest hypotheses and then attempt to refute them. In this view it is almost correct to say that language learning by the child consists in finding the transformations which will derive the surface structures of sentences in his language from the universal set of base structures.

If this third hypothesis is correct, then it cannot be the case that Nootka, Japanese, and English, for example, differ in having one, two, or three major lexical categories, respectively. George Lakoff and Paul Postal have argued that the classes of adjectives and verbs in English are in actuality merely two subclasses of one lexical category, thus making English look more like Japanese.[14] Traditional Indo-European grammar,

---

[11] This is one of the positions outlined in Chomsky (1965, pp. 117 f).

[12] This is the position represented in Bach (1967) and suggested as one of several alternatives in Lakoff (1965). Lakoff stated it more positively as a hypothesis at the La Jolla conference mentioned above.

[13] I am referring here especially to the work of Ross and Lakoff presented at the La Jolla conference and during and after the Texas conference.

[14] See Lakoff (1965, Appendix A) and Prideaux (1966); for a recent discussion of 'parts of speech' see Lyons (1966). The main difference between the view presented here and that of Lyons, in so far as I understand him, is that he considers the category Noun to be a basic one, whereas I consider it to be derived and that the functional notion of being a term or argument (NP) for a predicate is more basic.

on the other hand, has generally lumped together nouns and adjectives (largely, to be sure, because of morphological characteristics). I shall now present some arguments which seem to me to indicate that all three categories are represented by one in the base component. We might call this category 'contentives' ('predicates' would be a suitable term except that it has been preempted in linguistic terminology for another usage— *contentives* are quite like the *predicates* of logic or the 'full words' of traditional Chinese grammar).

Under current conceptions of English grammar the following pairs of sentences have quite different underlying structures, since 154 and 156 are composed of two underlying sentences, but 153 and 155 of only one:

153. The man is working.
154. The one who is working is a man.
155. The man is large.
156. The one who is large is a man.

In the system of rules which I have suggested, the underlying structures would be much more similar:

157. The one who is a man is working.
158. The one who is working is a man.
159. The one who is a man is large.
160. The one who is large is a man.

These sentences happen to be translations of examples given by Morris Swadesh (1939) to illustrate the fact that there are no distinctions between these sorts of stems within the major lexical class of Nootka. In the order given we have

161. *mamo·kma qo· ?as?i* ('is working, the man')
162. *qo· ?asma mamo·k?i* ('is a man, the working one')
163. *?i·ḥma· qo· ?as?i* ('is large, the man')
164. *qo· ?asma ?i·ḥ?i·* ('is a man, the large one')

My claim, which of course must be justified in detail, is that the asymmetries of the English sentences result from transformational rules and are not to be attributed to the deep structures. Under my conception, the base rules will include the categories *term* (=NP, more or less), various operators as indicated before, variables, S, and *contentive*. A full justification of this proposal would take us well beyond the bounds of this paper. I can only sketch out here some of the reasons which lead me to consider this idea correct.

I   Many transformations mention the element NP in their structure index; however, hardly any mention the element *noun,* and these all seem to be quite late transformations which might be assumed to operate after the rules which (in languages like English) introduce the surface-structure differences between nouns and adjectives, for instance. (Examples are agreement rules, rules which rearrange nouns and adjectives, and so on. Note that there must be rules which rearrange different classes of adjectives also.)

II   Chomsky has claimed that the difference between nouns, on the one hand, and adjectives and verbs is reflected in their behavior with respect to selectional rules (see 1965, pp. 113 f.). That is, inherent features are developed in nouns. Then selectional rules on adjectives and verbs are formulated in terms of these noun-inherent features. This cannot be true. On the one hand, we have nouns which must contain selectional features in terms of which their 'subjects' are selected:

165. That he had killed the sparrow was a fact.
166. * That he had killed the sparrow was a pencil.

On the other hand, the occurrence of the crucial noun may be embedded indefinitely far down:

167. The one that seemed most likely to turn out to be a friend was anxious to go.
168. * The one that seemed most likely to turn out to be a table was anxious to go.[15]

III   In English and many other languages it is necessary for phonological rules to be able to refer to a class consisting precisely of nouns, adjectives, and verbs (and possibly adverbs) and excluding pronouns, articles, and the like. The notion of lexical category, which might be called on here, is not very helpful, since it is often quite arbitrary whether we set up our rules so that items like tense, for instance, are lexical categories or not.

IV   Many transformations which have been formulated so as to depend on the presence of some feature of verbs (either a subclassificational feature as in early transformational studies or a rule feature as in Lakoff, 1965) must, in a full description of English, include such

---

[15] I was made aware of these problems by cases presented by Ross and Lakoff at the La Jolla conference.

a feature or subclassification in nouns as well as verbs (and adjectives). Thus there are not only stative verbs and adjectives (Lakoff, 1965, 1966), which cannot occur in the progressive, have imperatives, and so on, but also stative nouns:

169. Don't be a fool.
170. * Don't be a mammal.
171. He's being a fool.
172. * He's being a mammal.

So also some complement transformations:

173. He's crazy to go.
174. * He's tall to go.
175. He's an idiot to go.
176. * He's a cook to go.

So also the comparative transformation:

177. He's more of a fool than I am.
178. * John was more of a corpse than Bill was.

5 In positing a universal base component it is, of course, necessary to exclude the lexical component. It is precisely in the set of lexical elements that the famous 'arbitrariness' of the linguistic sign becomes most obvious. Not only do the actual phonological shapes of words vary from language to language, but the particular sets of meanings and syntactic features which are given lexical status can vary widely (though not without limit). The final suggestion I wish to make has to do with the conception of the lexicon and its operation in a linguistic theory.[16] The hypothesis which I would like to entertain is that the base component does not actually add a phonological representation to the complex symbols of deep structures but merely develops the sets of semantic and syntactic features, which are then mapped into phonological shapes *after* the operation of the transformational rules (or some part of the

[16] Gruber (1965) suggests a system which is very close to the one outlined here. I was not aware of Gruber's work when this paper was first written. Gruber discusses many examples of the sort considered under V below. His proposals differ from mine mainly in that he considers part of the semantic reading of a sentence to be contributed by the lexical entry. The lexicon is called into play after the operation of certain pre-lexical transformations which have both a syntactic and a semantic role. At the moment it is difficult to see what sort of evidence would be required to decide between the two alternatives. In any case I must relinquish claims for priority and at the same time express pleasure that similar results were arrived at independently.

transformational rules). This idea is independent of the previous suggestions which I have made, but it helps to explain certain problems remaining in the above account and also, it seems to me, makes the notion of a universal base much more plausible. I shall outline some of the arguments which seem to speak for this idea and make some suggestions about the kind of cases which would strengthen the hypothesis.

I In present analyses pronouns can result from independent selection in the base or from the operation of transformational rules on embedded sentences and the like. If the phonological shape of the pronoun is part of its lexical entry, then the results of pronominalization via transformation must be given a phonological shape for each pronoun which is exactly the same as that of the base-derived pronoun. Clearly, it is undesirable to give such information twice in a grammar. Alternatively, we could make a second pass through the lexicon to pick up the phonological representation for such items. If all phonological representations are made late in the transformations, then no such change in the theory is needed.

II Some phonological representations are already spelled out in the transformational component, and the number of such cases seems to be increasing. This was true in the earliest analyses for such items as *do* and *self,* and it has been suggested for *one,* the articles, *have, be,* and various kinds of conjunctions, and is clearly appropriate for all sorts of inflectional and derivational material (on such 'segmentalization' rules see Lakoff, 1965, Postal, 1966).

III A very strong case could be made for this idea if we could find instances where conditions of identity had to exclude precisely the phonological representation of two items. Bates Hoffer III (in a seminar at the University of Texas) has reported on what looks to be such a situation in Japanese, involving classifiers. Some classifiers occur as independent nouns, and some have several alternants which are selected by morpheme features of the co-occurring nouns or numerals. In general, when a number phrase involving a classifier like $(y)en$ ('unit of money') is construed with an identical noun (in the identical interpretation) the second occurrence is deleted. But this deletion seems to take place regardless of the phonological shape of the second noun. These are the crucial examples:

179. *san-en no en > san-en* 'three Yen'
180. *samba no suzume* 'three sparrows' (*wa ~ ba* 'classifier for birds')
181. *samba no tori* 'three chickens' (*tori* 'chicken/bird')

182. *samba no tori* > *samba* 'three birds'
183. *sannin no kodomo* 'three children' (*nin* 'classifier for humans')
184. *sannin no hito* > *sannin* 'three people' (*hito* 'person')
185. *sambako no hako* > *sambako* 'three boxes' (*hako* ~ *bako* 'box')

One can develop a similar argument for English on the basis of examples like the following:

186. The man next door met the man next door.
187. The fellow next door met the guy next door.

It seems as if these are interpreted in exactly the same way, namely that identity of reference is excluded (because of *meet,* an irreflexive verb). With another verb, say *kill,* if identity of reference is intended (and it cannot be excluded) both will reduce to reflexives:

188. The man next door killed himself.
189. The fellow next door killed himself.

IV Suppletive forms like *went* versus *go* could simply be listed with appropriate entries to get them into the right contexts. An argument similar to that about pronouns shows that this cannot be done under the present conception of the lexicon. That is, some occurrences of the marker or feature for past tense are introduced in the base, while others must come from the operation of transformational rules (such as the rules for sequences of tenses, indirect discourse, and the like). Thus we either have to introduce the form *went* from *go* by a unique rule or go back through the lexicon after the operation of the transformations.

V The most compelling reasons for this conception of the nature and placement of the lexicon are, however, of a different sort. Recall the cases which seemed to show that the interpretation of indefinite noun phrases depended on the scope of a quantifier or operator and the presence of an embedded sentence:

190. She wants to marry a man with a big bank account.

Now it happens that we get exactly the same kind of ambiguity in some sentences which do not have an embedded sentence in their surface structure nor, in current analyses, in their deep structure:

191. She's looking for a man with a big bank account.

Let us next note a paraphrase of 191 which does in fact have such an embedded sentence and hence can be explained in the same way as 190:

192. She's trying to find a man with a big bank account.

It seems to me that there is a significant generalization here which we are prevented from stating just because of the present conception of the lexicon, its position and operation in a grammar. Once we change our conception of the lexicon as a set of entries which can be inserted in the place of individual complex symbols occurring in the deep structures of sentences to that of a set of transformational mappings of parts of phrase markers into phonological representations, there is nothing to prevent us from assigning the same deep structure to 191 and 192 and noting the fact in our lexical mappings that a structure underlying the phrase *try to find* has an alternate representation as a single lexical item, *look for*. It seems to me that present theory is making the same mistake as taxonomic phonemics makes. The insistence on a separate phonemic level between the 'morphophonemic' and the phonetic precludes the statement of a single generalization about devoicing of final obstruents in languages like Russian or Dutch, which happen to have some gaps in their set of voiced and voiceless obstruents (that is, biunique-phonemic obstruents). Similarly here, the current conception of the lexicon prevents us from stating a single generalization about the interpretation of sentences like 190 and 191, where a language like English does not happen to have a regular formation for desiderative or 'attemptative' verbs, or does not happen to have a verb, say *shmarry,* meaning 'try to marry'.

   In general, many of the relationships between different syntactic structures currently expressed by transformations have their counterparts in the relations between lexical items. Klima (1964) has discussed inherently negative verbs like *doubt,* which can be treated exactly like strings containing an overt negative element. Chomsky (1965, pp. 162 f) has raised the question of accounting for relationships between verbs like *buy* and *sell, strike* and *regard, like* and *please,* some of which can be explicated as partaking in the active-passive relationship. Many verbs are best considered the causatives or inchoatives formed from other verbs, even if there does not happen to be a regular way of deriving such forms from each other and the only relation seems to be a lexical one (Lakoff, 1965). One can speculate about such pairs as *tall* and *short, parent* and *child:* 'Bill is shorter than John' is in a sense the passive of 'John is taller than Bill'. Compare the paraphrase (representing the usual way of expressing such relations in many languages):

193. John surpasses Bill in tallness (height).
194. Bill is surpassed by John in tallness.

Note that these examples bear directly on the idea that there is one category underlying the classes of nouns, verbs, and adjectives. Recent research by John R. Ross and George Lakoff has shown that deep structures are much more abstract than has been thought. One part of this research has resulted in the positing of many kinds of abstract pro-verbs which receive only indirect phonological representation. What I am proposing is, I believe, a natural extension of this line of work.

To summarize, I have argued on the basis of many pieces of evidence that it is reasonable to suppose that all nouns come from relative clauses based on the predicate nominal constituent. Further I have proposed that the referential indices assumed to occur with nouns in current theory be replaced by a system of operators and variables much like those used in logic but clearly different in detail, and that these elements rather than actual pronouns or the like be used to tie together the sentences underlying a single complex utterance. I have tried to show that the distinctions between such parts of speech as nouns, adjectives, and verbs have no direct representation as such in the base, but are the results of transformational developments in one or another language. Finally, I have suggested that the current theory of grammar be modified so that the role of the lexicon is to map into phonological shape structures derived via the major transformations.

The base component suggested here looks in some ways very much like the logical systems familiar from the work of modern logicians like Rudolf Carnap, Hans Reichenbach, and others. In particular, such systems do not have any subdivision of 'lexical items' into nouns, verbs, and adjectives. Much more basic is the distinction between variables, names,[17] and general 'predicates' which can be n-placed with respect to the number of terms that can occur as their arguments. It should not be surprising that a system of universal base rules should turn out to be very close to such systems, which are after all the result of analyzing the most basic conceptual relationships that exist in natural languages. Such a system

[17] Within the framework suggested here, names could be treated in two ways: They could be allowed to occur as alternatives to variables within sentences, or they could be derived from embedded sentences involving the predicate 'is called _____' or the like. If the latter course is followed, one could deal with the semantic content of names in a way parallel to that of other 'nouns'. In any case, it is clear that names have to have special treatment because of their behavior with respect to relative clause formation and the like. Note the following examples: 'John, which is my brother's name . . .', but * 'John, who is my brother's name. . .'.

expresses directly the idea that it is possible to convey any conceptual content in any language, even though the particular lexical items available will vary widely from one language to another—a direct denial of the Humboldt-Sapir-Whorf hypothesis in its strongest form.

THE
ROLE OF SEMANTICS
IN A
GRAMMAR[1]

James D. McCawley *The University of Chicago*

[1] I am grateful to Noam Chomsky, Jerrold Katz, George Lakoff, Leonard Linsky, Lester Rice, and John Robert Ross for valuable discussions of some of the topics covered in this paper; needless to say, none of them swallows whole everything I say.

A portion of this paper was read under the title 'The Syntax and Semantics of Plural Noun Phrases' at the annual conference of the New York Linguistic Circle, March 19, 1967.

I wish to dedicate this paper to the memory of Uriel Weinreich, whose untimely death has taken from linguistics one of its most productive scholars; his influence will be apparent at many places in this paper.

My conscience demands that I begin by pointing out that I am writing under false pretenses. I do not purport to have any universals in semantics to propose and indeed feel that linguists at present are as ill-equipped to propose universals of semantics as pre-Paninian linguists would have been to propose universals of phonology. Accordingly, let me for the bulk of this paper forget that this is a conference on language universals and simply talk about semantics as it relates to English.

There is an uncomfortable similarity between the way that semantics has generally been treated in transformational grammar and the way that syntax was treated in the 'phonological grammar' of Trager and Smith. In either case the subject is a nebulous area which cannot be dealt with on its own ground but is accessible only through the more manageable field of syntax or phonology. This similarity is made especially clear in Katz and Fodor's dictum (1963) that 'linguistic description minus grammar equals semantics', which in effect asserts that semantics is (by definition) the hairy mess that remains to be talked about after one has finished with linguistics proper. Both phonology and syntax have progressed immeasurably as a result of the realization by linguists that phonology and syntax are two interrelated areas, each of which leads its own kind of existence and neither of which can be defined in terms of the other with a minus sign in front of it. I will present evidence in support of my belief that the corresponding realization regarding the roles of syntax and semantics may have an equally great effect on the progress of both these areas of linguistics.

As a prerequisite to the rest of what I will say about semantics, I must take up one aspect of the notions 'dictionary entry' and 'lexical item'. Katz and Fodor (1963) treat a polysemous item such as *bachelor* as a single lexical item with a single dictionary entry containing four subentries, one for each of the four meanings of *bachelor* which they recognize ('1. A young knight serving under the standard of another knight; 2. one who possesses the first or lowest academic degree; 3. a man who has never married; 4. a young male fur seal when without a mate during the breeding time'). Katz and Fodor's position, like that of most professional lexicographers, is to group together in a single dictionary entry all the readings which can be associated with a given phonological shape and belong to a single syntactic class. However, there is no a priori reason why the information in the dictionary must be grouped together on the basis of phonological identity rather than on the basis of some other identity, say, identity of semantic representation or (to take an absurd case) identity of the list of transformations and phonological rules which the item is an exception to. Moreover, there is no a priori reason for grouping items together in a dictionary at all: one could perfectly well take the notion 'lexical item' to mean the combination of a single semantic reading with a single underlying phono-logical shape, a single syntactic category, and a single set of specifications of exceptional behavior with respect to rules. Under this conception of 'lexical item', which was proposed by Weinreich (1966), there would simply be four lexical items pronounced *bachelor* rather than a single four-ways ambiguous lexical item. There are a number of compelling reasons for believing that language operates in terms of Weinreich lexical items rather than Katz-Fodor lexical items, the chief reason being that transformations which demand the identity of a pair of lexical items demand not merely the identity of their Katz-Fodor dictionary entries but indeed the identity of the specific readings involved. An instructive example of this is the following problem, which is discussed incon-clusively in Chomsky (1965). What is the source of the anomaly of the following sentences (Chomsky, 1965, p. 183)?

1. * John is as sad as the book he read yesterday.
2. * He exploits his employees more than the opportunity to please.
3. * Is Brazil as independent as the continuum hypothesis?

Since each of these sentences is a comparative construction arising from a deep structure which Chomsky would represent along the lines of the figure on p. 127.

Through a transformation which deletes in the embedded sentence an adjective identical to that of the main sentence, the obvious place to look for the source of the anomaly is the identity condition on the ad-jectives. If different readings associated with the same phonological shape are considered to be different lexical items, the problem is immediately solved. There are, then, two different lexical items: sad_1, meaning 'ex-periencing sadness, said of a living being', and sad_2, meaning 'evoking sadness, said of an esthetic object'. This means that the above diagram could represent any of four conceivable deep structures, depending on whether the two items labeled *sad* are occurrences of sad_1 or sad_2. Of these four deep structures, the one having sad_1 in both places would be anomalous because of a selectional violation in the embedded sentence, in which sad_1, which requires a living being as subject, is predicated of *that book;* the structure having sad_1 in the main sentence and sad_2 in the embedded sentence could not undergo the comparative transformation because the two adjectives are not identical; for exactly the same reason the structure having sad_2 in the main sentence and sad_1 in the embedded sentence could not undergo the comparative transformation and thus could not yield 'John is as sad as that book'; and finally, the structure which has sad_2 in both places would be anomalous because of a selectional violation in the main sentence, in which sad_2, which requires an 'esthetic object' as subject, is predicated of *John.* However, this solution to the problem of why Sentences 1 to 3 are anomalous is not available to a

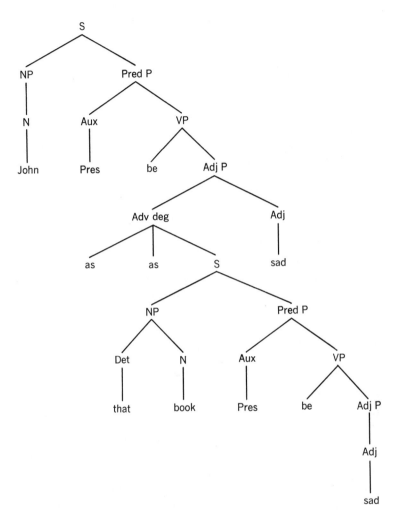

linguist who, like Chomsky (1965),[2] considers the terminal nodes in deep structures to correspond to single polysemous items such as Chomsky's undifferentiated *sad*. I thus will henceforth assume that each terminal node in a deep structure has exactly one semantic reading attached to it.

I should say a word here about the relation of the 'disambiguation' of polysemous lexical items in Katz and Fodor's theory to Weinreich's notion of lexical item. Katz and Fodor's semantic projection rules are of the following type: if an item consists of two constituents, one which

---

[2] Chomsky has since modified his conception of 'lexical item' (see fn. 6 of Chomsky, 1966b).

has a set of *m* readings attached to it (that is, is *m*-ways ambiguous) and one which has a set of *n* readings attached to it, the *mn* combinations of one reading of each constituent are formed, those combinations in which a reading for one constituent violates a selectional restriction in the reading for the other constituent are discarded, and from each of the remaining combinations a reading for the whole item is constructed in a manner specified by the projection rule. By applying the projection rules to successively larger constituents in the deep structure, one eventually ends up with a set of readings for the whole sentence. Disambiguation in Katz and Fodor's theory is effected solely by means of the discarding of combinations of readings which violate a selectional restriction. If Katz and Fodor's notion of lexical item is replaced by Weinreich's, disambiguation will consist in eliminating a certain subset of a set of deep structures which terminate in homophonous Weinreich lexical items; the projection rules would apply separately to each of these deep structures, each application of a rule consisting in attaching to a node a reading which is obtained by combining in some way the single readings attached to the nodes it directly dominates, and the entire deep structure would be judged anomalous or nonanomalous rather than combinations of readings discarded whenever a selectional violation is encountered.

There are several advantages of such an approach over Katz and Fodor's. First of all, certain sentences are nonanomalous even though they have a selectional violation in an embedded sentence, for example,

4. It is nonsense to speak of a rock having diabetes.
5. Rocks can't have diabetes.
6. John said that the rock had diabetes.

This means that the procedure given in Katz and Fodor (1963) whereby a pair of readings for two constituents is discarded if one violates a selectional restriction in the other must be refined so that a decision as to the anomalousness of a deep structure will require examination of the semantic representation of the whole deep structure. An assertion that something anomalous is anomalous is a tautology and thus semantically impeccable, and there is nothing anomalous about reporting that someone has said something anomalous. The latter facts are recognized by Katz, who states (1965, p. 161): 'We may observe that the occurrence of a constituent without readings is a necessary but *not* sufficient condition for a sentence to be semantically anomalous. For the sentence *We would think it queer indeed if someone were to say that he smells itchy,* which contains a constituent without readings—which is semantically anomalous —is not itself semantically anomalous'. However, the position that the constituent in question has no readings is untenable, since that would mean that

7. He says that he smells itchy.
8. He says that he poured his mother into an inkwell.
9. He says that his toenail sings five-part madrigals.

would be synonymous. Moreover, if the embedded sentence in something like 4 contains a polysemous item only one reading of which makes the sentence anomalous, then throwing away anomalies whenever they arise would give an incorrect reading to the sentence. For example, if *king* is assumed to have the two readings 'monarch' and 'chess piece', Katz's procedure would mark

10. It is nonsense to speak of a king as made of plastic.

as unambiguously meaning 'it is nonsense to speak of a chess king as made of plastic' and would exclude the normal interpretation, 'it is nonsense to speak of a monarch as made of plastic'.

Secondly, disambiguation actually involves not merely linguistic competence but also the language user's factual knowledge; indeed, it is merely a special case of the judgment of a speaker's intentions. In support of these contentions, I observe first that whether a speaker judges an expression such as Ziff's example 'the shooting of the elephants' [3] to be ambiguous depends on his knowledge of physics and biology and the strength of his imagination. Evidently my imagination but not Ziff's is up to the task of imagining the design of a gun with a trigger so large that an elephant could pull it; I suspect that the difference between my judgments and Ziff's may be the result of my having read *Babar* as a little boy and his not having done so. Similarly, Katz (1965, p. 158) states that the word *priest* has the semantic marker (Male) in its dictionary entry. However, this marker relates solely to factual information as to who current regulations allow to be priests, since the discussion going on in liberal Catholic circles as to whether women should be allowed to become priests relates to the changing of the regulations and not to whether women should be allowed to undergo sex-change surgery so as to qualify them to become priests. Thus the disambiguation of the sentence

11. The landlord knocked the priest up.

[3] The example but not the interpretation of it is taken from Ziff (1965).

in favor of the reading, 'The landlord awakened the priest by knocking on his door', is based on factual information rather than purely on meaning. Finally, there are many situations in which a sentence which Katz and Fodor's theory will disambiguate in favor of a certain reading will be understood as meaning something which their disambiguation procedure will reject as a possible reading. For example, Katz and Fodor's theory would mark *bachelor* in

12. My aunt is a bachelor.

as unambiguously meaning 'holder of the bachelor's degree', since the other three readings of *bachelor* would require a male subject. However, one can easily imagine situations in which this sentence would immediately be interpreted as meaning that the aunt is a spinster rather than that she holds an academic degree. I conclude from these considerations that the violation of selectional restrictions is only one of many grounds on which one could reject a reading as not being what the speaker intended and that it moreover does not hold any privileged position among the various criteria for deciding what someone meant.

The term 'lexical item' should not mislead one into thinking that every 'lexical item' of a language must appear in the lexicon of that language. On the contrary, probably all languages have implicational relationships among their lexical items, whereby the existence of one lexical item implies the existence of another lexical item, which then need not be listed in the lexicon. For example, Lester A. Rice has called to my attention the fact that in many languages the words for temperature ranges (*warm, cool,* and so forth) may be used not only to represent those temperature ranges but also to represent the temperature sensation produced by wearing an article of clothing. Thus, the English sentence

13. This coat is warm.

is ambiguous between the meaning that the coat has a relatively high temperature and the meaning that it makes the wearer feel warm. There is exactly the same ambiguity in the Hungarian sentence

14. *Ez a kabát meleg.*

I propose then that English has two lexical items *warm,* of which only one appears in the lexicon, the other being predictable on the basis of a principle that for each lexical item which is an adjective denoting a temperature range there is a lexical item identical to it save for the fact that it is restricted to articles of clothing and means 'producing the sensation corresponding to the temperature range denoted by the original adjective'. Note that while the derived lexical item involves the notion of causation, it is not derivable by the usual causative transformation because that transformation would not give rise to the restriction of the derived item to articles of clothing and because the causative transformation yields sentences in which the underlying subject of the 'basic' lexical item is present as the object of the 'derived' item (as in 'John opened the door', which is a causative in which the structure underlying 'The door opened' is embedded), whereas the derived adjective *warm* does not allow the overt presence of a noun phrase corresponding to the person or thing which is made warm.

A second example of lexical items whose presence in a language is predictable from other lexical items is given by the process which Lakoff calls *reification*. Note the difference in meaning between the two occurrences of *the score* in the sentences (based on examples of Lakoff's)

15. John has memorized the score of the Ninth Symphony.
16. The score of the Ninth Symphony is lying on the piano.

and similarly between the two occurrences of *John's dissertation* in

17. John's dissertation deals with premarital sex among the Incas.
18. John's dissertation weighs five pounds.

In the first member of each pair the noun phrase refers to a work of art or scholarship, in the second case to its physical embodiment. In this connection, note the difference in normalness between:

19. I am halfway finished with writing my dissertation, which deals with premarital sex among the Incas.
20. * I am halfway finished with writing my dissertation, which weighs five pounds.

Another case of reification is pointed out in Wierzbicka (1967), namely the difference in meaning between the proper names in

21. John thinks that the world is flat.
22. John weighs 200 pounds.

In 21 the proper name refers to the person, in 22 to his body. The distinction between these two meanings is made clear by Lakoff's example (1967)

23. * James Bond broke the window with himself.

Note that *James Bond* referring to the person and *James Bond* referring
to that person's body do not count as identical for the purposes of re-
flexivization.[4] Here also one may say that the existence of one set of
lexical items implies the existence of a parallel set of lexical items: that
each lexical item denoting a person implies the existence of an otherwise identical lexical item denoting that person's body, and only the
former lexical items need appear in the lexicon. Rules of a similar nature
to these lexical prediction rules figure in Weinreich's treatment of meta-
phor (Weinreich, 1966, Section 3.5). Weinreich's 'construal rules' amount
to rules which create a new lexical item by modifying the semantic
representation of an already existing lexical item so as to make it compatible with the semantic representation of a sentence in which the
original lexical item would be anomalous in some way. However, rules
of this type, which create lexical items that are all in some way 'deviant'
and whose use is restricted to highly specialized poetic ends, must be
distinguished sharply from the rules creating the derived senses of *warm,*
dissertation, and *John,* which give rise to lexical items that are no more
'deviant' than the items they are derived from.

I turn now to the question of selectional restrictions. In most of
the published literature on transformational grammar, selectional restrictions are treated as within the domain of the base component of a
grammar. For example, the treatment of selectional restrictions in Chomsky (1965) goes roughly as follows: the base component contains rules
which add 'inherent' features such as [+animate] or [−animate], [+hu-
man] or [−human], to each noun node; those rules are followed by
rules which mark each verb node with features such as [animate subject],
[nonhuman subject], and so on, depending on what features have been
added to the noun node of the subject, and similarly for direct object,
and other constituents, and then under each complex of features is
inserted a lexical item whose feature composition does not contradict
any of the features in the feature complex under which it is inserted.
One important point to note is that Chomsky treats a selectional restriction as a restriction between two *lexical items,* say, a verb and the
noun which is the head of its subject. An alternative conception of selectional restrictions appears in Katz and Fodor (1963), namely a conception of selectional restrictions whose fulfillment or violation is determined in the semantic component of the grammar rather than the
base component and which treats selection as operating not between

---

[4] However, the 'person' appears to include the body, as is shown by examples such as:
   24. James Bond hurled himself through the window.

two lexical items but rather between a lexical item and an entire syntactic constituent, say, between a verb and the entire noun phrase which serves as its subject. Specifically, the selectional restriction on the verb specifies a property which the semantic representation of the subject noun phrase must possess, and one determines whether the condition is met or violated by determining the semantic representation of that noun phrase and checking whether it possesses the required property. Katz and Fodor do not make clear whether they believe that these 'semantic selectional restrictions' would appear in the grammar instead of or in addition to 'syntactic selectional restrictions' such as appear in Chomsky (1965).

Remarkably little attention has been devoted to the question of whether an adequate theory of language requires only syntactic selectional restrictions or only semantic selectional restrictions, or both. Chomsky (1965, pp. 153–154) mentions the question briefly and dismisses it as if it were merely a matter of notation, which is surprising in view of the fact that the different answers to this question in fact have radically different empirical consequences. I will now present an argument that an adequate account of selection must be in terms of semantic selectional restrictions such as those of Katz and Fodor (1963) and that there is no reason to have the 'syntactic selectional features' of Chomsky (1965) nor the complicated machinery for creating 'complex symbols' which the use of such features entails.

Consider first the question of whether a selectional restriction imposed by a verb or adjective is a restriction on the entire noun phrase which serves as its subject, object, or what have you, or rather a restriction on the head of that noun phrase. The former appears to be the case in view of the fact that examples can readily be constructed of noun phrases which violate a selectional restriction because of a modifier rather than the head. For example, the sentence

25. * My buxom neighbor is the father of two.

violates the same selectional restriction as does

26. * My sister is the father of two.

but the violation of the selectional restriction in 25 has nothing to do with the head noun, since

27. My neighbor is the father of two.

contains no selectional violation. Moreover, there are no cases on record of a verb which will exclude a lexical item as the head of its subject but allow the subject to be a noun phrase which splits the same semantic-information between the head and a modifier; for example, there are no verbs on record which exclude *a bachelor* as subject but allow *an unmarried man*.[5]

This establishes that one must look at a representation of an entire constituent rather than its 'head' lexical item to determine whether it meets or violates a given selectional restriction. Consider now the question of just what information about that constituent is involved in determining whether it meets a selectional restriction. I maintain first that any piece of information which may figure in the semantic representation of an item may figure in a selectional restriction and secondly that no other information ever figures in selectional restrictions. As evidence for the former assertion, I will point out that on any page of a large dictionary one finds words with incredibly specific selectional restrictions, involving an apparently unlimited range of semantic properties; for example, the verb *diagonalize* requires as its object a noun phrase denoting a matrix (in the mathematical sense), the adjective *benign* in the sense 'noncancerous' requires a subject denoting a tumor, and the verb *devein* as used in cookery requires an object denoting a shrimp or prawn. Regarding my second assertion, that only semantic information plays a role in selection, I maintain that the various nonsemantic features attached to nouns, for example, proper versus common, grammatical gender, grammatical number, and so on, play no role in selection. All the verbs which have suggested themselves to me as possible counterexamples to this assertion turn out in fact to display selection based on some semantic properties. For example, the verb *name* might at first glance seem to have a selectional restriction involving the feature [proper]:

28. They named their son John.
29. * They named their son that boy.

However, there are in fact perfectly good sentences with something other than a proper noun in the place in question:

30. They named their son something outlandish.

The selectional restriction is thus that the second object denote a name rather than that it have a proper noun as its head. Regarding grammatical number, verbs such as *count* might seem to demand a plural object:

[5] This fact and the example were suggested by Lakoff and Ross (personal communication).

31. I counted the boys.
32. * I counted the boy.

However, there are also sentences with grammatically singular objects:

33. I counted the crowd.

The selectional restriction on *count* is not that the object be plural but that it denote a set of things rather than an individual. Similarly, there is no verb in English which allows for its subject just those noun phrases which may pronominalize to *she*, namely noun phrases denoting women, ships, and countries. I accordingly conclude that selectional restrictions are definable solely in terms of properties of semantic representations and that to determine whether a constituent meets or violates a selectional restriction it is necessary to examine its semantic representation and nothing else. Since if the base component were then to contain any machinery to exclude structures which violate selectional restrictions, that machinery would have to duplicate what already must be done by the semantic projection rules, I conclude that the matter of selectional restrictions should be totally separate from the base component and that the base component thus be a device which generates a class of deep structures without regard to whether the items in them violate any selectional restrictions.

Before leaving the topic of selectional restrictions I would like to comment briefly on something which appears at first glance to be a counterexample to what I said above. Specifically, the different vocabulary items used in sentences of different politeness levels in languages such as Japanese and Korean seem at first glance to exhibit selectional restrictions based on nonsemantic features of lexical items rather than on semantic features of larger constituents. For example, the Japanese verbs *aru* and *gozaru* both mean 'there is', but the latter is restricted to situations demanding honorific language. In such situations the informal pronouns are excluded, so that while

34. *Watakusi wa zidoosya ga gozaimasu.*

is a permissible way of saying 'I have a car' in a situation demanding honorific language and

35. *Ore wa zidoosya ga aru.*

is a permissible way of saying the same thing in a situation where highly informal language is allowed, *ore* and *gozaru* cannot be used together:

36. * *Ore wa zidoosya ga gozaimasu.*

It should be noted that there are many respects in which these co-occur-rence restrictions differ radically from what has hitherto been understood by 'selection'. First, there appears to be no nonarbitrary way of deciding which of the elements in question determines the choice of the other. Second, rather than relating to a specific pair of constituents, say, a verb and its object, the restriction here applies globally: the presence of an honorific verb such as *gozaru* precludes the presence of informal pro-nouns such as *ore, boku,* or *kimi* anywhere in the sentence, and indeed, anywhere in the entire discourse, for that matter. Third, unlike all other selectional restrictions that have ever been discussed, which remain the same regardless of whether the constituents belong to a main clause or to an embedded clause, some co-occurrence restrictions relating to po-liteness levels apply differently in independent clauses than in subordi-nate clauses. For example, the politeness morpheme *mas,* which is at-tached to verbs of the main clauses in formal and honorific discourses but not in informal speech, is absent from relative clauses regardless of the po-liteness level and thus regardless of what pronoun forms appear in the relative clause. I thus conclude that this phenomenon is of a different formal nature from either what is described by a theory of semantic selec-tional restrictions such as I have sketched above or a theory of syntactic selectional restrictions such as described in Chomsky (1965). As my choice of words in describing this phenomenon suggests, I believe that what is going on here is that the choice of pronouns and verbs is dependent on features attached to the entire discourse rather than to individual lexical items and that the politeness morpheme *mas* is attached by a transformation to the appropriate verbs if the relevant discourse features are present.

If the position I take here on selectional restrictions is adopted, most of the discussion which has appeared in print on the question of the 'delicacy' of syntactic subcategorization becomes totally vacuous. The dictionary entry of a lexical item must specify all semantic information needed to characterize exactly what it means and must contain a full specification of what transformations it is an exception to; nothing more is needed and in neither area does the linguist have any choice as to how finely lexical items are to be subcategorized.

I turn now to the topic of indices and their relation to syntax and semantics. The discussion here will be complementary to that of Bach's paper in this volume: his paper dealt primarily with indices used as vari-ables, whereas this paper will deal primarily with indices used as con-stants. Chomsky (1965, p. 145) observes that transformations which are contingent on the identity of two noun phrases require not merely that the noun phrases be syntactically identical but also that they have the same 'intended referent'. Thus,

37. A man killed a man.
38. A man killed himself.

are both English sentences, and in the former the speaker is understood as referring to two different persons by the two occurrences of *a man*. Chomsky's proposal for the incorporation of these observations into a formal description of English syntax is that the base component of the grammar supply each noun phrase[6] with an 'index' which marks its intended referent and that identity between constituents be interpreted as meaning identity of everything, indices included. Thus, 37 and 38 will each have a deep structure containing two occurrences of the noun phrase *a man*[7] and will differ only in that these two occurrences will have different indices in the case of 37 but the same index in the case of 38 (tense is ignored in these diagrams):

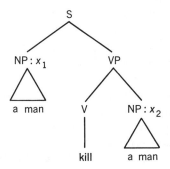 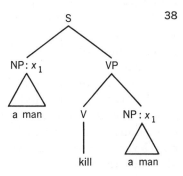

A man killed a man   A man killed himself

[6] Chomsky's actual proposal attaches the index to the head noun rather than to the entire noun phrase. However, the index must be attached to the noun phrase since transformations which require the identity of nouns rather than of noun phrases do not require coreferentiality: note the pronominalization of a repeated noun by *one* in sentences such as 'John has a blue hat and I have a brown one' even though two different hats are referred to. In Chomsky (1965), indices are only referred to informally; no rules are given for the insertion of indices, and no indices appear overtly in any diagrams. Chomsky (personal communication) indicates that he did not intend indices to mark intended referents *per se* but only that sameness of index mark sameness of intended referent, that is, he wishes 'John shot himself' to have the same deep structure regardless of who the speaker means by 'John'. I argue below against the autonomy of linguistics from psychology which Chomsky's position presupposes.

[7] I do not mean to imply that the article *a* will be present in deep structure. In fact, articles are to a large extent (though not completely) predictable on the basis of indices. However, since a full treatment of articles requires an adequate account of deixis, a subject which has so far been dealt with only in a fragmentary way, and since the points I am making here are not affected by the question of how articles are chosen, I will simply write *a man* to indicate a noun phrase which could be realized as *a man* and not commit myself as to whether its article would be present in deep structure.

Since these two sentences differ not only syntactically but also in meaning, this difference in index will have to be part of not only their syntactic representation but also their semantic representation. An obvious proposal in this regard is that the semantic representation of sentences should involve not the feature-like 'markers' of Katz and Fodor (1963) but rather predicates (in the symbolic logician's sense of the term). I thus propose that the most common reading of the word *man* be represented not as a set of markers {human, male, adult} but rather as an expression such as 'human(x) $\wedge$ male(x) $\wedge$ adult(x)', where x is a variable, and that the semantic projection rule which assigns a reading to a noun phrase containing that lexical item substitute the index of the noun phrase for that variable. Such a rule formalizes the notion that in a noun phrase such as *that man* the properties 'human', 'male', and 'adult' are not merely being referred to but are being predicated of the individual to which the noun phrase is intended to refer.

Some comments are in order here relating to both the status of indices and my use of the word *refer*. Throughout this paper I will use *refer* in connection with the 'intended referent' of a noun phrase rather than its 'actual referent', that is, indices will correspond to items in the speaker's mental picture of the universe[8] rather than to real things in the universe. This approach to indices is necessary if a theory of semantic representation is to cover such things as sentences dealing with imaginary objects and sentences based on misconceptions about the facts. It is of no relevance to linguistics whether a person has correctly perceived and identified the things he talks about; thus one need not know whether there are such things as guardian angels and heaven in order to assign a semantic representation to the sentence

39. My guardian angel is helping me to get to heaven.

With this understanding of 'intended referent', one could perfectly well say that the index does not represent the intended referent but indeed *is* the intended referent: one's current knowledge and beliefs about the world involve his having available for use in his thinking certain terms which he identifies (rightly or wrongly) as corresponding to individual entities in the world, and it is those terms to which the expression 'intended referent' applies and which function as indices in the semantic representation of the sentences that person uses. One consequence of this point of view would be that when one learns a proper name, the semantic information he has learned is an index, namely the term correspond-

---

[8] This remark of course applies only to constant indices and not to the variable indices of sentences such as 'No men have three ears'.

ing to the individual who he has learned possesses that name. The learning of proper names appears to be of the same nature as the learning of
a wide range of nonlinguistic knowledge: when one sees a person for
the first time, he adds a new·term to his conceptual repertoire and adds
to his set of knowledge and beliefs a set of predications about that
term which correspond to the things he has (correctly or falsely) observed
about that person; in learning a name, one has simply added one more
fact to his knowledge about the person. Thus indices are nonlinguistic
units which happen to play a role in linguistic representations. Since in
English many proper names can equally well be given to a girl as to a
boy and there is no name which in principle could not be given to a
member of either sex or to a horse or a boat for that matter, a sentence
such as

40. Gwendolyn hurt himself.

cannot be regarded as anomalous in itself, although it will be token-odd if
applied to virtually any of the persons who actually happen to bear
the name Gwendolyn; however, this token-oddity is in no way different
from the token-oddity of 'My neighbor hurt himself' when it is said of a
person who is actually a woman. A somewhat different situation holds in
Japanese, where not only may most first names be given only to a boy or
only to a girl, but indeed many names may only be given to a first son,
only to a second son, and so forth.[9] It is thus appropriate in this case (although not in English) to speak of personal names as having a semantic
representation which includes information such as 'male' and 'firstborn'.
      Indices and the knowledge in which they figure play a role in the
choice of pronominal forms. In English the choice between *he, she,* and
it or between *who* and *which* depends on one's knowledge of the intended
referent of the noun phrase rather than on the lexical items involved in
the antecedent noun phrase. Note the difference in relative pronoun in
the sentences

41. Fafnir, who plays third base on the Little League team, is a fine
     boy.
42. They called their son Fafnir, which is a ridiculous name.
43. * They called their son Fafnir, who is a ridiculous name.

The difference in pronoun choice relates to the different indices which
the noun phrases will have and the fact that the one index corresponds

---

[9] Occasionally other uses of these personal names are found. For example, in Miyadi
(1964) the names Taroo, Ziroo, Saburoo, and so on (normally reserved for first son,
second son, third son) are attached to the chief (Taroo) of a troop of monkeys which
Miyadi studied, the next highest monkey in the 'pecking order' (Ziroo), and so on.

to a person whereas the other corresponds to a name. Similarly, the different choice of pronouns in

    44. My neighbor hurt himself.
    45. My neighbor hurt herself.

corresponds to whether the speaker's knowledge about the index of the token of *my neighbor* in the sentence contains the information that that individual is male or is female. An alternative analysis of these sentences, proposed by Chomsky (1965), would have the base component of the grammar supply each noun with a full complement of specifications for the features which play a role in any syntactic or morphological rule (for example, pronoun choice), so that 44 and 45 would differ in deep structure by virtue of the noun *neighbor* having the specification [+male] in the one deep structure and [−male] in the other. However, that proposal is highly suspicious, since it would make sentences such as

    46. My neighbor is tall.

appear ambiguous, since they could be derived with either [+male] or [−male] on the noun *neighbor*. Moreover, the transformation which yields sentences such as

    47. The neighbors are respectively male and female.

would have to ignore the specifications of [+male] and [−male] which would be attached to the two occurrences of *neighbor* in the structure which would serve as input to that transformation:

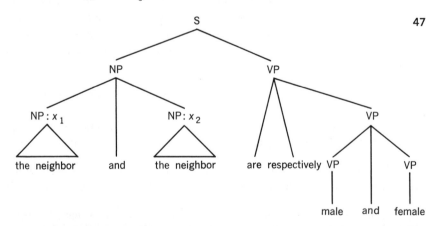

In view of these defects in the only alternative analysis with which I am familiar, I conclude that the difference between 44 and 45 corresponds not to a difference in deep structure but to a difference between the circumstances surrounding different tokens of the same deep structure. In support of this contention, I might mention that the sentence

48. My neighbor is a woman and has suffered an injury.

ought to be a paraphrase of 45 according to the analysis in which a feature of [−male] is attached to the occurrence of *neighbor* in the deep structure of 45. However, it does violence to the notion of paraphrase to say that 48 is a paraphrase of 45. While both convey the information that the individual named by *my neighbor* has suffered an injury, 48 and not 45 is what one would say if he wanted to convey to his hearer the information that that person is female. Sentence 45 is what one would say simply in order to convey the information that the person in question has suffered an injury, and in saying it one assumes that his hearer has prior information about that individual, among other things the information that she is a woman. To distinguish between the ways in which 48 and 45 convey information, it will be necessary to make a distinction between 'meaning' and 'presupposition': the information that the individual in question has suffered an injury is part of the meaning of both 45 and 48; however, the information that that individual is female is part of the meaning of 48 but only part of the presupposition of 45.

Actually, pronoun choice in English is not completely determined by presupposition, since one feature which plays a role in pronoun choice, namely number, is not completely predictable from knowledge about the intended referent. Note that there are cases where one and the same thing may be referred to by either a singular noun phrase or a plural noun phrase, and anaphoric pronouns must have the same number as the noun phrase actually used:

49. John gave me the scissors; I am using them now.
50. * John gave me the scissors; I am using it now.
51. John gave me the two-bladed cutting instrument; I am using it now.
52. * John gave me the two-bladed cutting instrument; I am using them now.

In languages having lexical gender, anaphoric pronouns generally must agree in that feature with the head noun of the antecedent noun phrase. In some languages (for example, German) the anaphoric pronoun always agrees in gender with the head of the antecedent noun phrase, whereas in other languages (for example, French and Yiddish) there is agreement with the head of the antecedent noun phrase except when it refers to a human being, in which case the pronoun form corresponds to the sex of that person regardless of the gender of the head of the antecedent noun phrase. In the case of nonanaphoric (that is, deictic) pronouns, the choice of gender is always made on the basis of presupposition concerning the intended referent: when a girl enters a room one may nudge his companion and ask '*Wie heisst sie?*' even though later in the conversation he may refer to the same girl with the noun phrase *das Mädchen* and then refer anaphorically to that noun phrase with the pronoun *es*. What is common to pronoun choice in German, French, and English is the attachment of certain grammatical features to a noun-phrase node on the basis of the noun (if any) which that node dominates (in French, this is done only for noun phrases which do not refer to a human being). Pronominalization consists in wiping out everything except the index and those grammatical features; the specific form of the pronoun is determined on the basis of the grammatical features on the NP node, with presupposition concerning the index providing any information needed for pronoun choice which is not contained among those grammatical features. In the case of a deictic pronoun, no grammatical features of number or gender will be attached to the node in question and the choice of pronoun will be made entirely on the basis of knowledge in which the index figures.

I have spoken so far as if an index could only be an item in a speaker's conceptual apparatus which he identifies as an individual. This is proper in the case of a singular noun phrase. However, a plural noun phrase usually refers not to an individual but to a set of individuals. Moreover, plural noun phrases will have to bear indices since they, just like singular noun phrases, may meet or fail to meet identity conditions by virtue of what their intended referents are. Since a plural noun phrase generally refers to a set, it can be expected that its index will behave like a set, and indeed there are syntactic phenomena which show that it must in fact be possible to perform set-theoretic operations on indices and that syntactic rules must be able to make use of the results of such operations.

Consider conjoined modifiers of the type illustrated by

53. the male and female employees
54. new and used books
55. the string quartets of Prokofiev and Ravel

Note that 53 refers not to employees who are simultaneously male and female but rather to an aggregate consisting of some employees who are male and some who are female. It may thus be paraphrased by

56. the male employees and the female employees

I maintain that conjoined modifiers of this type arise from deep structures which (neglecting tense) are of the form

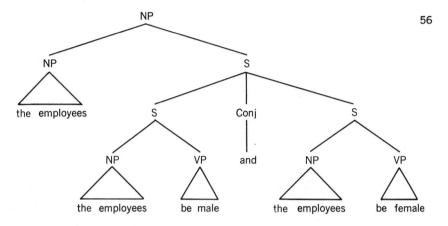

56

in which the two occurrences of *the employees* under the S node have different indices, say *A* and *B* respectively. The sentence which is adjoined
to the noun phrase meets the conditions for the *respectively* transformation, yielding

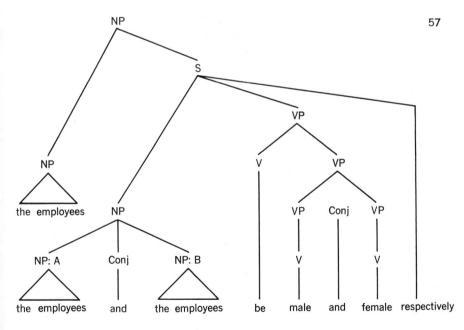

57

The material under the S node of this tree would appear to underlie the nonsentence

57. * The employees and the employees are male and female respectively.

There is a transformation which obligatorily collapses the conjoined subject *the employees and the employees* into a single occurrence of *the employees*. This collapsing transformation is necessary in a grammar of English because sentences such as

58. These boys are respectively Polish and Irish.

fill the semantic gap left by the nonoccurrence of *respectively* constructions with formally identical conjoined subjects. The resulting structure

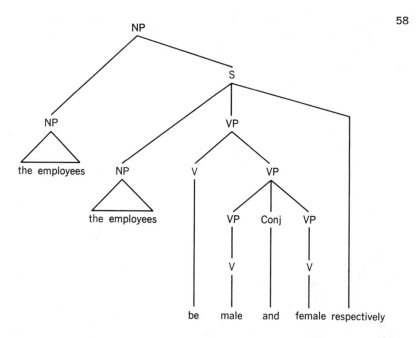

58

is subject to the relative clause transformation, which converts the occurrence of *the employees* in the embedded sentence into a relative pronoun, thus yielding a structure

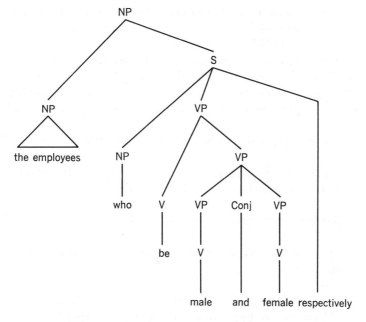

which could be realized as

  59. The employees who are male and female respectively.

The word *respectively* and the relative pronoun and copula may optionally be deleted, and if they are, then the conjoined predicate *male
and female* is obligatorily placed in front of the noun by the well-known
rule for forming prenominal modifiers (Smith, 1964; Lakoff, 1965), thus
yielding 53.

    The *respectively* transformation creates a conjoined noun phrase,
which must have an index attached to it since it participates in transformations requiring identity of index; for example, it may have a nonrestrictive clause attached to it. I propose that the index of a conjoined
noun phrase be the set-theoretic union of the indices of its conjuncts.
This principle would attach the index $A \cup B$ to the noun phrase *the
employees and the employees* in the second tree, and $A \cup B$ would remain
the index of that noun phrase after the collapsing rule applies to it.
Since the nonrestrictive clause transformation can attach a nonrestrictive
clause to 53:

  60. The male and female employees, who say they are dissatisfied,
      are actually very well paid.

and since that transformation requires identity of index, it thus must be possible to check whether the index of the noun phrase in the clause to be adjoined equals $A \cup B$.

The principle that a conjoined noun phrase has as index the union of the indices of its conjuncts provides an explanation of some interesting facts about conjunction and plurality. Because of extralinguistic knowledge I happen to know that the appropriate paraphrase of 55 is

61. The string quartets of Prokofiev and the string quartet of Ravel.

However, if I were presented with a similar expression containing the names of two composers I had never heard of, say,

62. The string quartets of Eierkopf and Misthaufen.

I would be at a loss to say which of four conceivable paraphrases was the appropriate one:

63. The quartet of Eierkopf and the quartet of Misthaufen.
64. The quartets of Eierkopf and the quartet of Misthaufen.
65. The quartet of Eierkopf and the quartets of Misthaufen.
66. The quartets of Eierkopf and the quartets of Misthaufen.

However, it is noteworthy that regardless of whether the appropriate paraphrase has two singulars, a singular and a plural, or two plurals, 62 has the plural noun *quartets*. This fact provides evidence that the plural morpheme is not present in deep structure but is rather inserted by a rule that is sensitive to whether a noun phrase has a set or an individual index, that is, a rule by which the plural morpheme is adjoined to any noun directly dominated by a noun-phrase node having a set index. This rule must apply later than the collapsing rule, so that when it applies *quartet* in 62 will always be directly under a noun-phrase node that has an index that is derived through the operation of union and is thus a set rather than an individual, which means that the plural morpheme will always be inserted. It should be remarked parenthetically that the notion of 'set' that functions here, in English syntax and semantics, is not exactly the same as the 'set' of mathematics, since the mathematical notion admits an empty set and one-member sets, whereas only sets of two or more members count for the purposes of the rules in question here. The 'set theory' involved here is one which ignores the difference between an individual and a one-member set and thus allows individuals to be combined by the union operation: $x_1 \cup x_2 = \{x_1, x_2\}$. The distinction between set and individual, thus understood, also allows a uniform treatment of number agreement. In published transformational descriptions (for example, Lees, 1960, p. 44), number agreement has generally been formulated as a rule that marks a verb as plural or singular depending on whether it is or is not preceded by the plural morpheme, with an extra clause whereby conjoined subjects require plural number agreement regardless of whether they contain the plural morpheme. However, what determines number agreement is clearly not the presence of the plural morpheme but rather something which may be called plurality of the whole subject and which corresponds very closely to the set/individual distinction. The correspondence is not exact because of *pluralia tantum* such as *scissors,* which take a plural verb even when they have an individual index. The following system of ordered rules is thus needed to derive number agreement:

(a) Mark a noun-phrase node [+plural] if it has a set index and [−plural] otherwise.
(b) Mark a noun-phrase node [+plural] if it directly dominates a noun marked as belonging to the class *'pluralia tantum'.*
(c) Mark a verb [+plural] or [−plural] depending on whether its subject is marked [+plural] or [−plural].

Note that the creation of a set index by the principle mentioned earlier is needed to derive the plural agreement of

67. John and Harry are Polish and Irish respectively.

and of the especially interesting example

68. John and Harry like the play and are disappointed by it respectively.

Here the two verbs take plural number agreement even though each of them applies semantically to a singular subject, but the conjoined subject created by the *respectively* transformation still demands plural number agreement. Note the ungrammaticality of

69. * John and Harry likes the play and is disappointed by it respectively.

One interesting consequence of these facts is that the rule making the verb agree in number with the subject cannot be formulated by any formula of the type presently used to represent transformations, since it must attach the agreement feature simultaneously to all the finite verbs

of a conjoined verb phrase rather than to a single verb: the transformation which creates the source of the plurality (the conjoined subject)
simultaneously creates a conjoined verb phrase.

So far I have considered conjoined noun phrases which arise through
the *respectively* transformation. What about other conjoined noun
phrases? Chomsky (1957, pp. 35–37) contains the proposal that all conjoined constituents are derived from pairs of simple sentences, so that

70. John and Harry are erudite.

would be derived by a conjoining transformation from structures which
underlie the two sentences 'John is erudite' and 'Harry is erudite'. This
idea appears in slightly revised form in Chomsky (1965, p. 225), where
it is suggested that (all?) conjoined elements are derived from underlying
conjoined sentences, so that 70 would arise through a 'conjunction reduction' transformation from a structure which also underlies

71. John is erudite and Harry is erudite.

It has been recognized that some conjoined constituents cannot plausibly
be derived from underlying conjoined sentences, for example,

72. John and Harry are similar.
73. John and Mary embraced.

Note the deviance of the putative source sentence

74. * John is similar.

except when it arises through ellipsis as in

75. Max is a fool; John is similar.

and the total inadmissibility, ellipsis or not, of

76. * John embraced.

Lakoff and Peters (1966) have proposed that 70 has a conjunction of sentences as its deep structure but 72 has as deep structure a simple sentence
with a conjoined subject:

70

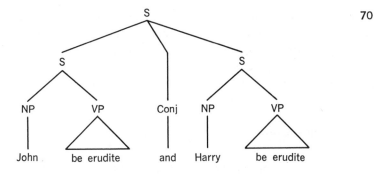

John and Harry are erudite.

72

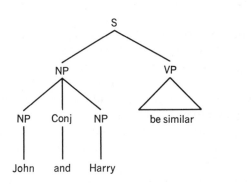

John and Harry are similar.

Noting that the sentences to which they assign deep conjoined subjects admit variants in which one of the conjuncts appears in the verb phrase, for example,

77. John is similar to Harry.
78. John embraced Mary.

Lakoff and Peters propose that the latter sentences arise from the same deep structures as 72 and 73 through the application of a 'conjunct movement' transformation which optionally shifts one of the conjuncts of a conjoined subject into the verb phrase.

In both types of sentences, a simple noun phrase may appear in place of the conjoined noun phrase, as in

79. Those men are erudite.
80. Those men are similar.

Consider what restriction must be placed on the subject of *similar* to exclude * 'John is similar'. An obvious suggestion would be that *similar* demands a plural subject, whether it be conjoined as in 72 or simple as in 80. However, that formulation of the restriction is not correct, since *pluralia tantum* may not function as the subject of *similar* unless interpreted as referring to a set:

81. These scissors are similar.

is admissible only when *these scissors* is paraphrasable by *these pairs of scissors* and not when it is paraphrasable by *this pair of scissors*. Evidently the restriction is that the subject must have a set index rather than an individual index. However, that restriction is a logical consequence of the semantic representation of *similar* as contrasted with *erudite*. The meaning of 79 is that each of the men in question has the property denoted by *erudite;* that is, eruditeness is a property of an individual. Thus the semantic representation of *erudite* has an individual variable in it and the semantic representation of sentences such as 79 is derived by a projection rule that allows the variable to range over the set serving as index of the subject. But the property denoted by *similar* is a property not of an individual but of a set. The semantic representation of *similar* contains not an individual variable but a set variable,[10] and to obtain the semantic representation of a sentence such as 80, it is necessary to substitute for that variable the set which functions as index of the subject noun phrase. But to carry out that operation it is

---

[10] The set variable in the semantic representation of *similar* is necessary for the following reasons. *Similar* may be followed by *in that S*, as in

82. Those men are similar in that they play tennis well.

The meaning of this sentence can be represented as $\bigwedge_{x \epsilon M}$ [*x* plays tennis well], where *M* is the set of men in question. Thus *similar in that* can be viewed as an operation performed on a set and a propositional function. *Similar* when used without *in that S* appears to be identical in meaning to *similar in that S* except that the respect in which the items are similar is not expressed. This will correspond in some cases to the semantic representation having a 'pro-propositional function' in place of the S of *similar in that S;* however, I conjecture that a sentence such as 'John is a fool; Max is similar' should be derived from a structure paraphrasable as 'John is a fool; Max and John are similar in that they are fools' and that *similar* results through ellipsis from *similar in that S*. Note that in this sentence the similarity must be interpreted as relating to their both being fools rather than, say, to their both having mustaches. One important problem about *similar* is that of specifying what propositional functions may combine with it; it is odd to say

83. John and Harry are similar in that I met their respective sisters on a prime-numbered day of the month.

This problem appears to be identical to that of specifying when a sentence can be said to express a property of a particular thing mentioned in it.

necessary that there be such a set, and there is not in the case of a subject with an individual index. Thus the restriction of *similar* to subjects with a set index follows from the fact that if the subject does not have a set index then one of the semantic projection rules needed for the interpretation of the sentence is unable to operate. This example, incidentally, shows that semantic projection rules affect the generative power of a grammar. If a grammar is taken to be a device specifying how semantic representations are paired with phonetic representations, then semantic projection rules exclude from this pairing any structure on which their functioning is blocked.

I wish now to reconsider the deep structure of 70. In light of the above discussion, there is no longer any reason to consider 70 to be derived from an underlying conjoined sentence. The differences between 70 and 72 are accounted for by the difference in the semantic representation of the adjective, and the conjunct movement transformation could perfectly well be made contingent on that difference rather than on the presence of a deep, rather than a derived, conjoined subject. Since there is good reason why 72 may not be derived from a conjoined sentence and no reason for the deep structure of 72 to differ in shape from that of 70, I propose that in both cases the deep structure is a simple sentence with a conjoined subject and thus that no rule of conjunction reduction is needed to derive either conjoined noun phrase.

The evidence which has been adduced for saying that 70 is derived by the conjoining of two sentences is rather slight, namely, the facts that conjuncts have the same selectional restrictions as do simple constituents and that sentences such as 70 are paraphrasable by sentences such as 71. These two facts are just as easily explainable under my proposal. Let x_1 be the index of *John* and x_2 the index of *Harry* in the sentence 'John and Harry are erudite'. Then *John and Harry* has for its index their union, that is $\{x_1, x_2\}$. By exactly the same semantic projection rule which gave the semantic representation of 'Those men are erudite', 'John and Harry are erudite' will receive the semantic representation $\bigvee_{x \in \{x_1, x_2\}}$ [erudite x]. If semantic representations are assumed to be subject to the principle of symbolic logic that a universal quantifier over a finite set is equivalent to the conjunction of the formulas obtained by substituting each of the members of that set,[11] this formula will be equiva-

---

[11] Russell (1920) points out that this principle, strictly speaking, is not correct: 'The apostles all had beards' is not equivalent to 'Peter had a beard, and John had a beard, and . . . , and Judas Iscariot had a beard', since the former cannot be deduced from the latter without the additional information that that is all the apostles there are. However, that observation does not affect the argument here, since the condition that 'that's all there are' holds by definition if the set is defined by enumerating its elements.

lent to 'erudite(x_1) $\wedge$ erudite(x_2)'. But that is simply the semantic representation of 'John is erudite and Harry is erudite', which explains why it is a paraphrase of 'John and Harry are erudite'. If my earlier conclusion that selection is based on the semantic representations of the relevant constituents is accepted, then this also explains why the conjuncts in a sentence such as 70 have the same selectional restrictions as a simple subject, as in 'John is erudite'. Note also that conjuncts are all subject to the same selectional restrictions, even in cases like 72 or 73 where the sentence cannot be derived from conjoined simple sentences.

Consider now another class of sentences which has been proposed as an argument for deriving some conjoined noun phrases from conjoined sentences, namely sentences such as

84. John and Harry went to Cleveland.

This sentence is ambiguous, allowing the two paraphrases

85. John and Harry each went to Cleveland.
86. John and Harry went to Cleveland together.

The former reading of 84 could plausibly be assigned the deep structure of a conjoined sentence and the latter of a simple sentence with conjoined subject. However, there is a strong argument against that proposal, namely the fact that sentences such as

87. Those men went to Cleveland.

have exactly the same ambiguity as 84, and the Lakoff-Peters proposal allows no obvious way of letting the two readings of 87 differ in a fashion parallel to the two readings of 84. The only way I know of assigning deep structures to these sentences in such a way as to make the ambiguity of 87 parallel to that of 84 is to subcategorize noun phrases which have set indices into two types, which I will call joint and nonjoint. Joint noun phrases allow adjuncts such as *together;* nonjoint noun phrases allow adjuncts such as *each*. Attached to each set index in deep structure will be a specification of [+joint] or [−joint]. Some verbs allow only a nonjoint subject, for example, *erudite:* some allow either a joint or a nonjoint subject, for example, *go;* and some allow only a joint subject, for example, *similar*. Semantically, the distinction between joint and nonjoint relates to the order of quantifiers. In the one reading (joint) of 87, the meaning is that there was an event of 'going to Cleveland' in which each of the men participated; in the other reading (nonjoint), the meaning is that for each man there was an event of 'going to Cleveland' in which he participated; symbolized very roughly,

Joint: $\underset{y \ x\epsilon M}{\exists \ \forall}$ 'go to Cleveland' (x, y)

Nonjoint: $\underset{x\epsilon M \ y_x}{\forall \ \exists}$ 'go to Cleveland' (x, y_x)

The notion of joint and nonjoint is involved in the problem of the semantic interpretation of the sentence

88. These men and those boys are similar.

or alternatively,

89. These men are similar to those boys.

In the deep structure which I have proposed for this type of sentence, a noun-phrase node would dominate two noun-phrase nodes which had the indices A of *these men* and B of *those boys*, respectively:

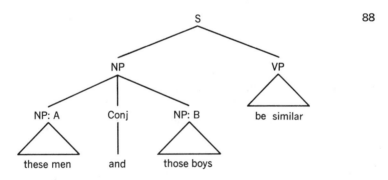

88

This ought to mean that the whole subject has index $A \cup B$ and that the meaning of 88 and 89 is that the property *similar* applies to the set $A \cup B$. However, that is incorrect, since 'similar$(A \cup B)$' means that the men are similar not only to the boys but also to each other, which is in fact not part of the meaning of 88. What is going on here is that, as mentioned in the last paragraph, the quantifier corresponding to a nonjoint NP takes the 'outside' position in the semantic representation. The meaning of 88 is actually that 'similar$(\{x_1, x_2\})$' is true, where x_1 ranges over A and x_2 over B. This example shows English to have at least two kinds of universal quantifier: if $\forall$ is interpreted as in symbolic logic, then ' $\underset{x_1 \epsilon A}{\forall}\ \underset{x_2 \epsilon B}{\forall}$ similar($\{x_1,\ x_2\}$)' would represent not the meaning of 88 but that of

90. Every one of the men is similar to every one of the boys.

The meaning of 88 involves two 'universal quantifiers' whose combination implies not that the predicate holds of all pairs of an element of A and an element of B but rather that the pairs of elements for which the relation holds exhaust or almost exhaust A and B. I will call this quantifier the 'set exhaustion quantifier' and write ' $\underset{x_1 \epsilon A}{X}\ \underset{x_2 \epsilon B}{X}$ similar($x_1,\ x_2$)' to symbolize the meaning of 88. The set exhaustion quantifier is also involved in such sentences as

91. The men courted the women.

which does not imply that every man courted every woman but rather that every (or almost every) man courted one or more women and that every (or almost every) woman was courted by at least one man.

Recall my assertion that *similar* requires a [+joint] subject. All apparent counterexamples to this restriction appear to arise through ellipsis from a deep structure with a [+joint] subject, for example,

92. John is stupid and Bill and Harry are similar.

Here *similar* has a nonjoint surface subject, but the clause arises through ellipsis from 'Bill and Harry are similar to John', which has a deep structure in which *Bill and Harry* is not the whole subject but merely one conjunct of the [+joint] noun phrase *Bill and Harry and John*:

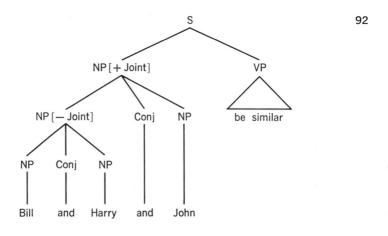

92

A consideration of the restriction that *similar* have a [+joint] subject provides the death blow to the theory which derives conjoined noun phrases from conjoined sentences by a conjunction reduction transformation. According to that theory it ought to be possible to reduce the conjoined sentence

93. These men are similar and those boys are similar.

into 88. However, 88 in fact does not permit the paraphrase in 93, which it ought to permit if conjunction reduction applied to conjoined sentences differing only in subject. Thus there appears to be no non-ad-hoc way in which the theory with conjunction reduction could prevent 88 from being analyzed as having an ambiguity which it in fact does not have.

Another matter in which set operations and set relations play a role is person. To discuss this topic it will be necessary for me first to summarize a recent proposal by John Robert Ross. Various descriptions of English have involved elements such as a 'question formative' which is to be present in the deep structures of all questions and an 'imperative formative' which is to be present in the deep structures of all imperatives (Katz and Postal, 1964; Thorne, 1966). The meaning of these formatives can be paraphrased as 'the speaker asks his listener whether . . .', 'the speaker asks that his listener do . . .'. They thus have the meaning of a verb with first person subject and second person indirect object. Ross proposes that these items indeed be analyzed as verbs and that the deep structures of not only questions and imperatives but indeed all sentences have in their topmost S a first person subject, a second person indirect object, and a verb of the type which J. L. Austin (1962) called 'performative verbs': a verb that specifies the illocutionary force of the sentence it heads, that is, a verb that specifies the relationship the utterance mediates between speaker and person spoken to. Examples of overt performative verbs are found in the sentences

94. I *promise* to give you ten dollars. (This sentence is a promise by the speaker to the hearer.)
95. I hereby *order* you to open the door. (This sentence is an order by the speaker to the listener.)
96. I hereby *declare* that I will not pay this bill. (This sentence is a declaration by the speaker to the listener.)

In Ross's proposal, all sentences which do not have an overt performative verb, as these do, have a deleted performative which in deep structure appears in the topmost S:

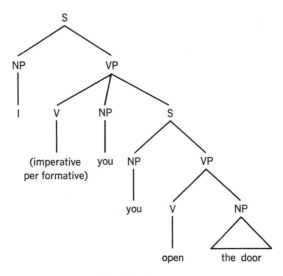

Open the door!

There is a fairly large body of facts which support Ross's proposal. Consider first the fact that imperatives behave as if they had a subject, *you* (for example, NP's are reflexivized in imperatives if and only if they are in the second person: 'wash yourself', * 'wash himself', * 'wash you'), and that that *you* is absent from the surface form of the sentence. If Ross's proposal is accepted, then these facts, rather than requiring ad hoc rules, as in all previous descriptions, become consequences of some very general mechanisms which the grammar must have anyway. Specifically, all verbs of 'ordering' must be followed in deep structure by a noun phrase and an embedded sentence, and the subject of that sentence must be identical with the preceding noun phrase; furthermore, the equi-NP-deletion transformation of English deletes the subject of an embedded sentence if it is preceded by an identical noun phrase. These principles are needed to explain the syntax of sentences such as

97. I ordered John to open the door.

Since the performative verb which Ross sets up in the deep structures of imperatives is a performative, its indirect object must be *you;* since it is also a verb of 'ordering', the subject of the embedded sentence must also be *you;* and just as with other verbs of 'ordering', the subject of the embedded sentence will be deleted by the equi-NP-deletion transformation. Thus the loss of the subject in imperatives is simply a special case of equi-NP-deletion and requires no special transformation. A second fact which supports Ross's analysis is the defective distribution exhibited by some of the overt performative verbs: certain verbs may appear as overt performatives when accompanied by the word *hereby* but not without it:

98. I hereby tell you to open the door.
99. * I tell you to open the door.
100. I hereby ask you where you were last night.
101. * I ask you where you were last night.
102. I hereby tell you that Lyndon Johnson is an imperialist butcher.
103. * I tell you that Lyndon Johnson is an imperialist butcher.

(there are of course also performatives which may appear without *hereby*, as in Sentence 94). Moreover, with one exception which I will discuss below, for each of the deleted performatives that Ross's analysis demands, I have been able to find a verb that has this hole in its distribution. Temporarily leaving aside the one exception I mentioned, one could explain this hole in the pattern by proposing that the deleted performatives in Ross's analysis are not the abstract bundles of features he initially treated them as but, indeed, are real lexical items such as *tell* and *ask*, that the performative deletion rule is a minor rule which these items are marked as undergoing, and that that rule is formulated so as to apply when the sentence consists of subject, verb, indirect object, and embedded sentence (that is, the rule is inapplicable when there is any additional item such as *hereby*). Thus, 99, 101, and 103 correspond to deep structures which actually yield

104. Open the door!
105. Where were you last night?
106. Lyndon Johnson is an imperialist butcher.

via the performative deletion transformation. The exception to which I referred above is the performative verb which would be needed as the topmost verb in 'echo questions' such as

107. You saw *who?*

by Ross's analysis. There is no lexical item overtly occurring in English which has the above hole in its paradigm and which is synonymous with the echo-question performative. But there is no verb in English by which one can report echo questions at all; that is, there is no verb such as * *bnick* which could be used in a sentence

108. * John bnicked me what I beat my wife with.

which would be a report of John's having asked me the echo question

109. You beat your wife with $\overgroup{what}$?

Thus, this discrepancy from the correspondence noted above between deleted performatives and overt performatives which may not appear alone does not impair the above analysis; what it means is that the echo-question performative is constrained so that it may only appear in the environment in which it will be deleted.

In Ross's analysis the deep structure of any sentence must have a performative verb as its topmost verb and that verb must have *I* for its subject and *you* for its indirect object. Thus the person of the noun phrases in the topmost sentence is predictable. Accordingly, one could simply not specify these noun phrases for person and have a rule which would add the specifications 'first person' and 'second person' to them; that is, one could take the configurations 'subject of performative' and 'indirect object of performative' as *defining* the notions 'first person' and 'second person'.[12] If this approach is adopted, then person specifications need not appear in deep structures at all. One undifferentiated personal pronoun type will become specified for person on the basis of its index and the indices of the subject and indirect object of the performative. However, the conditions for specifying a noun phrase as first or second person relate not to identity of indices but rather to the subset relation between indices. If the index of the subject of the performative is contained in the index of a given noun phrase, that noun phrase is marked 'first person'; then if the index of the indirect object of the performative is contained in the index of a given noun phrase which has not yet been specified for person, that noun phrase is marked 'second person'. The effects of these rules can be seen in sentences such as

110. You and I like our work.
111. You and John like your work.
112. John and Harry like their work.

where *our, your, their* correspond to indices containing respectively that of *I,* that of *you* but not *I,* and neither.

This treatment of person makes unnecessary some totally ad hoc restrictions on person which would otherwise be needed. Note what hap-

[12] This treatment is a generalization of an idea of J. P. Thorne, who states (1966, p 76), '*You* is not a different pronoun from *he, she,* and *they* but a different form—the vocative form—of them'.

pens when an echo question corresponds to something with an overt
performative and *hereby*. One may respond to the sentence 'I hereby order
you to open the door' with either of the echo questions

   113. You hereby order me to do *what?*
   114. *Who* hereby orders me to open the door?

Hereby appears in these questions with the subjects *you* and *who* but
may not otherwise take such subjects:

   115. * You hereby order me to open the door.
   116. * Who hereby orders me to open the door?

The echo-question performative verb is unique in that the sentence embedded below it must be of the form which would correspond to the
deep structure of a whole sentence, right down to the performative; this
corresponds to the fact that what an echo question asks relates to the
utterance which has just been produced rather than to its content. The
noun phrase which is the subject of the clause containing *hereby* is
marked for person by the above rules, and in the normal situation where
one asks an echo question of the person who has supposedly just uttered
the stimulus to it, it will be identical in index to the indirect object
of the performative and thus will be marked 'second person', thus yielding 113. Except in the case of echo questions it is impossible for the
subject of a clause with *hereby* to meet the conditions for being labeled
'second person'. For another example, consider sentences such as

   117. Shall I open the door?

This is to my knowledge the only type of question in English to which
the appropriate answer is an imperative rather than a declarative sentence.[13]

   118. Yes, open the door.
   119. No, don't open the door.
   120. * Yes, you shall open the door.

---

[13] The frequently encountered argument that imperatives must have an underlying
auxiliary *will* because of 'tag imperatives' such as 'Open the door, won't you?' is in-
valid, since the tag of the 'tag imperative' is totally different in meaning from the
tag of the tag question (while 'Mary is pretty, isn't she?' requests an answer such as
'Yes, she is', the tag imperative does not request an answer such as 'Yes, open it')
and thus is probably the result of quite different rules. Further evidence for this
conclusion is given in Bolinger (1967).

Note that the question has a first person subject and the answer a (deleted) second person subject. In the case of a first person plural subject whose index includes the index corresponding to the hearer (that is, an inclusive first person plural), the answer is a first person plural imperative with *let's:*

    121. Shall we go to dinner now?
    122. Yes, let's go.
    123. No, let's not go yet.
    124. * Yes, we shall go.

These facts are explained if 117 and 121 are in fact analyzed as interrogated imperatives. A first person plural results in 121–123 since the noun phrase in question will have the index $\{x_1, x_2\}$, where x_1 and x_2 are the indices corresponding to the two persons involved. In 121 this noun phrase will be marked 'first person' because its index contains x_1, and in 122 and 123 it will be marked 'first person' because its index contains x_2. If *we* had been used in an exclusive sense in 121, that is, if the index of *we* there had included the index of the speaker but not that of the listener, the appropriate answers would have been

    125. Yes, please go.
    126. No, don't go yet.

since in the answer the index of the noun phrase in question would now contain the index corresponding to the person addressed but not that corresponding to the speaker. *Let's* requires an inclusive first person subject, as is shown by Lakoff's examples

    127. Let's you and me go to the movies.
    128. * Let's John and me go to the movies.

The Hungarian equivalent of 'Shall I come?' is *'Menyék?'*, that is, a first person singular imperative with question intonation; here an analysis as an interrogated imperative is unavoidable. The treatment of person proposed above again makes it unnecessary to state person restrictions that would otherwise be needed to exclude sentences such as * *'Menyék'* (with declarative intonation). Note, however, that an uninterrogated first person singular imperative occurs in dependent imperative constructions such as

    129. *János azt mondta, hogy menyék.* 'John told me to come.'

Finally, there are a small number of examples (all to my knowledge obscene) of idioms which require both an imperative and a reflexive.[14] These exhibit only a second person reflexive when used in independent sentences but are not restricted to second person in embedded imperatives such as 'I told John to . . .'. The treatment of person which I propose makes it unnecessary to impose any person restriction on these idioms. They are simply required to have a subject identical to the indirect object of the next higher sentence, and if the next higher sentence happens to be the topmost sentence, then the conditions for introducing the 'second person' specification will always be met.

I will conclude by repeating the moral which I hinted at earlier, that a full account of English syntax requires a fairly full account of semantics to just as great an extent as the converse is true. I think that the examples which I have presented here give considerable justification for this position and thus feel that it is high time for linguists to grant to semantics the status as an integral part of linguistics which has hitherto been denied it by most.

A Postscript

Since writing the above paper, I have modified my thinking on certain points treated in it. First of all, I now feel that the feature [joint] on NP's is merely a makeshift device which will have to be supplanted by several distinct theoretical devices in an adequate account of the phenomena discussed. One of the devices which will supplant part of the function of this feature appeared implicitly in my discussion of the semantic representation of the different meanings of 87. The y's which appear in those representations can be considered (following a proposal of Postal's) as indices of the verb:

$$\text{Joint: } \mathop{\exists}_{y} \mathop{\forall}_{x \epsilon M} [x \text{ go}_y \text{ to Cleveland}]$$

$$\text{Nonjoint: } \mathop{\forall}_{x \epsilon M} \mathop{\exists}_{y_x} [x \text{ go}_{y_x} \text{ to Cleveland}]$$

Ross has called to my attention the fact that the 'joint' and 'nonjoint' readings of sentences such as 84 and 87 behave differently with respect to the action nominalization:

130. John and Harry's departure for Cleveland (joint)

---

[14] An idiom that has the surface appearance of belonging to this category but in fact does not belong to it is discussed in Quang (1966).

131. John's and Harry's departures for Cleveland (nonjoint)
132. The departures of John and of Harry for Cleveland (nonjoint)

The positing of verb indices explains the plurality of the nominalized verb: in the 'joint' case the verb has the individual index y, whereas in the 'nonjoint' case it has the set index $\{y_1, y_2\}$, where y_1 is the index corresponding to John's departure and y_2 that corresponding to Harry's departure. Thus, not only noun phrases but also verbs allow a distinction between set index and individual index. A set index on a verb is also involved in the adjuncts *twice, many times,* and so forth. Note the examples

133. John denied the accusation five times.
134. John's five denials of the accusation
135. *John's denials of the accusation five times

Semantically, *five times* is identical to the *five* of *five horses:* it specifies that the cardinal number of a certain set is *five;* these examples suggest that *time* is an 'empty' morpheme which is inserted to support a numerical adjunct to an unnominalized verb.[15]

The plurality of the noun in 131 seems very like that of the noun in:

141. John and Harry love their wives.

Note that only in the case of a *ménage à trois* would it be appropriate to use the singular noun *wife.* Moreover, the word *respective* may appear in 141 without any change of meaning:

142. John and Harry love their respective wives.

as well as in 131 and 132:

---

[15] It will be necessary to distinguish between different types of verb indices. Note that 'the many similarities between John and Harry' corresponds not to

136. * John and Harry are similar many times.

but to

137. John and Harry are similar in many ways.

There will be a different 'empty' morpheme corresponding to each type of verb index. Different index types may contrast with each other:

138. John criticized the book many times.
139. John criticized the book in many respects.

Both of these examples nominalize to

140. John's many criticisms of the book.

143. John's and Harry's respective departures for Cleveland
144. The respective departures of John and Harry for Cleveland

Since *respective* and *respectively* are identical in meaning and are in complementary distribution (*respective* appears only as an adjunct to a noun and *respectively* only as an adjunct to a larger constituent), one is forced to say that the same transformation which produces the sentence

145. John and Harry love Mary and Alice respectively.

is involved in the derivation of 142 and that 142 and 145 differ in deep structure only to the extent that where 142 has *John's wife* and *Harry's wife,* 145 has *Mary* and *Alice.* I conclude from all these considerations that the 'nonjoint' sense of 84 must arise through the *respectively* transformation from

146. John go$_{y_1}$ to Cleveland and Harry go$_{y_2}$ to Cleveland.

and that the *respectively* transformation is thus responsible for the set index on *go* in that reading of 84. However, here a problem arises: corresponding to all the examples discussed so far there are examples which involve not conjoined singular noun phrases but simple plural noun phrases:

87. Those men went to Cleveland.
147. Those men's respective departures for Cleveland
148. The respective departures of those men for Cleveland
149. Those men love their respective wives.

If *respective* is to arise through the *respectively* transformation, which I have hitherto assumed to apply to conjoined structures differing at two places, how is it to arise in examples such as these, which have no conjoined constituent in them? There are two possible solutions to this problem: one is to generalize the *respectively* transformation in some way and the other is to derive all plural noun phrases from underlying conjoined noun phrases. The latter, which has been proposed by Postal, seems attractive in view of the fact that there are already some plural noun phrases (for example, that of 58) which must be derived from conjoined singular noun phrases. However, there are compelling reasons why this proposal must be rejected. First, for this proposal to yield deep structures which are suitable for correct semantic interpretation, the number of conjuncts underlying a plural noun phrase would have to equal the number of individuals being talked about (for example, 'The

63,428 persons in Yankee stadium' could not have merely two conjuncts underlying *persons*), but on the other hand one is not always talking about a definite number of individuals:

150. He has written approximately 50 books.
151. There were very few persons at the football game.
152. There were an enormous number of persons at my party.
153. How many times have you failed your French examination?

Moreover, one could not even represent these plural noun phrases as disjunctions of all the conjunctions which have a number of terms in the range specified by *approximately fifty,* and so on, because the range which these expressions denote may vary with what is being talked about (for example, *very few* in 151 may be 5000 and *an enormous number* in 152 may be fifty) and because there are cases in which an indefinite numeral may not be used but a definite numeral within the range denoted by the indefinite numeral may be:

154. Those five men are Polish, Irish, Armenian, Italian, and Chinese, respectively.
155. * Those several men are Polish, Irish, Armenian, Italian, and Chinese, respectively.

Thus, in order to explain 141–149, it will be necessary to change the formulation of the *respectively* transformation so as to make it applicable to cases where there is no conjunction but there are plural noun phrases, or rather, noun phrases with set indices: *pluralia tantum* do not allow *respectively* unless they have a set index, so that

156. The scissors are respectively sharp and blunt.

can only be interpreted as a reference to two pairs of scissors and not to a single pair of scissors. The correct formulation of the *respectively* transformation must thus involve a set index. That, of course, is natural in view of the fact that the effect of the transformation is to 'distribute' a universal quantifier: the sentences involved can all be represented as involving a universal quantifier, and the result of the *respectively* transformation is something in which a reflex of the set over which the quantifier ranges appears in place of occurrences of the variable which was bound by that quantifier. For example, the semantic representation of 149 is something like $\bigvee_{x \in M}$ [x loves x's wife], where M is the set of men in question, and 142 can be assigned the semantic representation $\bigvee_{x \in \{x_1, x_2\}}$

[x loves x's wife], where x_1 corresponds to *John* and x_2 to *Harry;* the resulting sentence has *those men* or *John and Harry* in place of one occurrence of the bound variable, and the corresponding pronominal form *they* in place of the other occurrence. Moreover, *wife* takes a plural form, since after the *respectively* transformation the noun phrase which it heads has for its index the set of all wives corresponding to any *x* in the set in question. The difference between 142 and 145 is that the function which appears in the formula that the quantifier in 142 binds is one which is part of the speaker's linguistic competence ($f(x) = x$'s wife), whereas that in 145 is one created ad hoc for the sentence in question ($f(x_1) = $ Mary, $f(x_2) = $ Alice).

I conclude from these considerations that the class of representations which functions as input to the *respectively* transformation involves not merely set indices but also quantifiers and thus consists of what one would normally be more inclined to call semantic representations than syntactic representations.

We thus arrive at the second major point on which my views have changed since writing the preceding paper, namely, the status of deep structure as a level of linguistic description. In the paper, while quarreling with many of the details of the conception of a grammar presented in Chomsky (1965), I accepted its general outlines and, in particular, the hypothesis that the components of a grammar of a language include a base component, which specifies the membership of a class of potentially well-formed deep structures, a semantic component, which correlates deep structures with their semantic representations, and a transformational component, which correlates deep structures with their surface syntactic representations. Of the three levels of linguistic representation just alluded to, there is no question about the need of positing the existence of semantic and surface syntactic representation, which have indeed figured at least implicitly in virtually every system of linguistic description that has been conceived of. However, it is necessary to provide some justification for the hypothesis of an intermediate level (deep structure) between those two levels: there is no a priori reason why a grammar could not instead consist of, say, a 'formation-rule component', which specifies the membership of a class of well-formed semantic representations, and a 'transformational component', which consists of rules correlating semantic representations with surface syntactic representations in much the same fashion in which Chomsky's 'transformational component' correlates deep structures with surface syntactic representations. Moreover, the burden of proof in choosing between these two conceptions of linguistic competence rests with those who posit the existence of the extra level, just as in phonology the burden of proof rests with those who posit the existence of a 'phonemic' level intermediate between lexical phonological representation (often called 'systematic phonemic' or 'morphophonemic' representation) and phonetic representation. Transformational grammarians have largely ignored the problem of providing such justification, much in the same way as phonemicists largely ignored the problem of providing justification for a phonemic level, and for similar reasons: just as phonemicists have largely treated phonemics as home ground and morphophonemics as *terra quasi incognita* and have rarely attempted to give a general account of the latter, the attempts being largely programmatic and anecdotal (for example, Chapter 14 of Harris, 1951), so also transformational grammarians have largely stuck to their home ground of syntax and thus have been in no position to take an overall view of the relationship between semantic and surface syntactic representation such as would be necessary to decide whether that relationship is decomposable into two component relationships which could be identified with a system of semantic projection rules and a system of syntactic transformations.

When Halle, Lees, and others took such an overall view of the relationship between lexical phonological representation and phonetic representation, they found unitary phenomena which could not be treated as unitary phenomena within a grammar having separate systems of 'morphophonemic' and 'allophonic' rules which met at a 'phonemic' level (for example, the voicing assimilation in Russian, whose effect is 'allophonic' in the case of [c, č, x] but 'morphophonemic' in the case of all other obstruents, and which thus would have to be treated in a grammar with a phonemic level as two separate rules of limited generality which belonged to separate components of the grammar); accordingly, the question must be asked whether similar phenomena will be found when an overall view of syntax and semantics is taken. I claim to have exhibited just such a phenomenon earlier in this postscript, namely the *respectively* transformation. It has in part the effect of specifying a relationship between a representation involving quantifiers and bound variables and a representation involving ordinary noun phrases, that is, the effect of what in Chomsky (1965) is called a semantic projection rule. However, as pointed out by Paul Postal (personal communication, May 8, 1967), it also subsumes much of what has been regarded as a syntactic transformation of conjunction reduction, for example, the derivation of 84 from a conjoined sentence. Postal points out that if the restriction of conjunction reduction to conjoined structures with only one difference were dropped, all conjunction reduction would be a special case of *respectively;* he observes that the difference between

157. That man loves Mary and Alice.
158. Those men love Mary and Alice respectively.

is simply whether two underlying occurrences of *that man* have the same index or different indices: both can be said to arise from an underlying structure of the form

159. That man loves Mary and that man loves Alice.

by the *respectively* transformation; in either case a conjoined subject *that man and that man* would arise and would be subject to the noun phrase collapsing rule; if the two occurrences of *that man* had the same index, the set-theoretic union of the indices would be simply the original index: $x_1 \cup x_1 = x_1$, and 157 would result. I accordingly conclude that *respectively* cannot be treated as a unitary phenomenon in a grammar with a level of deep structure and that that conception of grammar must thus be rejected in favor of the alternative suggested above, which was proposed in Lakoff and Ross (1967).

If this conclusion is accepted, then the syntactic and semantic components of the earlier theory will have to be replaced by a single system of rules which convert semantic representation through various intermediate stages into surface syntactic representation. An obvious question to raise at this point is whether this component would not in fact consist of two radically different kinds of rules, one defined on semantic representations and one defined on syntactic representations, rather than of a single homogeneous system of rules. To answer this question, it will be necessary to discuss the extent to which semantic representation and syntactic representation are different in their formal nature. At the Texas universals conference, Lakoff pointed out that there is much less difference between these supposedly different kinds of representation than has been hitherto assumed. He observes that there is an almost exact correspondence between the more basic syntactic categories and the primitive terms of symbolic logic and between the rules which he and Ross have proposed as base component universals and the formation rules for symbolic logic which various authors have proposed (for example, the 'relative clause rule' NP → NP S corresponds to the rule that from a 'term' x and a 'predicate' f one may form the term $\{x: f(x)\}$, to be read 'the x's such that $f(x)$'). Moreover, semantic representations involve constituents which are grouped together by parentheses and thus can be represented by trees. Since the categories of the operations and operands which appear in symbolic logic (which I hypothesize to supply the basis for semantic representation) correspond to syntactic categories, semantic representations can be regarded as trees labeled with syntactic category symbols. Furthermore, there is nothing a priori to prevent one from treating semantic representation as involving a linear ordering of constituents. Much confusion in this regard has been created by the mistaken belief that things which are identical in meaning must have identical semantic representations. The notion 'identity of meaning' can perfectly well be regarded as referring to an equivalence relation defined on semantic representations and two sentences said to be identical in meaning if their semantic representations are equivalent even if not identical. For example, the sentences

160. I spent the evening drinking and singing songs.
161. I spent the evening singing songs and drinking.

might be assigned semantic representations which differed in the order of two conjoined propositions but which would be equivalent by virtue of the principle $p \wedge q \equiv q \wedge p$. Thus, semantic representations can perfectly well be regarded as ordered trees whose nodes are labeled by syntactic category symbols, so that the only formal difference between semantic and syntactic representations would be the type of constituents which appear as terminal nodes in the trees. Thus, the system of rules which converts semantic representation into surface structure will be a system of rules which map ordered labeled trees onto ordered labeled trees, and among these rules will be not only the adjunctions, deletions, and permutations which are familiar from the theory of Chomsky (1965) but also 'lexical insertion' transformations, which insert lexical items in place of portions of labeled trees. However, 'lexical insertion' transformations must be part of the machinery of a grammar even within the framework of the theory of Chomsky (1965), since such processes as pronominalization involve the insertion of lexical material under nodes which originally dominated other lexical material. Moreover, some lexical insertions must take place extremely late in the grammar, as is shown by the following two examples. (1) The selection of the pronominal noun phrases *the former* and *the latter* cannot be made until after all transformations which move noun phrases have been carried out. (2) If, after the selection of pronouns, two conjoined pronouns are identical in form, then noun-phrase collapsing must be performed and then a new pronoun selected (this fact was pointed out to me by John Robert Ross):

162. He and she live in Boston and Toledo respectively.
163. * He and he live in Boston and Toledo respectively.
164. They live in Boston and Toledo respectively.

Chomsky (1965) in effect asserts that all lexical insertion takes place in the base component unless triggered by other transformations, as in the above examples. This view has been challenged in two ways: Gruber (1965) argues that related pairs such as *buy/sell* and *send/receive* arise through transformations which precede lexical insertion, and Lakoff and Ross (1967) argue that the insertion of many idioms takes place after various transformations have applied; in the one case it is argued that some transformations come earlier in the grammar than the theory of *Aspects* would allow, in the other case that some lexical insertion occurs later than it would allow.

One interesting consequence of the conception of grammar which I am advocating here is that it allows lexical items to be inserted in place of constituents which are created by transformations. A great many transformations proposed in recent years can now be viewed as transformations which combine semantic constituents before lexical insertion, for example, the various nominalization transformations and the transformations forming derived causative and inchoative verbs (Lakoff, 1965). The distinction between 'transformationally derived' and 'lexical', which many linguists have placed great importance on (see especially Chomsky, forthcoming), thus appears to be a false dichotomy.

LINGUISTIC UNIVERSALS AND LINGUISTIC CHANGE

Paul Kiparsky *Massachusetts Institute of Technology*

I would like to thank J. R. Ross and W. G. Moulton for suggesting to me many improvements for this paper. But they do not necessarily agree with me, and the responsibility is mine alone.

1. The Psychological Reality Problem[1]

Suppose that someone succeeds in writing a grammar which correctly enumerates the sentences of a language and assigns them the right structural descriptions. Such a grammar would ipso facto correctly represent the substance of a fluent speaker's knowledge of this language. But it would not necessarily represent the form of this knowledge in the sense of actually corresponding to the system of rules which is internalized by the speaker and constitutes part of what enables him to produce and understand arbitrary utterances in the language. Similarly, the knowledge of someone who has learned arithmetic, that is, the infinite set of correct arithmetical computations, could be defined by many different systems of rules, including both psychologically incorrect ones, such as certain axioms of set theory, computer programs, and so on, and the psychologically correct one, namely whatever knowledge is actually used in arithmetical performance, such as the rules of school arithmetic and the multiplication table. How do we know that generative grammar is not psychologically as wrong a model of linguistic competence as set theory is of arithmetical competence?

The linguistic universals which linguistic theory specifies include fixed notations in which grammars are written and an evaluation measure, which together establish a hypothesis about which of the innumerable grammars that might characterize the sentences of a language possesses psychological reality in the sense of representing the form rather than just the substance of a fluent speaker's competence. From among the pile of generalizations that might be made about the sentences of a language they select certain ones as being linguistically significant and corresponding to the generalizations that a child hearing such utterances would actually arrive at in constructing his grammar. The question, then, is how the various aspects of this hypothesis are justified.

For many features of universal grammar there is justification enough in the fact that without them it would simply not be possible to write grammars that account for the sentences of a language. Particularly in syntax, as Chomsky has pointed out, the typical problem is not choosing the right one among various theories that work but finding even one that will work at all. But with conventions which are essentially abbreviatory in nature, such as braces and parentheses, among others, real problems of empirical justification can arise. A grammar can always be replaced by

[1] This work was supported in part by The National Institutes of Health (Grant MH 13390–02).

171

another, descriptively equivalent one, in which any one of these abbreviatory notations is not made use of. There could not be a language whose sentences could be enumerated one way but not the other. Then what is the empirical force, if any, of such notational conventions?

For example, most linguists would agree that two rules of the form

$$X \rightarrow Y$$
$$Z \rightarrow Y$$

if not separated in the ordering by any other rule, should be combined by factoring out their common right hand side as follows:

$$\left\{ \begin{array}{c} X \\ Z \end{array} \right\} \rightarrow Y$$

We would say that the braces represent a linguistically significant generalization about these two rules. But how do we know that they do? How would we justify this convention to some linguist A who maintained that it was wrong and that the two rules should be kept separate? Or, to take a more likely contingency, how would we justify it to another linguist B who maintained that neither theory makes any verifiable truth claim as against the other, that since they are mutually convertible notational variants of each other, they represent equivalent hypotheses about the speaker's internalized grammar?

There are no conscious a priori ideas of generality that we can appeal to here in the way that we can appeal to intuitions that reflect features of structural descriptions, such as ambiguity and synonymy. The processes of normal language learning being unconscious, we have absolutely no ideas about the form of grammars, though we have clear ideas about the forms of sentences which grammars account for. It is true that the practicing linguist soon acquires ideas about the form of grammars and such concepts as generality. But these ideas are somehow the result of his work on languages, and we would like to know what the ideas are based on.

Nor is the fact that a generalization can be stated enough to show that it is real. All sorts of absurd notational conventions can easily be dreamed up which would express the kinds of spurious generalizations that we would want to exclude from grammars. It is necessary to justify conventions by showing that the generalizations they allow one to express do not hold accidentally. One might try to do this by arguing that a convention which can be used frequently in grammars cannot represent an accidental fact about language. But many presumably spurious conventions would come in handy very often in linguistic descriptions. For example, what about a linguist C who says that the brace notation should be extended to collapse rules of the form

$$X \to Y$$
$$Z \to X$$

into the form

$$Z \to \left\{ X \right\} \to Y$$

He will be able to show us just as many cases where such braces could be used in grammars to group rules together. Or, to cite an actual linguist, Pāṇini often makes use of an abbreviatory convention which corresponds to the following kind of use of braces, ruled out in generative grammar:[2]

$$A \to B \atop D \to \left\{ {E \atop F} \right\} / \_\_ C \atop / \_\_ G$$

What seems wrong about this is that it allows collapsing rules which represent heterogeneous processes. Of the rules combined here, two have absolutely nothing in common with each other: the top rule

$$A \to B / \_\_ C$$

and the bottom rule

$$D \to F / \_\_ G$$

But we would like the rules in a grammar to form blocks whose parts are related in some sense that goes beyond just partial identity. Ideally, the

[2] The reason is that abbreviatory conventions in the Indian grammatical tradition, originally an oral one, were not graphic devices such as braces, parentheses, or anything directly equivalent to them, but rather resembled the conjunction-reduction processes of natural language. In the following three sutras, for example, the bracketed words are omitted and understood as carried over from the previous sutra.

6.1.77   *iko yaṇ aci* (high vowels become glides before vowels)
6.1.78   *eco'yavāyāvah [aci]* (e, o, . . . → ay, av, . . . before vowels)
6.1.79   *[eco] vānto yi pratyaye* (o, au → av, āv before y)

It is hardly possible to collapse these three rules into one rule by any extensions of the conventions of generative grammar.

rules should be grouped into natural blocks whose parts represent different aspects of the same basic process.

Can psycholinguistics provide experimental evidence on the form of grammars? Recent psycholinguistic experiments designed to test the psychological reality of generative grammar have been concerned mainly with two questions. One group of experiments has sought behavioral correlates to the structural descriptions postulated by generative grammar. Bever, Fodor, and Garrett have, for example, carried out a series of experiments in which they found that the location at which a burst of sound is perceived in a synchronously presented sentence differs from its objective location in a way that can be predicted from the surface constituent structure of the sentence. The goal of another group of experiments was to find evidence bearing on the claim that a system of rules such as that postulated by generative grammar is involved in producing and understanding utterances. In contrast with the successful experiments concerned with the psychological reality of structural descriptions, those concerned with the psychological reality of grammars have on the whole been a failure (Fodor and Garrett, 1967). It is true that there was an initial spate of successes in which a clear relationship seemed to emerge between the grammatical complexity of a sentence, as measured by the number of rules of the grammar that contribute to its formation, and its perceptual complexity, as measured by various experimentally obtained performance parameters. But in recent experiments with more complex linguistic material this relationship has all but disappeared. It stands to reason that the utilization of the speaker's internalized grammatical rules is a highly complex process involving elaborate ways of tracking down the relevant rules and processing sentences in such a way that parameters which tap performance directly are not going to be related at all directly to such crude grammatical properties of sentences as the number of rules involved in their derivation. The fact that grammars are not performance models presumably means that the answer to the question of whether they are correct competence models is not likely to be forthcoming by any currently known experimental techniques until the contributions of competence can be separated out from the facts about performance.

What we really need is a window on the form of linguistic competence that is not obscured by factors like performance, about which next to nothing is known. In linguistic change we have precisely such a window.

2. The Form of Linguistic Change

We can think of linguistic change in roughly the following terms. Grammars are subject to changes of two kinds: the addition of new rules to them and simplification of them. In phonology, the addition of rules corresponds roughly to the concept of 'sound change' (Halle, 1962; Postal, 1968). For example, the sound change whereby final obstruents in words became voiceless in German and many other Germanic languages is the addition of the rule

1. $[+\text{obstruent}] \rightarrow [-\text{voiced}] / \underline{\hspace{1cm}} \#$

Through alternations such as [bunt]:[bunde] (versus [bunt]:[bunte]), in which this rule is reflected, it is learned anew as part of the language by each generation of speakers, and even in modern German the underlying representations of most words retain the medially pronounced voiced segment. Yet the addition of Rule 1 does not leave the lexicon entirely unaffected. Words like *ab, ob,* and *weg,* which never came to stand before an inflectional ending that would cause the reappearance of an underlying voiced obstruent, are never heard after the sound change with anything but a voiceless final obstruent; in these isolated forms, succeeding generations of speakers therefore have no reason to set up underlying forms with voiced obstruents. The change thus brings about a restructuring in a tiny corner of the vocabulary.

I hope that this use of the term *generation* will not convey the absurd picture of a society horizontally segmented into a number of discrete age groups, each with its own grammar. The point is simply that a language is not some gradually and imperceptibly changing object which smoothly floats through time and space, as historical linguistics based on philological material all too easily suggests. Rather, the transmission of language is discontinuous, and a language is recreated by each child on the basis of the speech data it hears. Nor should the term *restructuring* be understood as denoting a change of some speaker's grammar into another grammar, for it refers just to a discontinuous linguistic change arising from the difference between the grammar constructed by a child and the grammar of those whose speech constituted his linguistic experience. In discussing linguistic change in these elementary terms we are, of course, missing a number of important factors which cannot in the long run be ignored. For example, as Jakobson has pointed out, metalinguistic information concerning such things as the social value of different speech forms is an important part of what a speaker knows, and Labov's recent studies (1963, 1965) show its diachronic relevance very clearly. A conception of grammar in which these broader aspects of competence are explicitly accounted for will hopefully provide a general basis for the study of their role in linguistic change.

A sound change that I will frequently refer to is umlaut in Germanic. By this rule, vowels were fronted before *i* (for example, Old High German *wurmi* > *würmi* 'worms', *tāti* > *tǣti* 'deeds', *nōti* > *nō̄ti* 'needs'). Short *a* was not only fronted but also raised to *e* (for example, *slagi* > *slegi* 'strokes', *gasti* > *gesti* 'guests'). The original umlaut rule, then, was the following:[3]

2.
$$\begin{bmatrix} V \\ <-\text{long}> \end{bmatrix} \rightarrow \begin{bmatrix} -\text{back} \\ <-\text{low}> \end{bmatrix} / \underline{\hspace{1cm}} C_o i$$

In modern German we encounter this rule in a somewhat different form. In the majority of dialects what we find as the productive umlaut of *a* is not *e*, as originally, but *æ*. For example, in the Low German dialect of Prignitz (Mackel, 1905–1907) we have *gast:gæst, kraft:kræftig* with a low front vowel in the umlauted forms, rather than the expected *gast:gest, kraft:kreftig*. But the only *e*'s that have thus gone to *æ* are those that were productively umlauted from *a*. Phonemic *e*'s have remained unchanged. These include not only original Germanic *e* in words like *nest* but also *e* from historically umlauted *a* in words like *bet* 'bed', *net* 'net' where *e* has become phonemic since there was no reason to derive it synchronically from an underlying *a*. Analogous facts hold true in Old English as well. In terms of the grammar, this widespread change is a simplification of the umlaut rule from its original form of 2 to the form in 3:

3. V → [− back] / . . .

(I leave open here the question of what exactly the environment of umlauting in modern German is, which is irrelevant for present purposes.)

The change from 2 to 3 is an instance of the second basic type of linguistic change, simplification.[4] I shall merely illustrate this type for the moment but hope to justify it in more detail later. Simplification is a generalized and reinterpreted version of the traditional concept of analogy (Matthews, forthcoming; Kiparsky, 1965, 1967). This is particularly evident in its simplest form, namely morphological regularization as in changes of the type *brought* > *bringed*, which amount to loss of the special mark associated with lexical entries like *bring* that singles

---

[3] The rule must be complicated somewhat to include secondary umlaut.

[4] The term *generalization* is sometimes confusing, and I will not use it here. It is applicable in the natural sense of the word only to simplification in the structural analysis of a rule; simplification in the structural change is hardly generalization in this same sense. Even regarding the structural analysis, it is hard for some people to get used to the idea that a rule applying to stops and to *f* is less general than one applying just to stops.

them out as morphological exceptions and specifies the nature of their exceptional behavior. Much more interesting in many respects are cases in which the simplification affects the rules of the grammar rather than the lexicon. Quite commonly, such simplification leads to the loss of parts of rules from the grammar, as in the change of the umlaut rule just cited, where what is lost is the part of the rule which raises *a*. The process may even lead to the loss of entire rules. For example, Rule 1, which devoices word-final obstruents and once was common to all dialects of German, has been lost in some dialects of Northern Switzerland as well as in some varieties of Yiddish. In place of *bunt:bundes* they have *bund:bundes,* with the morphophonemic distinction of voicing now again appearing phonetically in word-final position. We know that these languages once possessed Rule 1, as it has permanently affected the handful of isolated words like *(a)vek* 'away', *ap* (Yidd. *op*) 'away', which had a voiced final obstruent but lost it even morphophonemically after the phonetic devoicing took place because retention was not motivated by any inflected forms. Hence there was also no basis for reintroducing the voicing in these words once Rule 1 had dropped out of the language by simplification.

It is also evident that the *order* of rules in a grammar is subject to historical change. Later, I will try to show that this is a special case of simplification; right now a few examples will do. By a historically fairly old rule of Finnish, underlying long mid vowels are diphthongized, for example, *vee > vie*. Subsequently, the loss of certain medial voiced continuants introduces new long mid vowels, for example, *teγe > tee*. In standard Finnish, these new long mid vowels stay, and the rule introducing them must therefore follow the diphthongization. That is, the order is

a. diphthongization
b. loss of medial voiced continuants

Yet in many dialects of Finnish the new long mid vowels have subsequently come to join in the diphthongization, for example *teγe > tee > tie*. What this means is that the order of the rules has changed to

a. loss of medial voiced continuants
b. diphthongization

Notice also what it does *not* mean. It does not mean what anyone coming from traditional historical linguistics automatically tends to think it means, namely, that in standard Finnish, where *tee* from *teγe* does not diphthongize, the diphthongization rule is not 'productive'. On the contrary, it is perfectly productive since it must apply to underlying forms like *vee*, in which the underlying long mid vowel must be assumed because of morphophonemic rules such as those for past formation, for example, *vee + i > vei* like *saa + i > sai*, as McCawley (forthcoming *a*) has shown. The difference between the two kinds of dialects has nothing to do with the productivity of the diphthongization rule but simply with its order with respect to the loss of medial voiced continuants.

An example of reordering which once again involves the umlaut is the following. In the dialects of Northeastern Switzerland the back midvowel *o* becomes lowered to *ɔ* if it immediately precedes a dental or palatal (nongrave, or what Halle now calls a coronal) true consonant or *r*. Compare, in the Kanton of Schaffhausen (Wanner, 1941):

> Retention of *o:*
>> before *l:* foll, holts, gold
>> before labials: grob, ops, hobəl, xnopf, dobə, ofə, xopf
>> before velars: xoxxə, xnoxxə, rokx, kflogə, bogə.
> Lowering to *ɔ:*
>> before *r:* hɔrn, tɔrn, šɔrə
>> before dentals and palatals: rɔss, xrɔttə, lɔsə, ksɔttə, bɔdə, pɔšt.

The distribution of allophones is given by the rule

$$
4. \quad \begin{bmatrix} \text{V} \\ -\text{high} \\ +\text{back} \end{bmatrix} \rightarrow [+\text{low}]/\underline{\hspace{1cm}} \begin{bmatrix} +\text{consonantal} \\ -\text{grave} \\ -\text{lateral} \end{bmatrix}
$$

It is necessary to restrict 4 to the back vowels. The umlauted variant *ö* of the vowel *o* is not lowered. The plurals of *bogə* and *bɔ də* are *bögə* and *bödə,* both with a mid *ö*. Hence the relative order of 4 and umlaut must be

> *a.* Rule 3 (umlaut)
> *b.* Rule 4 (lowering)

This is the situation in some dialects on the northern fringe of Switzerland. Elsewhere a different state of affairs obtains.

I will take a dialect which in all other relevant respects is identical to that of the Schaffhausen area, namely that of Kesswil, in neighboring Oberthurgau (Enderlin, 1911). Rule 4 operates in unmodified form here too. All the vocabulary items cited above for the Schaffhausen dialects are found, with the same distribution of *o* and *ɔ*, in Kesswil. But the difference is that Kesswil, along with most of Northeastern Switzerland, has *ö* as the umlauted form of *o*, but *ɔ̈* as the umlauted form of *ɔ̈*. In these dialects the plural of *bogɔ* is *bögɔ*, but the plural of *bɔdɔ* is *bɔ̈dɔ*.

The solution which first might come to mind is that the lowering rule in 4 was simplified to apply to rounded vowels regardless of whether they are front or back. But this fails since phonemic *ö* does not lower to *ɔ̈* in the environment of 4. The crucial cases are such forms as *plötsli* and *fröšš* 'frog' (originally a plural form). The behavior of these isolated forms whose vowels are not lowered shows conclusively that we are in reality not dealing with a lowering of *ö* to *ɔ̈* at all, but rather with the umlauting of *ɔ* as well as of *o*. That is, the order of the rules has now become

> *a.* Rule 4 (lowering)
> *b.* Rule 3 (umlaut)

Applying to the same underlying forms as before, these rules now produce the segment *ɔ̈,* which did not arise under the old ordering.

3.   A Criterion for Psychological Reality

Returning after this brief survey of some main types of phonological change to the initial question about the justification for assuming the psychological reality of generative grammar, suppose that we now raise this question about some aspect of generative grammar, such as the requirement that grammars contain a certain level of representation, or that they be written with the use of certain notational conventions. The conception of linguistic change sketched out above, in which linguistic structure crucially figures at several points, suggests as one test for determining the answer that we ask the question: Do the levels, the kinds of rules, and so on, which are required by this theory ever play a role in linguistic change? Taking as our example again the simple case of the brace notation, we can ask: Do blocks of rules collapsed by braces form units of a kind which can undergo systematic change? If they do, this will be a powerful argument for this notation, and if not, we will have prima facie evidence that it is a spurious notation. On such questions, evidence of the following kind can be found.

In English, underlying long vowels, which are otherwise realized as diphthongs, are shortened in two main phonological environments: before two or more consonants (for example, *keep:kept*) and in the third syllable from the end of the word (for example, *vain:vanity, severe: severity*). The rules which bring these shortenings about are the following:

5'. $V \rightarrow [-\text{long}]/\underline{\quad}CC$
5''. $V \rightarrow [-\text{long}]/\underline{\quad}C \ldots V \ldots V$

The theory of generative grammar requires that 5' and 5'' be collapsed into a single rule as follows:

5. $V \rightarrow [-\text{long}]/\underline{\quad}C \begin{cases} C \\ \ldots V \ldots V \end{cases}$

It asserts that of the two descriptively equivalent grammars, one of which contains the two rules (5' and 5'') as separate processes, and the other as a single process combined into 5 by factoring out their common part and enclosing the remainder in braces, it is the latter which is the psychologically correct one.

Rule 5 arose in Early Middle English as a generalization of a much more restricted process of shortening. In Old English, vowels were shortened before *three* or *more* consonants (for example, *gōdspell* > *godspell, brǣmblas*) > *brǣmblas*) and in the third syllable from the end provided they were followed by *two* consonants (for example, *blēdsian* > *bledsian*).[5] The corresponding rules were:

6'. $V \rightarrow [-\text{long}]/\underline{\quad}CCC$
6''. $V \rightarrow [-\text{long}]/\underline{\quad}CC \ldots V \ldots V$

Again, these rules must be collapsed as before:

6. $V \rightarrow [-\text{long}]/\underline{\quad}CC \begin{cases} C \\ \ldots V \ldots V \end{cases}$

On comparing the Old English rule in 6 and the Early Middle English (and indeed Modern English) rule in 5 we see that the only difference between them is that the later rule (5) has lost one of the required consonants in its environment. It represents a simpler, more general form of the Old English vowel-shortening process. It will apply in all cases where 6 applied but also in cases where 6 would not have applied. Evidently the change from 6 to 5 is an instance of simplification, which we have seen to be one of the basic mechanisms of linguistic change. But in

[5] Luick (1921, pp. 204, 352–353). In isolated words the Old English shortening also applied before geminates. But in these isolated words it led to restructuring, and since there was no shortening in *derived* words in Old English, the (synchronic) phonological rule of Old English was as stated. This rule covers all cases where there was actual alternation between long and short vowels in Old English.

a linguistic theory in which the brace notation plays no role, the relation between the Old English and the Early Middle English shortening processes is a different one. If the brace notation were not part of linguistic theory we would have two separate changes—namely, $6' > 5'$ and $6'' > 5''$—on our hands and we would be faced with the very peculiar fact that two separate, unrelated rules have undergone an identical modification at the same point in the history of English. The linguistic theory on which traditional historical grammar was based is an instance of such a theory, and traditional historical grammar has in fact failed to see the regularity here and has treated the change as two separate processes.

In the same way, we can go on to ask whether rules of the form

$$\left\{ \begin{array}{c} X \\ Y \end{array} \right\} \rightarrow Z$$

can be added to grammars. On the assumption that sound changes are natural processes, and that the brace notation groups rules into natural blocks, we should predict that rules collapsed by braces should be capable of being added to grammars. There are of course numerous instances of this type of change. In fact, the addition of Rule 6 to the grammar of Old English is probably just such an instance. Similarly we should predict that rules collapsed by braces should participate in reordering as blocks.

The proposed test also has the virtue of rendering such notations eminently vulnerable to potential counterevidence from historical change. The counterclaim which would be made by the theory which excludes braces is that rules like $5'$ and $5''$, or $6'$ and $6''$, when found together in a grammar with no necessarily intervening rules forcing them apart, should be able to undergo simplification individually, in such a way that the resulting pair of rules could not subsequently be collapsed by braces. Such a change, which in this theory would be a legitimate simplification, would be neither a possible sound change nor a simplification in a theory which allows collapsing by braces, and it would therefore be excluded in the latter. If such changes could be found, they would be clear counterevidence against the brace notation and would suggest that the generalizations effected by means of braces are spurious ones. The position which excludes braces would also entail that a rule could be inserted between two rules collapsed by braces in such a way that they subsequently could no longer be so collapsed. And finally, it would also entail that the parts of rules collapsed in this way should be individually capable of reordering with other rules of the grammar. The fact that no such changes appear to exist is strong negative evidence which adds to the historical support for the essential correctness of this abbreviatory convention of generative grammar.

The aforementioned linguist C, who wanted to introduce abbreviations like

$$Z \to \left\{ \begin{matrix} \\ X \\ \\ \end{matrix} \right\} \to Y$$

and Pāṇini, who supported other conventions which generative grammar does not countenance, now both get a real opportunity to prove their points by showing that the blocks of rules resulting from such conventions act as units in simplification (for example, by showing cases in which the joint environment X is simplified) or by showing that they are added as units to grammars, or reordered as units with respect to other rules. There is no evidence in sight that I know of to encourage them in this search.

One answer, then, to the question concerning the empirical basis for the notational conventions of linguistic theory is that these conventions are an essential part of any attempt to characterize what is a possible linguistic change and what is not a possible linguistic change. It involves in a sense only systematically drawing the conclusions from Halle's idea (1962) that the class of possible sound changes (qua added rules) is the same as the class of possible phonological rules and bringing in the additional evidence of simplification, whose role in linguistic change Halle did not consider.

In many crucial respects this criterion for rule naturalness lends support to the assumptions which are currently made in the theory of generative grammar. But accepting the equivalence of possible sound change and possible rule commits one to placing many restrictions on the notations of grammatical descriptions which are not at present acknowledged, and on the other hand, it suggests the need for many new conventions and new extensions of notations which should be incorporated into linguistic theory. For example, by saying that braces are needed we have only told half the story. We would like to limit the use of braces in such a way as to combine only processes which are indeed in some sense related and can jointly produce a sound change. Suppose, for example, that we found a language with three phonological processes that all applied before vowels and that did not have to be separated by other rules:

 a. voiced stops become continuants
 b. *s* becomes *h*
 c. vowels drop

For all three processes to take place before vowels is quite natural, and examples for each of them could be cited from dozens of languages. Yet there would be something wrong about combining all three by virtue of their shared environment. It is evident that *a* and *b* are more closely related than either of them is to *c*, and that an adequate theory should require the combining of *a* and *b* but not *c*. The basis for this feeling is, I think, nothing but the fact that *a* and *b* characteristically occur together in linguistic change and thus form a natural block of phonological processes. In fact, their relatedness has really nothing to do with the fact that they share a common environment but follows from an essential kinship of the phonetic processes involved. Thus they should be grouped together in a grammar even if they both were context free. To determine the natural groupings of rules was a goal of traditional historical linguistics which has been abandoned to a large extent in structuralism, at least in America. For example, *a* and *b* would have been considered *weakenings*. Probably phonology would profit by attempting to develop further and to make precise such concepts, which traditional grammars use to introduce an organization into their treatments of diachronic phonology.

4. Diachronic Evidence Concerning Phonological Levels

The psychological reality of levels of representation which emerge in different linguistic theories is subject to verification and falsification by diachronic evidence along the same lines. A question to be asked whenever some level of representation is proposed as linguistically relevant is whether this level functions in linguistic change. For example, it would be a striking and, to my mind, conclusive piece of evidence for the reality of autonomous ('taxonomic') phonemics if it could be shown that there were sound changes whose conditioning environment could be stated naturally only at precisely this level. It should be made clear just what such a demonstration would involve. It would involve showing both that the environments of this sound change were not morphophonemic and (the crucial part) that they could not be reformulated in terms of the phonetic level without restating exactly the rules that relate the phonetic and phonemic level. Of course, it is always by definition possible to reformulate a phonemic environment in terms of phonetic representations, and what would have to be shown is therefore that such a restatement of the conditioning environment of a sound change would lose a significant generalization. A hypothetical example of what to look for would be a change in some Russian dialect which affected all voiced obstruents except [ž̌] and [ǯ], the two voiced obstruents in Russian which are not phonemic but always come about only by automatic voicing assimilation of /č/ and /c/. As far as I know, no one has ever presented any instance of this kind, and there is therefore no basis for the claim that the facts of sound change somehow support a level of autonomous phonemics. And as has been repeatedly argued (Halle, 1962; Chomsky and Halle, 1968, Postal, 1968, Kiparsky, 1965, 1967), the facts of sound change do provide clear evidence for a deeper level of representation in phonology.

The contention has often been made that the level of autonomous phonemics is relevant to sound change in a somewhat different way. The suggestion is that the direction of sound change is determined by tendencies toward a symmetry of phonological units. What is important for our present discussion is that these units are often held to be specifically autonomous phonemes. Much the same comments again apply: if the level in question were demonstrably the relevant one here, and the tendencies in question could really be shown to exist, then this would decisively refute those who deny its existence. But once again, the necessary proof has, to my knowledge, never been provided.

Moulton had studied the vowel systems of Swiss dialects with the purpose of testing these concepts of 'phonological space'. He maintained (1961) that Rule 4—the lowering of *o* to *ɔ* before dentals, palatals, and *r*, whose relation to umlauting we discussed as an example of reordering —was caused by a drive towards symmetry through 'filling' the 'empty slot' in the systems which Moulton supposes that these dialects possessed before the lowering took place:

(A)	i	ü	u		(B)	i	ü	u
	e	ö	o			e	ö	o
	ɛ					ɛ		
	æ		a					a

But what is the justification for assuming that System *B* had this asymmetrical structure rather than the symmetrical structure, *C*, which one would have normally supposed it to have?

(C)	i	ü	u
	e	ö	o
	ɛ		a

Why did Moulton not assign *a* to the back vowels in these dialects as he did in the *A* dialects? Moulton has discussed the reason for his choice in another article (Moulton, 1960, p. 174), where the justification given for the asymmetrical System *B* is that these dialects underwent the lowering by Rule 4: 'The fact that the subsequent development of the vowel system of the North was parallel not to that of the West and Center but to that of the East confirms the belief that arrangement [*B* above] represents linguistic reality more faithfully, and suggests that arrangement [*C* above] would indeed be only a playful manipulation of symbols on paper.' In other words, these dialects had an asymmetrical system because they underwent lowering of *o* to *ɔ*, and they underwent lowering of *o* to *ɔ* because they had an asymmetrical system!

In sum, one prediction to which such theories lead is that certain phonological changes should be determined by whether or not pairs of certain sounds are contrastive in some phonetic environment and hence that isoglosses formed by phonological changes should characteristically be coextensive with boundaries between different autonomous phonemic systems. Other predictions are certainly also entailed, and the cases I have mentioned by no means constitute a full or even representative illustration of the range of predictions made, nor of the kind of evidence that is available to test them. But they nevertheless show how this theory and related ones do have very specific consequences which can be tested fully on historical material. I would guess that when this is done it will turn out that real enough tendencies towards phonological symmetry exist, but that they have nothing to do with the autonomous phonemic level for which they are often claimed. Rather they are probably brought about by simplificatory phonological changes such as rule simplification and rule reordering, and the symmetry they result in is phonetic rather than phonemic symmetry. This at any rate is what the Swiss German dialect material recently investigated by Moulton suggests.

5. Diachronic Evidence Concerning Features and Underlying Representations

The particular Swiss German example that I have talked about also raises a nest of further problems unrelated to that of the reality of the autonomous phonemic level, but highly relevant to the general topic of the relevance of linguistic change to linguistic universals. It will have been noticed that phonemic System *A* above, with four distinctive vowel heights, is a clear counterexample to Jakobson's distinctive feature system, which allows only three phonemic degrees of vowel height to exist in a language. First of all, the four degrees clearly contrast in simple, underived words and cannot be predicted by any general rules from some system with only three heights in any way that would not be ad hoc. For example,

ælf 'eleven'	gɛld 'money'	šelm 'rogue'	bild 'picture'
sæməl 'stool'	swɛbəl 'sulphur'	šnebəl 'sty (in	šwibəl 'grip'
hæks 'witch'	xrɛps 'crayfish'	the eye)'	blits 'lightning'
hællər 'small coin'	šellə 'bell'	nets 'net'	willə 'will'
		xellə 'scoop'	

In addition these dialects have a phonemic *a* which is quite distinct from all of these front vowels. Evidently, then, Jakobson's features compact and diffuse (low and high) should be replaced by two other features which allow four distinctive degrees of vowel height. A natural one would be the following:

	æ	ɛ	e	i
High	−	−	+	+
Mid	−	+	+	−

Yet if we shift our point of view somewhat and regard impossible systems simply as the end points of increasing scales of markedness, the proposed change to allow four heights is a relatively minor one. In a sense, these dialects, particularly if the historical evidence is brought in, support Jakobson's thesis in the modified form that vowel systems with four heights are complex, that is, highly marked systems, in the technical sense. For historically, a four-height system of this kind had to arise in all High German dialects. However, everywhere, with the exception of some tiny Swiss areas in Appenzell and Toggenburg, the four heights have been reduced to three by mergers either of the two mid vowels or of the two low vowels. These mergers have taken place quite independently in numerous dialects and thus have the character of drift or simplification rather than of normal sound changes. What this seems to indicate is that systems of four vowel heights are unstable because of their complexity, a conclusion which is indicated in any case by the rarity of such systems in the languages of the world.

The particular way in which these four-height systems have merged to three in the various dialects is itself a small piece of historical support for the feature system which I have proposed. The other possible alternative of characterizing four vowel heights by two features would be this:

	æ	ɛ	e	i
High	−	−	+	+
Raised	−	+	−	+

There would be no natural way of formulating the merger of mid vowels here since mid vowels do not make up a natural class under these features.

On the other hand, this alternative suggests mergers such as *æ* and *e* or *ε* and *i* which certainly do not occur. Vowel shifts of the type *ī* > *æi*, which are common in many languages, would also be expressed more simply in the system I have proposed. However, an alternative which may be even preferable and should in any case not be counted out yet is that vowel height is not broken down into two binary dimensions at all but forms a single dimension expressed by a feature which in underlying representations can assume at most four values (and must assume at least two).

Against the analysis which posits four heights of vowels in these dialects one might try to carry the argument that this analysis is implausible because closely related dialects have only three heights, and one would expect closely related dialects to differ not in their underlying phonemic system, but only in the rules which relate phonemic representations to phonetic representations. This would be a complete non sequitur. It is an empirical observation that related dialects often have the same phonemic system, but it is not a theoretical condition on related dialects that this should be the case. To say otherwise would be to credit children with historical or dialectological knowledge which they cannot possibly possess. The fact that the children of each generation in learning their language take a fresh look at the facts means that there is reason for underlying representations to be transmitted only when the synchronic facts of the language warrant it. The argument is just as irrelevant, and for just the same reason, as it would be to maintain that language *L* must have rule *R* in its grammar because *R* was a sound change in *L*.

A more difficult objection is based on the fact that *æ* in these dialects is the productive umlaut of *a*. To account for morphological umlaut in a language like German it is necessary to set up some abstract conditioning environment which will be a property of certain endings, such as plural *-er*. Whether this is a feature [±umlaut] as proposed by Zwicky (1967) or some phonological property of underlying representations will not matter here. Whatever this abstract environment is, generative phonology at present allows—and indeed probably requires—the trick of making it an obligatory part of isolated words like *schön, plötzlich, Tür*, which have umlaut vowels that correspond to no back vowels in any related forms. These words are then entered with underlying back vowels which undergo obligatory umlauting by virtue of this property of their underlying representations. The effect is to do away altogether with umlaut vowels in the phonemic system. In our case, then, *æ* would never be treated as phonemic and there would be only three phonemic vowel heights to worry about.

It is again the historical evidence which shows that this trick is wrong and that words like *schön, plötzlich, Tür* must have phonemic umlaut vowels. To see this let us go back to the example of reordering involving Rules 3 and 4 in Northeastern Switzerland. It will be recalled that as a result of the reordering, derived *ö* as in plural *böd*ə became *ɔ̈* but phonemic *ö* as in *plötsli* was not changed. There would be no way of accounting for a change like this (by no means an atypical case) in a theory which asserted that *all* umlaut vowels are underlying back vowels, for then we would have no natural way of telling apart those that are really so derived and do undergo lowering from those which are only fictitiously so derived and do not undergo lowering. This linguistic change cannot be accounted for unless phonological theory is tightened up in some way to exclude tricks of such a kind. It is interesting to note that whatever exactly the right way to do this turns out to be, it will bring the underlying representations of generative phonology a step closer to Sapir's descriptive practice (McCawley, 1967). And once this necessary move is made, the existence of systems with four vowel heights cannot be argued away.[6]

This last conclusion has the peculiar status of at present resting entirely on historical evidence, and of a fairly indirect kind at that. Whether or not we draw it depends on what we consider the subject matter of linguistics to be. We could not draw it if we regarded a grammar simply as a theory of the sentences of a language, and a linguistic theory as a theory of grammars. For this position would entail that linguistic change is no concern of linguistic theory, although it might of course be a pleasant bonus if linguistic theory could be usefully 'applied' to questions of linguistic change. But it would not cause us to demand of a linguistic theory that it must (in conjunction with a theory of linguistic change) provide an explanation of the linguistic regularities of diachrony. It is a very different matter if we regard a grammar as a theory of linguistic competence, and the field of linguistics as the study of universal grammar. On this view, which forms the topic of this conference and which I share, the facts of linguistic change assume a new relevance as empirical evidence on the nature of language. We must be prepared to allow them to bear on even purely synchronic questions and, for example, to let the fact that some phonological change is explainable by one linguistic theory but not by another carry weight in the choice between these two theories. The application of linguistic change to linguistic theory now becomes at least as important as the converse process.

The above rather scattered observations illustrate various types of inferences that can be made about grammatical form from the ways in

---

[6] David Stampe points out to me that the naturalness condition he proposes (at this same conference) requires exactly the underlying representations which we have seen to be justified on historical grounds.

which it shapes linguistic change. The reason I have dealt with phonological changes and not syntactic ones is partly that I know more about phonology, but also that the historical facts are here much easier to come by and the evidence they give is more needed in phonology than in syntax. I have been concerned not so much with establishing the virtues and faults of specific notations, levels, and so forth—much more evidence would be needed for that in almost every kind of problem dealt with above—as with making a case for the legitimacy and potential fruitfulness of certain general patterns of inference from linguistic change to the nature of grammar. In no case have the conclusions depended on very specific or controversial assumptions about linguistic change. The basic assumption from which these conclusions follow has been the very tame one that where grammar is involved in linguistic change it is involved in terms of its natural components and rules.

It is not so with another kind of inference from linguistic change to grammatical form to which I should now like to turn. This inference is based so heavily on the existence of grammatical simplification as a form of linguistic change that before proceeding to it I should like to outline the justification for assuming the existence of such a form of linguistic change.

6. Formal Justification for Simplification

The conclusion that such changes as simplification and reordering must exist does not and could not rest just on the fact that we observe related dialects to differ in the ordering of their rules, or to show minor differences in the details of essentially shared rules. That such differences are typical isoglosses is true but compatible with the position that addition of rules is the only form of phonological change. For as long as we look at dialects without knowledge of their historical origin we could explain any rule-ordering difference between them in a wave-theory fashion. For example, a spreading rule might be adopted at one position in the sequence of rules in one dialect and at some other position in another. There is another wave-theory effect which can cause pairs of rules to be differently ordered in different dialects. If Rule A spreads from West to East and Rule B spreads from East to West across some dialect area, then, if the two rules are critically ordered with respect to each other, the Western area will end up with the order A, B and the Eastern area with the order B, A. Undoubtedly these are both, in fact, quite common causes of ordering differences between dialects. Small differences in the form of rules can well occur in the course of their diffusion from one dialect to another. It has been observed that in such borrowing a narrowing down in the scope of rules often takes place. Thus the diphthongization of the long high vowels of Middle High German during its spread southward in Swiss territory was restricted to word-final position at a certain point before it stopped spreading altogether. Compare also the gradual curtailment of the High German consonant shift in the so-called Rhenish Fan.[7]

However, we find just the same types of minor differences in the form of rules and in their ordering when we compare successive stages of the same dialect rather than geographically adjacent dialects, and here the wave-theory and imperfect borrowing explanations are excluded. Furthermore, in such cases the form of rules almost always changes in the direction of greater simplicity. Can such changes be accounted for on the assumption that addition of rules is the only form of phonological change?

Consider the Finnish example cited in Section 2, in which the diphthongization rule was dialectally shifted down to follow loss of medial voiced continuants so as to apply to the long vowels which arose by this historically later rule (for example, *teγe* > *tee* > *tie*). Technically, it is not impossible to account for this change by means of added rules. There are even two ways of doing it. One is to assume that a rule of loss of medial voiced continuants, identical with the original one, was entered before diphthongization, causing the original one to become vacuous and to be dropped. The other is to assume that a diphthongization rule, identical with the original diphthongization rule, was entered *after* loss of medial voiced continuants. The optimal grammar for the resulting output would once again be the desired one. The unfortunate aspect of this is the arbitrariness of the choice between the two descriptions. It is hard to see how the distinction between them could correspond to any linguistic difference. The two distinct grammars containing an identical rule at two different points which are required as virtual intermediaries seem to be mere artifacts of a theory which excludes reordering as a mechanism of change and therefore must make an inappropriate extension of rule adding to account for a quite different kind of process.

The difficulties become considerable in such a case as the loss of word-final devoicing in Swiss German and Yiddish. We cannot, clearly, simply suppose that a late rule which made final obstruents voiced was added. Such a rule could not distinguish between morphophonemically voiced and voiceless stops and would wrongly turn into *bund* not only the *bunt* that is related to *bunde* but also the *bunt* that is related to *bunte*. In desperation we would take recourse to an ad hoc rule which somehow

---

[7] E. Bach has pointed out to me that these examples are not certain. If, as he suggests, rules are never narrowed down in borrowing, the case for simplification becomes even stronger.

would provide morphophonemically voiced stops with a diacritic feature before they got devoiced and later would use this diacritic feature as an environment for revoicing, after which the diacritic feature could be deleted again. Obviously this bears not the faintest resemblance to what actually happened, and no one would want to salvage a theory at the price of such an absurd analysis.

Chomsky and Halle (1968) discuss a convention for handling exceptions to rules which might be used in this particular example. The idea is that grammars can contain rules of the form

$$X \rightarrow [-\text{next rule}]$$

where X is a specification of the special cases in which some rule must not apply. Then it would be possible to say that a rule

$$[\quad] \rightarrow [-\text{next rule}]$$

was placed directly before the devoicing of word-final obstruents, thus preventing everything from undergoing it. The inoperative devoicing rule would then simply not be incorporated into the grammars of the next generation.

The difference here is not merely notational. The exception-rule solution generalizes neither to the reordering example that was just cited nor to cases like the simplification of the umlaut rule from 2 to 3 which was mentioned earlier. Since what was deleted here was *part* of a rule and the Chomsky-Halle convention for handling exceptions does not allow items to be exceptions to parts of rules, the solution which the convention made possible in the previous case is not available here. The best we can do is to say that the change consists of two separate but simultaneous events: first, the rendering inapplicable of the old umlaut rule (2) by the placement of a Chomsky-Halle exception rule before it, and second, the entering of the new umlaut rule (3) in its stead. That is, we are forced to treat this event as a composite product of two simultaneous changes, one of which alone would have far more spectacular consequences than the two have together. This leaves us completely in the dark as to why so many dialects (quite independently of each other, as is clear from the geographical distribution) should have undergone such a complicated pair of changes.

We see that to account for such examples by added rules, we would be forced to relax the proposed restriction that a sound change is the addition of a rule to the grammar to the extent of allowing a single historical change to involve the addition of *two* rules. In that case all arguments like those in Section 3 about sound change as a criterion for rule naturalness at once go out the window. And if this is done we also prepare a welcome for innumerable absurd descriptions of other changes. For example, in the case of the Finnish reordering of diphthongization and loss of medial voiced continuants (see Section 2 above) there are now two further alternatives which add to the general arbitrariness: the change might consist of simultaneously making diphthongization inapplicable and adding an exact replica of it after the loss of medial voiced continuants, or of simultaneously making loss of medial voiced continuants inapplicable and adding an exact replica of it before diphthongization.

Also, it is now just as easy to express the reverse change, that is, a change as a result of which the order

    a. loss of medial voiced continuants
    b. diphthongization

changes into

    a. diphthongization
    b. loss of medial voiced continuants

The effect of this would be that all *ie* diphthongs derived by way of *ee* from *eγe* would revert to their intermediate respresentation *ee,* while the *ie* diphthongs derived from basic *ee* would stay unchanged. There is no doubt that a theory of linguistic change should either completely exclude the possibility of such a change or at least reflect the obvious fact that it would be a far more complex and unlikely historical event than what actually happened. But the version to which the theory that rule addition is the only form of linguistic change has been driven at this point is completely incapable of doing so. As the brute necessity of somehow accommodating one set of data has forced it to be relaxed and extended more and more, it has lost the capacity of expressing the facts about sound change that originally motivated it.

7. Simplification and
Language Acquisition

To avoid this hopeless mess, the concept of simplification would be necessary even if we were concerned merely with characterizing the possible ways in which successive stages of a language could differ (which would be enough for purposes of linguistic reconstruction). But we also would like to find an explanation for why languages can change in the ways that they do. In that case, the reasons for assuming that simplification is a form of linguistic change become more compelling still. We cannot, then, close our eyes to the fact that the kind of driftlike changes which rule addition fails to handle without the special acrobatics of which samples were performed in Section 6 result in just the kind of grammars that appear spontaneously as intermediate stages in the course of the child's language-learning process.

I am not thinking just of the fact that instances of morphological analogy (*oxes, bringed*) are as characteristic of child language as they are of historical change, although this is perhaps the most evident instance of the correspondence. The parallelism goes deeper than that. For example, there is in many languages a drift toward multiple negation, as in substandard English 'I don't see nothing nowhere'. Such multiple negation has developed in the Romance languages and elsewhere in Europe too. Jespersen tried to attribute this drift to some vague tendency toward redundancy which he thought governed the direction of linguistic change. But this can hardly be true, for in other languages, such as Finnish, no comparable drift toward multiple negation is observed. Then it cannot be true that multiple negation is simply a general target in the direction of which all languages develop. In fact I think it is true that multiple negation appears only in those languages that have the equivalent of Klima's *neg*-incorporation rule which produces negative quantifiers such as in English *nobody, nothing* and French *rien*.[8] Surely this is related to the facts about the development of negation in child language found by Bellugi (cited from McNeill, 1966). She discovered that at the point at which the child's sentences like

I didn't see something.
You don't want some supper.

give way to sentences with negative quantifiers like *nobody, nothing, no supper,* a period of multiple negation at first sets in. As the child first formulates his *neg*-incorporation rule, it has not the form of standard English but of substandard English (which he very well may never have heard); and instead of producing the 'normal' sentences like

I saw nothing.
Nobody likes me.

he at first comes out with

[8] Finnish has indefinite pronouns such as *kukaan, mikään,* corresponding to English *anybody, anything,* but a negative cannot be incorporated into them to form any equivalents of *nobody, nothing.*

I didn't see nothing.
Nobody don't like me.

Thus some relationship between 'substandard' *neg*-incorporation and 'standard' *neg*-incorporation may be responsible for the fact that the former is the natural predecessor of the latter in the development of a child's linguistic system and also the natural result of the latter by linguistic change.

These facts begin to add up when we think of language acquisition as a process in which the child arrives at adult grammar gradually by attempting to match to the speech it hears a succession of hypotheses of an increasing order of complexity (in the linguistic sense of complexity) as these increasingly complex hypotheses become available to the child through maturational change. For phonology this was clearly shown by Jakobson's spectacular discovery that the child learns phonemes in a largely fixed order, which is determined not externally by the order or frequency with which they are heard, but internally by their relative linguistic complexity, as reflected also in the rules governing the possible phonemic systems of the languages of the world (Jakobson, 1942). Thus the child first produces the maximally unmarked, unvoiced, unaspirated stops, even if these, as in English, happen not to occur (except in some special environments) and only then splits up this first stop series into two series. In phonology, then, the order in which a child incorporates a particular piece of data into his internalized grammar is determined not by frequency or order of presentation, but by the readiness of the child to assimilate the kind of structure that underlies it. If we assume that the order in which the syntactic rules of the child unfold is internally determined in the same way, we can think of the child's multiple negation as analogous to his unvoiced, unaspirated stop in the sense that both are necessary prior structures which can be discarded only after the full structure develops. This is reasonable in view of the fact that multiple negation is produced by a version of *neg*-incorporation which is in two respects simpler than the adult version of this transformation. In the first place, the adult rule not only adds a *neg* to the quantifier, but it also deletes the original *neg* after the tense; this additional operation of deletion is absent from the child's first version of the rule. Secondly, the adult rule adds a *neg* to just one single quantifier in the sentence, whereas the child spreads the *neg* over all quantifiers that appear in the sentence, producing such specimens as the following:

I can't do nothing with no string.

Normally these oversimplified intermediate grammars which the child constructs on its way to adult language eventually give way to the full complexity of the adult system. The linguistic change of simplification takes place on those relatively rare occasions when some feature of these intermediate grammars survives into adulthood and becomes adopted by the speech community as a new linguistic norm. See Jakobson's remark (p. 332 of the 1962 reprinting):

> 'Die Sprachveränderung ist kein äusserer Beitrag, den die Kinder dem Sprachgebilde aufzwingen, sondern sie antizipieren dessen innerlich vorherbestimmte, sozusagen in der Luft schwebende Umwandlungen.'

That such survival is possible is not quite so surprising when we consider the extreme imperviousness of children to adult correction of their speech, as illustrated for multiple negation by the following dialogue (McNeill, 1966, p. 69):

CHILD: Nobody don't like me.
MOTHER: No, say 'nobody likes me'.
CHILD: Nobody don't like me.

(eight repetitions of this dialogue)

MOTHER: No, now listen carefully; say *'nobody likes me'*.
CHILD: Oh! Nobody don't likes me.

Thus we can relate the concepts of rule addition and simplification to adult and child language, respectively. The typical form of rule addition is the borrowing of rules among adults; simplification typically occurs in the learning of language by children. An interesting consequence of this is that isoglosses formed by the spread of rules over a speech territory should form large, coherent dialect areas, whereas those formed by simplification should be characteristically discontinuous because of independent development of the same change in several speech communities. The historically interesting isoglosses, therefore, should be based on the presence versus absence of rules, and not on differences in the form and order of shared rules. Indeed, this is what dialectologists have always implicitly assumed. The boundaries between the major dialect areas of Germany are drawn according to the rules they have, such as the consonant shifts. The isogloss between the two forms of the umlaut rule, 2 and 3 (that is, between e and $æ$ as the productive umlaut of a), would form a useless patchwork of no historical significance. Nor would anyone suppose a historical relationship between Yiddish and Swiss German on the grounds that they share the loss of the word-final devoicing rule. Very schematically, the two types of isoglosses would look like this (shaded areas are the innovating ones):

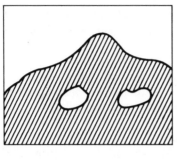

Spread of rule   Simplification

8.   Reordering as Simplification

Reordering resembles simplification both in the negative property that rule addition miserably fails to do justice to it and in the positive property of its driftlike character. I shall now claim that reordering is in fact a special case of simplification, and that the direction of reordering is predicted by general principles which assign certain types of order a higher value than others. If this can be established, then current phonological theory, which does not distinguish different kinds of linear order, is wrong and must be revised to account for this asymmetry.

To be convinced that reordering is a one-way affair, much as other simplification is, it is enough to examine the individual examples. For instance, many Swiss dialects have put the umlaut rule (3) after $o > ɔ$ (Rule 4), but none of these have made the reverse switch, and we could not easily imagine it taking place. And a dialect of Finnish in which *tie* from *teγe > tee* becomes *tee* again but *vie* from *vee* retains the diphthong, that is, a dialect in which diphthongization reverts to its original position before the loss of medial voiced continuants (which I will now call $γ > Ø$ for short) is inconceivable. The question is how this asymmetry, intuitively evident enough in each particular case, can be given a general characterization.

Of the various functional relationships that can hold between rules, two are of relevance here. One way in which two rules, *A* and *B*, can be functionally related is that the application of *A* creates representations to which *B* is applicable. That is, the application of *A* converts forms to which *B* cannot apply into forms to which *B* can apply; schematically:

A. [   ] > [φ]
B. [φ] > [   ]

Such a relationship holds for example between $\gamma > \emptyset$ (*teγe* > *tee*) and diphthongization (*tee* > *tie*) in our Finnish example. If the rules are applied in that order, $\gamma > \emptyset$ supplies a set of new cases (namely those derived from *eγe*) to which diphthongization can apply. In such a situation, call *A* a *feeding rule* relative to *B* (for example, $\gamma > \emptyset$ is a feeding rule relative to diphthongization). Call this relationship between rules a *feeding relationship* (for example, $\gamma > \emptyset$ and diphthongization are in a feeding relationship) and the linear order in which the feeding rule precedes a *feeding order* (for example, 1. $\gamma > \emptyset$, 2. diphthongization is a feeding order). Then one of the principles that determine the direction of reordering is

    I. Feeding order tends to be maximized.

Schematically:

    A. $[\varphi] > [\ \ ]$ *B*. $[\ \ ] > [\varphi]$
    B. $[\ \ ] > [\varphi]$ >   *A*. $[\varphi] > [\ \ ]$

    A further example of I involves the several palatalizations in Slavic. By the so-called first palatalization, *k* and *g* became *č* and *ǯ*, respectively, before front vowels and *y*, for example, **kĭto* > *čĭto* 'what', **givŭ* **ǯivŭ* 'alive'.[9]

7. $\begin{bmatrix} +\text{consonantal} \\ -\text{diffuse} \end{bmatrix} \rightarrow \begin{bmatrix} -\text{grave} \\ +\text{strident} \end{bmatrix} / \underline{\hspace{1cm}} \begin{bmatrix} -\text{consonantal} \\ -\text{back} \end{bmatrix}$

But the resulting voiced affricate *ǯ* has become a continuant *ž* in all Slavic languages by the rule

8. $\begin{bmatrix} +\text{voiced} \\ -\text{grave} \\ +\text{strident} \end{bmatrix} \rightarrow [+\text{continuant}]$

For example, **ǯivu* > *živŭ*.
    Subsequently new front vowels came to stand after velars by the rule

    9. ai → ě

By the so-called second palatalization *k,* and *g,* derived from *k* and *g* by

[9] Other aspects of the Slavic palatalizations are dealt with by Halle and Lightner in a forthcoming study. My knowledge of the rules is based entirely on their work. I state the rule here with the Jakobsonian features rather than any of the recent alternative proposals which have greatly improved the system.

an earlier rule) became c and $\mathfrak{z}$ before these new front vowels, for example, $*k_{\iota}\check{e}na > c\check{e}na$ 'price', $*g_{\iota}\check{e}lo > \mathfrak{z}\check{e}lo$ 'very':

10. $$\begin{bmatrix} +\text{obstruent} \\ -\text{grave} \\ -\text{strident} \\ -\text{diffuse} \end{bmatrix} \rightarrow \begin{bmatrix} +\text{strident} \\ +\text{diffuse} \end{bmatrix}$$

The resulting affricate $\mathfrak{z}$, unlike the earlier $\check{\mathfrak{z}}$, is retained in Old Church Slavic and in modern Polish. The grammars of these languages have Rules 7–10 as phonological rules in an order that matches their relative chronology. But elsewhere in Slavic, $\mathfrak{z}$ also has been replaced by its corresponding continuant, namely z, for example, $\mathfrak{z}\check{e}lo > z\check{e}lo$. These languages have the same four rules, but 8 must here follow 10, in order to apply to the affricate produced by the second palatalization as well. It is these two rules between which the feeding relationship obtains. Rule 10 is the feeding rule and the reordering establishes a feeding order between 10 and 8.

It should be noted that this relationship is a matter of the function and not of the form of the rules. In the Slavic example there is, as is often the case elsewhere too, a formal similarity between the related rules in that they mention some of the same features, and so on. But it would not be possible to define the correct relationship on the basis of the form of the rules. The two Finnish rules previously cited have very little in common, and the relationship is simply based on properties of the derivations the language has.

Another possible functional relationship between two rules is that A removes representations to which B would otherwise apply:

A. [ ] $> [\sim\varphi]$
B. $[\varphi] > [$]

Such a relationship holds for example between umlaut (A) and $o > \mathfrak{o}$ (B) in the example of Section 2. Thus the application of umlaut turns o into $\ddot{o}$, a front vowel to which the lowering rule is no longer applicable. If the lowering rule comes first in the ordering, it applies, turning o to $\mathfrak{o}$, and umlaut can then still apply. In the terms of the Indian grammatical tradition, umlaut is here the *nitya* or 'constant' rule. Call A a *bleeding rule* relative to B, the relationship between A and B a *bleeding relationship,* and the ordering in which A precedes B a *bleeding order.* The principle which underlies the asymmetry of order in this case is the following:

II. Bleeding order tends to be minimized.

$$A. \begin{array}{c} A. \; [\;\;] > [\sim\varphi] \\ B. \; [\varphi] \;\; > [\;\;] \end{array} > \begin{array}{c} B. \; [\varphi] \;\; > [\;\;] \\ A. \; [\;\;] > [\sim\varphi] \end{array}$$

In this way the original order, in which umlaut preceded lowering, became switched around into the new order, in which the bleeding did not take place.

As another illustration of the effect of II, consider the relation of two rules pertaining to voiced obstruents in German. One of them, which is historically the older, is the devoicing of obstruents in word-final position (for example, *bund* > *bunt*, *tāg* > *tāk*). This is Rule 1, which has come up in the discussion several times already. The other, found only in a certain group of dialects (Schirmunski, 1962, p. 302), is the spirantization of postvocalic voiced stops, for example, *tāgə* > *tāγə*, *sāgt* > *sāγt* (>*sāxt*). Originally, devoicing preceded postvocalic spirantization. Since, with this order, morphophonemic final voiced stops lost their voicing before spirantization applied, they remained stops and the contrast of *tāk:tāγə* resulted. This bleeding order, in which word-final devoicing deprives spirantization of some of the voiced stops to which it would otherwise apply, is still retained in some Alsatian, Bavarian, and Middle German dialects. More frequently the reverse ordering is found, with final voiced stops undergoing first spirantization (*tāg* > *tāγ*) and then devoicing (*tāγ* > *tāx*.) This order is widespread and especially common in the Low German dialects. We know that this order is a secondary development because some words like *(a)wek* (Standard German *weg*), where the voicing of the stop had no morphophonemic support, failed to spirantize even in the reordering dialects. This would be inexplicable unless we suppose that the devoicing was historically earlier even in these dialects in spite of the fact that it is synchronically later.

Another example can be cited from this same familiar area. A very widespread sound change in German dialects (Schirmunski, 1962, p. 212) is the rounding of *ā* to *ɔ̄*. As *ǣ*, the umlaut of *ā*, is unaffected by this change, it brings about alternations between *ɔ̄* and *ǣ* such as *šwɔ̄n* 'swan'. *šwǣn* 'Pl.', *špɔ̄t* 'late':*špǣtər* 'later'. Hence there is a bleeding order between the rules

a. umlaut
b. ā > ɔ̄

Many modern German dialects have just this system (see Rabeler, 1911, and Hotzenköcherle, 1934, for a Low German and Swiss German dialect, respectively). In others (for example, Wanner, 1941) the system has changed in that the umlauted form of *ɔ̄* is *ȫ*, for example, *šwȫn, špȫter*. The grammatical difference is that umlaut now applies after rather than before the rounding of *ā*. As phonemic *ǣ* in words like *tsǣ* 'tough' and *lǣr* 'empty' stays unrounded (more proof of the correctness of the argument is in Section 5) it is clear that the possibility of a simplification of the rounding rule to all long compact vowels is excluded and we are again faced with a case of reordering, which conforms perfectly to Principle II.

There is a more general principle underlying the two reordering tendencies (I and II) which combines them under a single wider concept of fuller utilization and makes their nature intuitively much clearer:

> III. Rules tend to shift into the order which allows their fullest utilization in the grammar.

If I am right that such a principle determines the direction in which reordering proceeds, then it follows that the order toward which rules gravitate in this way is linguistically simpler than its opposite. It is hard to see what other explanation there could be for such a consistent tendency toward a specific kind of order in linguistic change. As a convenient designation for the order types which are shunned and preferred according to Principles I–III, I suggest *marked* and *unmarked* order, respectively. It may well be that marking conventions analogous to those which assign the unmarked feature values in segmental phonology are the appropriate device for reflecting the asymmetry of ordering relations as well.

9. Leveling and Extension

As further justification for my assertion that unidirectional reordering tendencies exist and that they obey Principles I–III, I want to adduce an unexpected parallelism which obtains between reordering, if so constrained, and rule simplification. We can begin with a distinction drawn in traditional and structural historical grammar between two types of analogy, one called *leveling* and the other called *polarization* or *extension*. By leveling was meant roughly that existing alternations are either curtailed or eliminated altogether, with the result that allomorphs of some morphemes become more similar to each other or merge completely. Thus the change of *bunt:bunde* to *bund:bunde* would have been regarded as a leveling of the alternation of voiced and voiceless stops in word-final position. The simplification of the umlaut rule (2) to its other version (3), which replaced *kraft:kreftig* by *kraft:kræftig* would have been regarded as a leveling of the height alternation in favor of the low vowel throughout the paradigm.

Polarization, or extension, on the other hand, refers to a type of analogical change in which existing alternations spread to new instances. Here linguistic contrasts come to be more fully implemented than before, whereas leveling has precisely the opposite effect. We would presumably be dealing with extension if, for example, the alternation of medial voicing and final voicelessness in obstruents as in *tāge:tāk, bunde: bunt,* instead of being eliminated altogether, had become extended beyond its original domain to the sonorants, as has in fact happened in Icelandic. The change of the limited Old English vowel shortening rule (6) to its present more general form (5) is another instance of extension.

This distinction, implicit in traditional historical studies, though rarely drawn systematically (but see Hoenigswald, 1960, pp. 63, 108), is a useful one, partly for reasons that have to do with linguistic reconstruction. Leveling will often be recoverable by historical reconstruction, because of the relic forms which reflect older linguistic stages that leveling leaves behind. Extension, however, will in general not be so recoverable because, with certain very interesting exceptions, it cannot leave relic forms behind. The difference between these two types of analogy can be defined in terms of the formal differences of two kinds of rule simplification in a very straightforward manner. Rules consist of two parts, a structural analysis, which specifies to what forms the rule applies, and a structural change, which says what happens to these forms. In the customary notation for phonological rules, the structural change is the part between the arrow and the slash and the structural analysis is everything else. Then any rule simplification which modifies the structural change of a rule (whether or not it also modifies the structural analysis) is a *leveling,* and any rule simplification which does not modify the structural change of a rule is an *extension.* Thus the loss of final devoicing (Rule 1) and the simplification of Rule 2 to Rule 3 affect the structural change of the rule and are hence levelings, but the change of the shortening rule in English did not affect its structural change and is hence an extension.

It is a fairly surprising fact that the two kinds of reorderings we have found, namely those governed by I and II, correspond pairwise to these two kinds of rule simplifications and in turn to the traditional distinction between extension and leveling. Reordering by II results in leveling and thus corresponds to simplification in the structural change of a rule. For example, the effect of placing umlaut after $o > \vartheta$ is that the height alternation in *bɔdə:bödə* and innumerable similar cases is leveled and the resulting forms, *bɔdə:bödə,* retain the low vowel throughout the paradigm. So, too, the reordering of spirantization and word-final devoicing results in the dropping of a two-feature alternation, *tak:taγə* (with change of both voicing and continuance), in favor of a simpler one-feature alternation, *tax:taγə* (with a continuant throughout the paradigm), that is, again in leveling. In their effect on surface forms and on the relation of surface forms, leveling by simplification in the structural change of rules and leveling by reordering in accordance with Principle II have similar effects in that they make more alike the different shapes in which morphemes appear. But they bring this effect about in different ways because leveling by rule simplification brings the forms closer to the base forms, whereas leveling by reordering takes forms farther away from their base forms. But both types share the property that they can leave behind relic forms which make the recovery of these processes by linguistic reconstruction a possibility. What guarantees us the earlier grammar in each of these cases are the forms like *weg* (in the case where the devoicing rule is lost and in the case in which it is reordered with spirantization), *plötsli* (in reordering of umlaut and *o > ɔ*), and so on.

On the other hand, reordering by I results in extension (polarization) and so corresponds to simplification which affects only the structural analysis of rules. In the case of the Slavic palatalizations (see Section 8), for example, the voiced stop:voiced affricate alternation is polarized into a voiced stop:voiced continuant alternation. It is clear that in this case any forms which undergo the old form of the rules are also going to undergo them after the reordering, so that relic forms which would allow reconstruction of the change could not be created.

These relationships are summarized in the following table.

Reordering	Corresponds to simplification of	Reconstructible by relic forms?	Surface effect
by I	Structural analysis only	No	Extension (polarization)
by II	Structural change	Yes	Leveling

REFERENCES

Abaev, V. I. 1964. *A grammatical sketch of Ossetic*. Indiana University Research Center in Anthropology, Folklore, and Linguistics, Publication 35 (identical with *International Journal of American Linguistics*, XXX, No. 4, Part II). Bloomington, Indiana.

Austin, John L. 1962. *How to do things with words*. Oxford.

Babcock, Sandra S. 1966. "Syntactic dissimilation." Unpublished. Ohio State University.

Bach, Emmon. 1965. "On some recurrent types of transformations." *Report of the Sixteenth Annual Round Table Meeting on Linguistics and Language Studies* (identical with *Georgetown University Monograph Series on Languages and Linguistics* 18), pp. 3–18. Ed. Charles W. Kreidler. Washington, D.C.

———. 1967. "*Have* and *be* in English syntax." *Language* 43:462–485.

Baker, C. Leroy. 1966. "Definiteness and indefiniteness in English." Unpublished M.A. thesis. The University of Illinois.

Bally, Charles. 1926. "L'expression des idées de sphère personnelle et de solidarité dans les langues indoeuropéenes." *Festschrift Louis Gauchat*, pp. 68–78. Aarau.

Bazell, C. E. 1949. "Syntactic relations and linguistic typology." *Cahiers Ferdinand de Saussure* 8:5–20.

Bennett, Charles. 1914. *Syntax of Early Latin, II: The cases*. Boston.

Benveniste, Emile. 1962. "Pour l'analyse des fonctions casuelles: Le genetif latin." *Lingua* 11:10–18.

Blake, Frank. 1930. "A semantic analysis of case." *Curme volume of linguistic studies* (identical with *Language Monograph No. 7*), pp. 34–49. Eds. James Taft Hartfield, Werner Leopold, and A. J. Friedrich Ziegelschmid. Baltimore.

Bolinger, Dwight. 1967. "The imperative in English." *To honor Roman Jakobson*, I, 335–362. The Hague.

Cassidy, Frederick G. 1937. " 'Case' in Modern English." *Language* 13:240–245.

Chomsky, Noam. 1957. *Syntactic structures*. The Hague.

———. 1965. *Aspects of the theory of syntax*. Cambridge, Mass.

———. 1966a. *Cartesian linguistics*. New York.

———. 1966b. "Topics in the theory of generative grammar." *Current trends in linguistics*, III, 1–60. Ed. Thomas A. Sebeok. The Hague.

———. Forthcoming. "Remarks on Nominalization." To appear in *Readings in English Transformational Grammar*. Eds. Roderick Jacobs and Peter S. Rosenbaum. Boston.

———, and Morris Halle. 1968. *The sound pattern of English*. New York.

Diver, William. 1964. "The system of agency of the Latin noun." *Word* 20:178–196.

Enderlin, Fritz. 1911. *Die Mundart von Kesswil im Oberthurgau. Beiträge zur schweizerdeutschen Grammatik* 5. Ed. Albert Bachmann. Frauenfeld.

Fillmore, Charles J. 1966a. "Toward a modern theory of case." *The Ohio State University project on linguistic analysis, Report No. 13*, pp. 1–24.

———. 1966b. "A proposal concerning English prepositions." *Report of the Seventeenth Annual Round Table Meeting on Linguistics and Language Studies* (identical with *Georgetown University Monograph Series on Languages and Linguistics* 19), pp. 19–33. Ed. Francis P. Dinneen, S.J. Washington.

———. 1967. "The syntax of English preverbs." *Glossa*, 1:91–125.

Fodor, J., and M. Garrett. 1967. "Some reflections on competence and performance." *Psycholinguistics Papers*, pp. 135–154. Eds. J. Lyons and R. J. Wales. Chicago.

Fodor, J., and Jerrold J. Katz, eds. 1964. *The structure of language*. Englewood Cliffs, N.J.

Frei, Henri. 1939. "Sylvie est jolie des yeux." *Mélanges de linguistique offerts à Charles Bally*, pp. 185–192. Geneva.

———. 1954. "Cas et dèses en français." *Cahiers Ferdinand de Saussure* 12:29–47.

van Ginneken, Jacques. 1939. "Avoir et être du point de vue de la linguistique générale." *Mélanges de linguistique offerts à Charles Bally*, pp. 83–92. Geneva.

Gleitman, Lila. 1965. "Coordinating conjunctions in English." *Language* 41:260–293.

Gonda, J. 1962. "The unity of the Vedic dative." *Lingua* 11:141–150.

Greenberg, Joseph H. 1963. "Some universals of grammar with particular reference to the order of meaningful elements." *Universals of Language*, pp. 58–90. Ed. Joseph H. Greenberg. Cambridge, Mass.

———. 1966. "Language universals." *Current Trends in Linguistics*, III, 61–112. Ed. Thomas A. Sebeok. The Hague.

Grimes, Joseph E. 1964. *Huichol syntax*. The Hague.

de Groot, A. Willem. 1956. "Classification of uses of a case illustrated on the genitive in Latin." *Lingua* 6:8–66.

Gruber, Jeffrey. 1965. "Studies in lexical relations." Unpublished dissertation. M.I.T.

———. 1967. "Topicalization in child language." *Foundations of Language* 3:37–65.

Hall [Partee], Barbara. 1965. "Subject and object in English." Unpublished dissertation. M.I.T.

Halle, Morris. 1959. *The sound pattern of Russian*. The Hague.

———. 1962. "Phonology in generative grammar." *Word* 18:54–72. Reprinted in Fodor and Katz (1964, pp. 324–333).

Halliday, Michael A. K. 1966. "Some notes on 'deep' grammar." *Journal of Linguistics* 2:55–67.

Hamp, Eric P., Fred W. Householder, and Robert P. Austerlitz, eds. 1966. *Readings in linguistics II*. Chicago.

Harris, Zellig. 1951. *Methods in structural linguistics*. Chicago.

———. 1957. "Co-occurrence and transformation in linguistic structure." *Language* 33:283–340.

Hashimoto, Mantaro J. 1966. "The internal structure of basic strings and a generative treatment of transitive and intransitive verbs." Paper read before the 1966 Tokyo International Seminar in Linguistic Theory.

Havers, Wilhelm. 1911. *Untersuchungen zur Kasussyntax der indogermanischen Sprachen*. Strasbourg.

Hays, David G. 1964. "Dependency theory: A formalism and some observations." *Language* 40:511–525.

Heger, Klaus. 1966. "Valenz, Diathese und Kasus." *Zeitschrift für romanische Philologie* 82:138–170.

Hjelmslev, Louis. 1935, 1937. "La categorie des cas." *Acta Jutlandica*, VII, No. 1; IX, No. 2.

Hockett, Charles F. 1958. *A course in modern linguistics*. New York.

Hoenigswald, Henry M. 1960. *Language change and linguistic reconstruction*. Chicago.

Hotzenköcherle, Rudolf. 1934. *Die Mundart von Mutten. Beiträge zur schweizerdeutschen Grammatik* 19. Ed. Albert Bachmann. Frauenfeld.

Ivić, Milka. 1962. "The grammatical category of non-omissible determiners." *Lingua* 11:199–204.

———. 1964. "Non-omissible determiners in Slavic languages." *Proceedings of the Ninth International Congress of Linguists,* pp. 476–479. The Hague.

Jakobson, Roman. 1936. "Beitrag zur allgemeinen Kasuslehre." *Travaux du Cercle Linguistique de Prague* 6:240–288. Reprinted in Hamp, Householder, and Austerlitz (1966, pp. 51–89).

———. 1942. "Kindersprache, Aphasie und allgemeine Lautgesetze." *Språkvetenskapliga Sällskapets i Uppsala förhandlingar, 1940–1942* (identical with *Uppsala Universitets Årsskrift* 1942, Vol. 9), pp. 1–83. Reprinted in *Roman Jakobson Selected Writings,* I, 328–401. 1962. The Hague.

———. 1958. "Typological studies and their contribution to historical comparative linguistics." *Proceedings of the VIIIth International Congress of Linguistics,* pp. 17–25. Oslo.

Jespersen, Otto. 1924. *The philosophy of grammar.* New York.

Katz, Jerrold J. 1965. *The philosophy of language.* New York.

———, and Jerry A. Fodor. 1963. "The structure of a semantic theory." *Language* 39:170–210. Reprinted in Fodor and Katz (1964, pp. 479–518).

———, and Paul M. Postal. 1964. *An integrated theory of linguistic descriptions.* Cambridge, Mass.

Kiparsky, Paul. 1965. "Phonological change." Unpublished dissertation. M.I.T.

———. 1967. "On the history of Greek accentuation." *Langages,* in press.

———. Forthcoming. "Tense and mood in Indo-European syntax."

Klima, Edward S. 1964. "Negation in English." In Fodor and Katz (1964, pp. 246–323).

Kuipers, Aert H. 1962. "The Circassian nominal paradigm: A contribution to case theory." *Lingua* 11:231–248.

Kuryłowicz, Jerzy. 1960. "Le probleme du classement des cas." *Esquisses linguistiques,* pp. 131–150. Wrocław-Krakov.

———. 1964. *The inflectional categories of Indo-European.* Heidelberg.

Labov, William. 1963. "The social motivation of a sound change." *Word,* 19:273–309.

———. 1965. "On the mechanism of linguistic change." *Report of the Sixteenth Annual Round Table Meeting on Linguistics and Language Studies* (identical with *Georgetown University Monograph Series on Languages and Linguistics* 18), pp. 91–114. Ed. Charles W. Kreidler. Washington, D.C.

Lakoff, George. 1965. *On the nature of syntactic irregularity.* The Computation Laboratory of Harvard University Mathematical Linguistics and Automatic Translation, Report No. NSF-16. Cambridge, Mass.

———. 1966. "Stative adjectives and verbs in English." The Computation Laboratory of Harvard University Mathematical Linguistics and Automatic Translation, Report No. NSF-17, pp. I–1 to I–16.

———. 1967. "Instrumental adverbs and the concept of deep structure." Duplicated. Cambridge, Mass.

———, and Stanley Peters. 1966. "Phrasal conjunction and symmetric predicates." The Computation Laboratory of Harvard University Mathematical Linguistics and Automatic Translation, Report No. NSF-17, pp. VI–1 to VI–49.

———, and John Robert Ross. 1967. "Is deep structure necessary?" Duplicated. Cambridge, Mass.

Lane, George S. 1951. Review of Y. M. Biese, *Some notes on the origin of the Indo-European nominative singular. Language* 27:372–374.

Langacker, Ronald. Forthcoming. "On pronominalization and the chain of command."

Langendoen, D. Terence. 1966. "Some problems concerning the English expletive 'it'." *The Ohio State University Research Foundation Project on Linguistic Analysis*, Report No. 13, pp. 104–134.

Lee, P. Gregory. Forthcoming. "Some properties of *be* sentences."

Lees, Robert B. 1960. *The grammar of English nominalizations.* Indiana University Research Center in Anthropology, Folklore, and Linguistics, Publication 12 (identical with *International Journal of American Linguistics,* XXVI, No. 3, Part II). Bloomington, Indiana.

————. 1961. *The phonology of Modern Standard Turkish* (identical with *Indiana University Publications: Uralic and Altaic Series* 6). Bloomington, Indiana.

Lehmann, Winfred P. 1958. "On earlier stages of the Indo-European nominal inflection." *Language* 34:179–202.

Lévy-Bruhl, Lucien. 1916. "L'expression de la possession dans les langues mélanésiennes." *Bulletin de la Société de linguistique de Paris* 19:96–104.

Luick, Karl. 1921. *Historische Grammatik der englischen Sprache.* Leipzig.

Lyons, John. 1966. "Towards a 'notional' theory of the 'parts of speech'." *Journal of Linguistics* 2:209–236.

McCawley, James D. 1967. "Sapir's phonologic representation." *International Journal of American Linguistics* 33:106–111.

————. Forthcoming-a. *Finnish phonology.*

————. Forthcoming-b. "On the nature of the base component."

McKaughan, Howard. 1962. "Overt relation markers in Maranao." *Language* 38:47–51.

McNeill, David. 1966. "Developmental psycholinguistics." *The genesis of language,* pp. 15–84. Eds. Frank Smith and George A. Miller. Cambridge, Mass.

Mackel, E. 1905–1907. *Die Mundart der Prignitz. Niederdeutsches Jahrbuch,* 31, 33. Norden and Leipzig.

Manessy, Gabriel. 1964. "La relation génitive dans quelques langues mandé." *Proceedings of the Ninth International Congress of Linguists,* pp. 467–475. The Hague.

Martinet, André. 1955. *Économie des changements phonétiques.* Bern.

————. 1962a. *A functional view of language.* Oxford.

————. 1962b. "Le sujet comme fonction linguistique et l'analyse syntaxique du Basque." *Bulletin de la Société de linguistique de Paris* 57:72–83.

Matthews, G. Hubert. Forthcoming. "Proto-Siouan obstruents."

Meinhof, Carl. 1938. "Der Ausdruck der Kasusbeziehungen in afrikanischen Sprachen." *Scritti in onore di Alfredo Trombetti,* pp. 71–85. Ed. Ulrico Hoepli. Milan.

Miyadi, Denzaburo. 1964. "Social life of Japanese monkeys." *Science* 21:783–786.

Moulton, William G. 1960. "The short vowel systems of Northern Switzerland." *Word* 16:155–182.

————. 1961. "Lautwandel durch innere Kausalität: Die ostschweizerische Vokalspaltung." *Zeitschrift für Mundartforschung* 28:227–251.

Müller, C. F. W. 1908. *Syntax des Nominativs und Akkusativs im Lateinischen.* Leipzig.

Newmark, Leonard. 1962. "An Albanian case system." *Lingua* 11:312–321.

Oertel, Hanns. 1936. *The syntax of cases in the narrative and descriptive prose of the Brahmānas*. Heidelberg.

Pike, Kenneth L. 1943. *Phonetics*. Ann Arbor.

———. 1966. *Tagmemic and matrix linguistics applied to selected African languages*. Final Report, Contract No. OE-5-14-065, U.S. Department of Health, Education, and Welfare, Office of Education, Bureau of Research. Washington, D.C.

Postal, Paul M. 1963. "Mohawk prefix generation." *Proceedings of the Ninth International Congress of Linguists*, pp. 346–355. The Hague.

———. 1966. "On so-called 'pronouns' in English." *Report of the Seventeenth Annual Round Table Meeting on Linguistics and Language Studies* (identical with *Georgetown University Monograph Series on Languages and Linguistics* 19), pp. 177–206. Ed. Francis P. Dinneen, S.J. Washington, D.C.

———. 1968. *Aspects of phonological theory*. New York, Evanston, and London.

Prideaux, Gary Dean. 1966. "The syntax of Japanese honorifics." Unpublished dissertation. University of Texas at Austin.

Quang Phuc Dong. 1966. "English sentences without overt grammatical subject." Duplicated.

Quine, W. V. 1961. "Logic as a source of syntactical insights." *Structure of language and its mathematical aspects* (identical with *Proceedings of Symposia in Applied Mathematics* 12), pp. 1–5. Ed. Roman Jakobson. Providence.

Rabeler, Th. H. F. 1911. "Niederdeutscher Lautstand im Kreise Bleckede." *Zeitschrift für deutsche Philologie* 43:141–202, 320–377.

Redden, James E. 1966. "Walapai II: Morphology." *International Journal of American Linguistics* 32:141–163.

Robins, Robert H. 1961. "Syntactic analysis." *Archivum linguisticum* 13:78–89. Reprinted in Hamp, Householder, and Austerlitz (1966, pp. 386–395).

Rosén, Haiim. 1959. "Die Ausdrucksform für 'veräusserlichen' und 'unveräusserlichen' Besitz in Frühgriechischen." *Lingua* 8:264–293.

Ross, John Robert. 1967. "On the cyclic nature of English pronominalization." *To honor Roman Jakobson*, III, 1669–1682. The Hague.

Russell, Bertrand. 1920. *Introduction to Mathematical Philosophy*. London.

Saint-Jacques, Bernard. 1966. *Analyse structurale de la syntaxe du japonais moderne*. Paris.

Salzmann, Zdeněk. 1965. "Arapaho VI: Noun." *International Journal of American Linguistics* 31:136–151.

Sapir, Edward. 1917a. Review of C. C. Uhlenbeck, "Het identificeerend karakter der possessieve flexie in talen van Noord-Amerika." *International Journal of American Linguistics* 1:86–90.

———. 1917b. Review of C. C. Uhlenbeck, "Het passieve karakter van het verbum transitivum of van het verbum actionis in talen van Noord-Amerika." *International Journal of American Linguistics*, 1:82–86.

Schirmunski, V. 1962. *Deutsche Mundartkunde*. Deutsche Akademie der Wissenschaften zu Berlin, Veröffentlichungen des Instituts für deutsche Sprache und Literatur 25. Berlin.

Sommerfelt, Alf. 1937. "Sur la notion du sujet en géorgian." *Mélanges de linguistique et de philologie offerts à Jacques van Ginneken*, pp. 183–185. Paris.

Smith, Carlota S. 1964. "Determiners and relative clauses in a generative grammar of English." *Language* 40:37–52.

Swadesh, Morris. 1939. "Nootka internal syntax." *International Journal of American Linguistics* 9:77–102.

Tesnière, Lucian. 1959. *Éléments de syntaxe structurale*. Paris.

Thorne, James P. 1966. "English imperatives." *Journal of Linguistics* 2:69–78.

Trager, George L., and Henry Lee Smith, Jr. 1951. *An outline of English structure*. *Studies in Linguistics: Occasional Papers* 3. Norman, Oklahoma.

Trubetzkoy, Nikolai S. 1939. "Le rapport entre le déterminé, le déterminant et le défini." *Mélanges de linguistique offerts à Charles Bally*, pp. 75–82. Geneva.

Uhlenbeck, C. C. 1901. "Agens und Patiens im Kasussystem der indogermanischen Sprachen." *Indogermanische Forschungen* 12:170–171.

Vaillant, André. 1936. "L'ergatif indo-européen." *Bulletin de la Société de linguistique de Paris* 27:93–108.

Velten, H. V. 1962. "On the functions of French *de* and *à*." *Lingua* 11:449–452.

Wanner, Georg. 1941. *Die Mundarten des Kantons Schaffhausen. Beiträge zur schweizerdeutschen Grammatik* 20. Ed. Albert Bachmann. Frauenfeld.

Weinreich, Uriel. 1966. "Explorations in semantic theory." *Current trends in linguistics*, III, 395–477. Ed. Thomas A. Sebeok. The Hague.

Whorf, Benjamin Lee. 1965. "A linguistic consideration of thinking in primitive communities" (c. 1936). *Language, thought and reality: Selected writings of Benjamin Lee Whorf*, pp. 65–86. Ed. John B. Carroll. Cambridge, Mass.

Wierzbicka, Anna. 1967. "Mind and body from the semantic point of view." Duplicated. Cambridge, Mass.

Winter, Werner. 1965. "Transforms without kernels?" *Language* 41:484–489.

Ziff, Paul. 1965. "What an adequate grammar can't do." *Foundations of Language* 1:5–13.

Zwicky, Arnold M., Jr. 1967. "Umlaut and noun plurals in German." *Studia Grammatica*, 6:35–45.